FOOD LOVERS'
GUIDE TO
LOS ANGELES

FOOD LOVERS' SERIES

FOOD LOVERS'
GUIDE TO®
LOS ANGELES

The Best Restaurants, Markets
& Local Culinary Offerings

1st Edition

Cathy Chaplin

Guilford, Connecticut

To Vernon Chaplin—you're the best.

Illustrations: Jill Butler with additional art by Carleen Moira Powell and MaryAnn Dubé
Maps: Melissa Baker © Rowman & Littlefield

ISBN 978-0-7627-8112-6

Printed in the United States of America

Distributed by NATIONAL BOOK NETWORK

All the information in this guidebook is subject to change. We recommend that you call ahead to obtain current information before traveling.

Contents

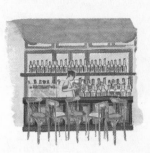

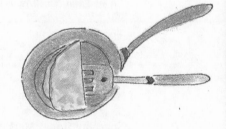

Recipes, 293

Appendices

About the Author

Cathy Chaplin was born in La Mesa, California, educated in Swarthmore, Pennsylvania, and cultured in Saigon, Vietnam. Now based in Los Angeles, she documents all things delicious on GastronomyBlog.com. Her writing and photography have appeared in numerous publications including *Saveur* magazine, *National Geographic*, and *Condé Nast Traveller*. When she isn't planning her next meal or reflecting on a previous one, she's lacing up her kicks and going for a run. Follow her bite-by-bite on Instagram and Twitter at @GastronomyBlog.

Acknowledgments

It takes a hungry and inquisitive village to uncover the hidden gems in this expansive town full of concrete nooks and crannies, and I could not have written this book nearly as well without the direction, contributions, and advice I received from my friends in the Los Angeles food community. Thank you to Alice Hom, Amy Luu (@theroaming belly), Amy Shuster (backyardbite.com), Anjali Prasertong (@anjaliruth), Anna Abatzoglou (bananawonder.com), Anne Alderete (@tunatoast), Bill Esparza (streetgourmetla.com), Christina Gilmour (@gilmoureats), Christine Choi (@olivejina), Danny Chen (@kungfoodpanda), Darin Louie (darindines.com), Diana Hossfeld (@dianatakesabite), Diep Tran (@goodgirldinette), Evelina Giang (@evelinag), Fiona Chandra (gourmet pigs.blogspot.com), Hadley Tomicki (LATaco.com), Helen Kim (@nele helen), Javier Cabral (@theglutster), Jenn Fujikawa (justjennrecipes .com), Joshua Lurie (foodgps.com), Julian Fang (@djjewelz), Kat Nguyen (@beo_meo), Lien Ta (@lientigre), Louise Yang (@NakedSushi), Matt Kang (@mattatouille), Misty Oka (@NomsNotBombs), Nastassia Johnson (@letmeeatcake), Remil Mangali (@limer35), Sam Kim (@samkimsam kim), Sree Roy (saagahh.com), Steve Graines (@infinitefress), Thien Ho (@XoiaEats), Tomo Kurokawa (@drtomostyle), Tsz Chan (gastrophoria .com), Valentina Silva-Charson (eastsidefoodbites.com), and Wesley Wong (@eatsmeetswes).

Also, thank you to veteran food writers Barbara Hansen, Jonathan Gold, and Linda Burum for laying the foundation and always digging deep. Your wealth of knowledge and far-reaching archives were immensely valuable every step of the way.

Introduction

In the very early days of developing this book, I saw that it was available for preorder on Amazon. Curious as to what the front cover of my yet-to-be-written book looked like, I clicked on the accompanying image. While the text read the same as the version you're holding in your hands, the photo was something totally different. Instead of the lush heap of *som tam*, it was a bowl of salad—mesclun topped with sliced radishes to be exact. Perplexed by the image that was chosen to tease and entice would-be readers, I inquired of my editors whether it was the real deal or just a mockup. The salad was just a placeholder . . . whew!

While there's certainly a contingent of Angelenos who eat leafy greens at every meal, topped with skinless grilled chicken breast if a splurge is to be allowed, this fragment of the local food scene hardly scratches the surface of what Los Angeles has to offer. The restaurants, bakeries, and mobile operations that I know, love, and explore in this book hail from vibrant communities, rich in culinary traditions, that feed each other well and inexpensively. Greens are mostly garnishes 'round here.

With nearly 10 million inhabitants calling this 4,752-square-mile metropolis home, eating in the City of Angels is a gut-busting adventure like no other. In the city center you'll find regional fare from Thailand, Korea, and Japan. Travel east for Chinese, Mexican, and Central American delights. South of the city is an "only in L.A." mash-up of Indian, Hawaiian, and soul food. The west side of town is home to some of the city's hottest tables, handsomest chefs, and brilliant Persian cuisine. Head north for throngs of Middle Eastern, South American, and Armenian eateries. Punctuating all regions of the dining landscape are hawkers of L.A.'s beloved classics like hot dogs, doughnuts, and hamburgers.

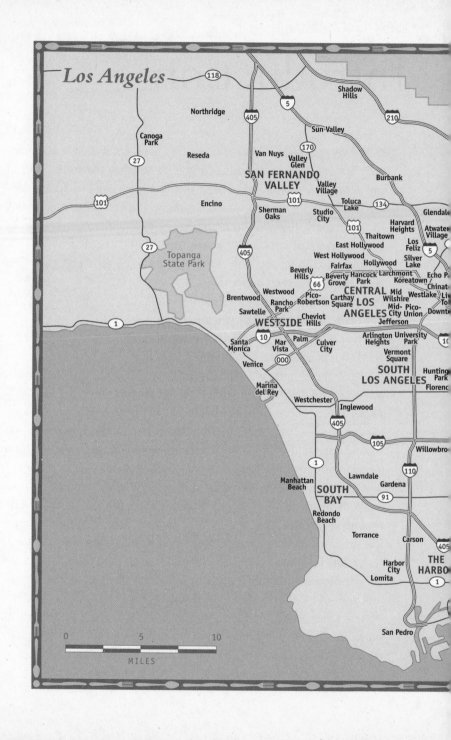

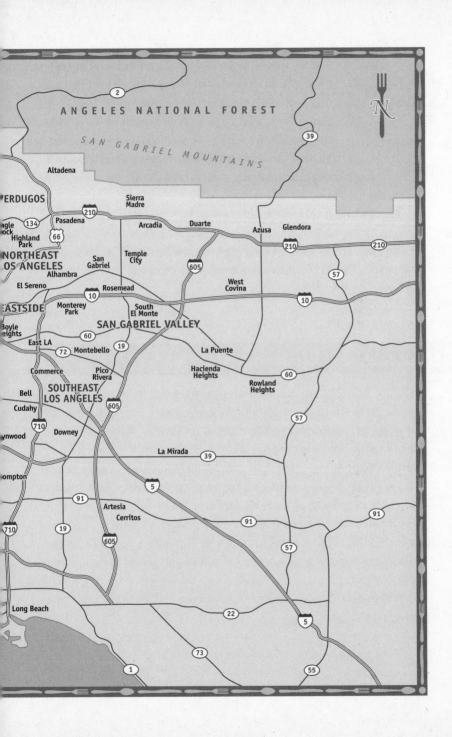

While a wide range of cuisines can be found in every major city in America, what's special about the food here is that it's made by the people, for the people. In place of one-stop shops that serve a country's greatest hits, you'll find a kind of regionalization and specialization that can only happen when there's a local audience large enough to recognize and appreciate the uniqueness of what's on the stove.

There really is something delicious to be eaten in every direction, so long as the traffic isn't too discouraging. The restaurants included in this book are the best in their class, quintessentially L.A., and most importantly, worth the drive. Put down your salad fork and grab your car keys—it's time to take a real bite out of this city.

How to Use This Book

Dividing nearly 5,000 square miles of freeways, hills, valleys, and coastal terrain into digestible chunks was no easy feat, but it had to be done for organization's sake. The chapters that follow are separated into the following regions: Central Los Angeles, Eastside, Harbor, Northeast Los Angeles, San Fernando Valley, San Gabriel Valley, South Bay, South Los Angeles, Southeast Los Angeles, Verdugos, and Westside.

At the beginning of each chapter is a list of neighborhoods that are included in the region (e.g., Koreatown, West Hollywood, and Echo Park are listed under Central Los Angeles). Flip to the appendices in the back of the book for a complete list of restaurants sorted by cuisine and neighborhood.

Within each chapter, listings are organized alphabetically under the following categories:

Foodie Faves

These restaurants deliver the kind of memorable meals that demand to be repeated. Service and ambiance may or may not be a strong suit, but you're guaranteed to find dependably delicious cooking.

L.A. Landmarks

These restaurants built the foundation of the city's dining scene and are considered institutions due to their longevity, contributions, nostalgia, or a combination of all three.

Sublime Sweets

These confectionaries deliver the finest sugar high in town, whether it's cakes, cookies, ice creams, or *churros*.

Specialty Stores, Markets & Producers

These establishments and artisans go above and beyond to bring truly unique edibles and products such as rare cookbooks, imported sushi knives, and made-from-scratch burrata cheese to Angelenos and beyond.

Every listing includes basic information (name, address, phone number, website, cuisine, and price range), as well as insights about ambiance, history, and specialties. For hours of operation, handicap access, dietary concerns, and other such matters, contact the establishment directly via phone or website.

Further Exploration

A number of restaurants include a subentry titled Further Exploration. These establishments are related to the main entry either by chef, genre, cuisine, or a combination of all three. As a general note, these destinations aren't quite as essential as the main entries, but they provide a solid jumping-off point for diners interested in digging deeper.

Restaurant Price Key

Price symbols are based on the average price for a single main course:

$	Under $10
$$	$10 to $20
$$$	$20 to $30
$$$$	Over $30

Recipes

Clear off your countertops and fire up the oven because the very last chapter contains a dozen recipes from local chefs who really know how to tickle those taste buds. Use these as a guide to re-create restaurant magic at home.

Keeping Up with Food News

From restaurant openings to chef departures and food policy, these online and print publications stay abreast of the latest news regarding the Los Angeles dining scene.

Eater L.A. (la.eater.com): Editor Kat Odell and her team of roving reporters cover up-to-the-minute restaurant openings, shutterings, "chef shuffles," and "rumor mongering."

L.A. Weekly: Grab the latest issue hot-off-the-press every Thursday or log on to the *Weekly*'s Squid Ink food blog (blogs.laweekly.com/squidink) for lively snippets edited by Amy Scattergood.

FOODIES TO FOLLOW

Follow these local food bloggers for a double dose of lively prose and screen-licking food porn: **Darin Dines** by Darin Louie (darindines.com), **Eastside Food Bites** by Valentina Silva-Charson (eastsidefoodbites.com), **Eat, Drink & Be Merry** by Dylan Ho (eatdrinknbmerry.com), **Eating L.A.** by Pat Saperstein (eatingla.blogspot.com), **Food GPS** by Joshua Lurie (foodgps.com), **Kevin Eats** by Kevin Hsu (kevineats.com), **Let Me Eat Cake** by Nastassia Johnson (theletmeeatcake.com), **Midtown Lunch: L.A.** by Zach Brooks (midtownlunch.com/los-angeles), **My Last Bite** by Jo Stougaard (mylastbite.wordpress.com), and **Street Gourmet L.A.** by Bill Esparza (streetgourmetla.com).

Los Angeles **magazine:** Food editor Leslie Barger Suter curates a strong food section each month, while restaurant critic Patrick Kuh tells it like it is. For restaurant recs at a glance, skim the magazine's restaurant listings.

Los Angeles Times: Turn to the paper's Saturday section for well-tested recipes, reviews by restaurant critic Jonathan Gold, wine recommendations, and much more, all edited by Russ Parsons. Snappier news is delivered on the Daily Dish (latimes.com/features/food/dailydish), the *Times'* food blog.

Tasting Table (tastingtable.com): A free e-mail daily uncovering food, dining, and drinking in Los Angeles edited by Garrett Snyder.

Food Events & Festivals

January

Dine L.A. (discoverlosangeles.com): Twice a year in January and July, the Los Angeles Tourism and Convention Board celebrates restaurant week with specially priced three-course menus at participating restaurants around town.

Lunar New Year: Ring in the Lunar New Year Downtown in historic Chinatown (chinatownla.com) and in Monterey Park (ci.monterey-park.ca.us) with dragon dances, firecrackers, and traditional foods.

February

Cupcake Challenge (drinkeatplay .com/cupcakechallenge): The city's best bakers face off at this annual event where attendees taste and vote on whose cupcakes reign supreme.

March

Planned Parenthood Food Fare (pplafoodfare.com): One of the oldest and most recognized food events, with over 150 of the city's best restaurants, caterers, wineries, and entertainers participating.

April

Grilled Cheese Invitational (grilledcheeseinvitational .com): It's all about "bread, butter, cheese, victory" at this quirky annual gathering where amateur and professional cooks dream up wildly creative grilled cheese sandwiches and compete for the title of grilled cheese champion.

***Los Angeles Times* Festival of Books (events.latimes .com/festivalofbooks):** Cookbook authors, including celebrity chefs, demonstrate recipes and discuss their latest releases on the Cooking Stage at this annual event.

Thai New Year's Day Songkran Festival (thainewyear .com): Centered on Hollywood Boulevard in the heart of Thaitown, this celebration includes a Miss Thai New Year pageant, a festive parade, and a virtual cornucopia of delicacies to sample.

May

Armenian Food Fare (armenianfoodfair.com): Pig out on kebabs, *piroshki* (baked or fried buns), and *sarma* (stuffed grape leaves) at this annual food and culture bonanza in Montebello.

Taste of the Eastside (tasteoftheeastside.com): A festival showcasing the evolving and diverse food scenes of the eastside neighborhoods of Silver Lake, Echo Park, Eagle Rock, Highland Park, Los Feliz, Atwater Village, and beyond.

June

Taste of the Nation (strength.org): The city's top chefs and mixologists come together in an effort to end childhood hunger in America at this annual fete benefiting Share Our Strength.

Vendy Awards (la.streetvendor.org): A yearly street food cook-off between Los Angeles' best sidewalk chefs.

July

Dine L.A. (discoverlosangeles.com): Twice a year in January and July, the Los Angeles Tourism and Convention Board celebrates restaurant week with specially priced three-course menus at participating restaurants around town.

East L.A. Meets Napa (altamed.org): East L.A.'s most iconic restaurants and chefs team up with Latino-owned wineries from Napa and Sonoma to raise funds for health-care nonprofit AltaMed at this annual gathering in Union Station.

L.A. Street Food Fest (lastreetfoodfest.com): Gourmet food trucks, local *loncheros,* and Baja culinarians take over Pasadena's historic Rose Bowl at this all-you-can-eat summer extravaganza.

Live & Dine L.A. (modernluxury.com/angeleno): *Angeleno* magazine celebrates the release of its annual Restaurant Issue by honoring notable chefs. Attendees are treated to plated bites, culinary demonstrations, and plenty to drink.

August

Chinatown Summer Nights (chinatownsummernights .com): A massive block party in the heart of historic Chinatown featuring cooking demonstrations by Chinese chefs, Chinese cultural activities, and gourmet food trucks.

L.A. *Weekly*'s Pancake Breakfast (laweekly.com): From *blinis* to *pajeon* to *okonomiyaki,* this event brings together some of the best pancakes around.

Los Angeles Food and Wine (lafw.com): A multiday celebration of all that is delicious in Los Angeles with tasting events and chef-driven restaurant demos, lunches, and dinners held at venues throughout the city.

Los Angeles Taco Festival (latacofestival.com): Enjoy some of the city's best tacos, from *birria* to *carne asada* to shrimp, as well as live mariachi music.

Lucky Rice Festival (luckyrice.com): A tasting event shining a spotlight on Asian culinary culture. The inaugural event included Spice Table's Bryant Ng, Good Girl Dinette's Diep Tran, and Kris Yenbamroong of Night + Market.

September

Good Food Pie Contest (kcrw.com): Enter a pie, cheer on the competitors, or just enjoy a slice at this annual contest hosted by KCRW's Evan Kleiman.

Greek Fest: An annual celebration of all things Greek including food, folk dancing, wine tasting, and a marketplace held in central Los Angeles (lagreekfest.com) and in Pasadena (pasadenagreekfest.org).

L.A. County Fair (lacountyfair.com): You'll find deep-fried Kool-Aid, Texas-size doughnuts, and all the funnel cake you can eat at this monthlong gustatory blitz held at the Pomona Fairplex.

L.A. Loves Alex's Lemonade (alexslemonade.org): The country's most talented chefs join forces to help end childhood cancer at this festive gathering hosted by Suzanne Goin, Caroline Styne, and David Lentz.

Los Angeles Times' "The Taste" (events.latimes.com/taste): A three-day food event designed both for and by locals featuring various themed tastings, panel discussions, and chef demonstrations.

October

Los Angeles magazine's "The Food Event" (lamag.com/thefoodevent): An annual tasting event featuring celebrity chefs, top restaurants, and wine and spirits tastings in the hills of Malibu at Saddlerock Ranch.

Mole Fair (feriadelosmoles.com): Celebrate this classic Mexican dish with food, music, dance, workshops, and a friendly competition.

Oktoberfest at Alpine Village (alpinevillagecenter.com): The oldest and largest Oktoberfest celebration in Southern California, held every Friday, Saturday, and Sunday in September and October.

November

Los Angeles Tamales Festival (losangelestamalefestival.com): An annual gathering of hot tamales featuring a cook-off, an eating contest, a tamale-making demonstration, and even a cornhusk fashion designing contest.

December

Artisanal L.A. (artisanalla.com): From caramels to chai to salumi and preserves, there is always plenty to ogle, taste, and buy at this gathering of local artisans.

Miscellaneous Events

Mitsuwa Market (mitsuwa.com): The Torrance branch of this Japanese market plays host to a number of food events throughout the year including the Umaimono Gourmet Fair, Summer Festival, and Hokkaido Fair.

626 Night Market (626nightmarket.com): The San Gabriel Valley's homage to Asia's bustling night markets with vendors hawking everything from dumplings to stinky tofu.

Central Los Angeles

Arlington Heights, Beverly Grove, Carthay, Chinatown, Downtown, East Hollywood, Echo Park, Fairfax, Hancock Park, Harvard Heights, Hollywood, Koreatown, Larchmont, Little Tokyo, Los Feliz, Mid-City, Mid-Wilshire, Pico-Union, Silver Lake, Thaitown, West Hollywood, Westlake

Foodie Faves

Angelini Osteria, 7313 Beverly Blvd., Los Angeles, CA 90036; (323) 297-0070; angeliniosteria.com; Italian; $$$. Gino Angelini, one of Los Angeles' most celebrated chefs, captures the flavors and spirit of Italy at this neighborhood *osteria*. After a hugely successful career in the old country cooking for everyone who's anyone including the pope and Pavarotti, Chef Angelini came to Los Angeles in 1995 as chef of Rex in Downtown and Vincenti Restaurant in Brentwood. He opened Angelini Osteria in 2001 after deciding to make the city his permanent home. Staying true to the spirit of an *osteria,* the restaurant isn't too fussy. The food is simple and thoughtfully executed, while the room is plain comfortable. Wines are encouraged by the glass or bottle. The Warm Tripe with Tomatoes and Cuttlefish transforms organ meats into a starter worth talking about. Other antipasti to consider include the sweet yet sharp shrimp salad tossed with celery, tomatoes, oregano, and *bottarga* (pressed dried caviar), and the exquisitely grilled octopus. Nonna Elvira's green lasagna made with a beef and veal *ragù* and scattered with fried baby spinach is the most popular *primi*. The *Bombolotti all' Amatriciana*, tubular pasta with shallow ridges, is paired with *guanciale* (unsmoked Italian bacon prepared from pig's cheeks), San Marzano tomatoes, and hot peppers to delicious effect. The whole branzino roasted in sea salt and herbs makes for a sensational *secondi*. Best of all, the fish is filleted tableside with a whole lot of finesse. This could very well be Los Angeles' best Italian restaurant.

Animal, 435 N. Fairfax Ave., Los Angeles, CA 90048; (323) 782-9225; animalrestaurant.com; New American; $$$. Anything goes so long as it's over the top at chefs Jon Shook and Vinny Dotolo's critically acclaimed and locally loved restaurant. The menu, which celebrates underappreciated parts like pig tails, veal brains, and beef belly, is not only fresh and exciting but also challenges wary diners to take a walk on the offal side. After all, who can resist crispy pig ears spiked with chili and lime and topped with a fried egg? The chefs' take on *poutine,*

FURTHER EXPLORATION: SON OF A GUN

The "Two Dudes" give fruits of the sea the Animal treatment at their second restaurant **Son of a Gun** (8370 W. 3rd St., Los Angeles, CA 90048; 323-782-9033; sonofagunrestaurant .com). The shrimp toast and lobster roll are buttery, creamy things that have a cultlike following. Ironically, it's the land-locked chicken sandwich that has emerged as the restaurant's signature dish; there's one on every table.

a Quebecois specialty of french fries, cheese curds, and gravy, has been popular with patrons since day one. Animal's version is heaped with rich oxtail gravy and tons of melted cheddar, all on a bed of golden spuds. Less adventurous eaters tagging along with their ballsier friends can treat themselves to balsamic pork ribs that literally fall off the bone or poached fish prepared as dictated by the season. A cool plate of *crudo* is also a terrific option if a break from the onslaught of flesh is desired.

Antojitos Bibi, 2400 W. 7th St., #109, Los Angeles, CA 90057; (213) 383-8595; Honduran; $$. Olga "Bibi" Cordon prepares Honduran specialties like fresh corn tamales and creamy coconut milk soups at Antojitos Bibi, a casual restaurant overlooking MacArthur Park Lake that could be mistaken for a shrine dedicated to the Honduran national *futbol* team. Locals gather here to catch the latest match over crunchy *enchiladas catrachas*, tostadas layered with a mixture of carrots and ground beef, shredded cabbage, tomatoes, hard-boiled egg, and a dusting of cheese. Pink pickled onions and a few lashings of Tapatio can be deployed as one sees fit. Creamy, beautifully seasoned soups like the *sopa de caracol* are popular with those whose eyes are glued to the screen, as well as their supportive companions. The orange-tinged chowder brimming with yucca, plantains, and chewy bits of *caracol* (conch meat) is reminiscent of a mild Thai curry. To eat, add a spritz of fresh lime juice and a sprinkling of onions and cilantro. The rice served alongside can be added to the bowl too. The *montuca,* a sweet tamale made with fresh corn instead of dried corn masa and eaten with cream, isn't available on a regular basis, but snatch one up if your visit coincides with a fresh batch.

A-Won, 913 S. Vermont Ave., Los Angeles, CA 90006; (213) 389-6764; Korean; $$. Everyone wins at A-Won, so long as there's plenty of raw fish, roe, and *gochujang* (fermented red chile paste) to go around. The stadium-size bowls of *hwe dup bap* are perfumed with sesame oil and prettily assembled with fresh halibut and salmon sashimi, nori (dried seaweed), bonito flakes, *tobiko* (flying fish roe), microgreens, sesame seeds, daikon radish, and shredded romaine. There's still a bit of work to be done once the *hwe dup bap* hits the table. Plop the warm rice that's served alongside into the larger bowl, along with as much *gochujang* as you can handle, then stir, mix, and meld until every component is tinged a fiery shade of red. Every bite is a study in contrasts—soft and crunchy, warm and cool. The *al bap,* a bowl of seasoned rice adorned with various eggs (sea urchin roe, smelt roe, salmon roe, and hen-egg omelet), seaweed, preserved fish, and pickled radish packs a beautiful wallop. The sensation of gnashing teeth on gentle eggs just can't be beat. If soupier, more adventurous sustenance is in order, the *al tang,* spicy cod stew with kimchee, roe, and sperm sacs, is all that and a bag of chips.

Bäco Mercat, 408 S. Main St., Los Angeles, CA 90013; (213) 687-8808; bacomercat.com; New American; $$$. Downtown's restaurant scene has been coming into its own these past few years, and much of the culinary credit goes to Chef Josef Centeno. He gained a loyal following with his imaginative small plates at Little Tokyo's **Lazy Ox Canteen** (p. 90) and struck out on his own with Bäco Mercat in 2011. Chef Centeno developed the "bäco," the restaurant's signature flatbread sandwich stuffed with crispy pork belly and beef *carnitas*, on the fly as a late-night snack for his staff at Lazy Ox. When word spread about this marvelously meaty creation, it evolved into an off-menu special reserved for friends and diners in the know. With the launch of Bäco Mercat, bäcos are finally available to the hungry masses for lunch, dinner, and weekend brunch. In addition to the original bäco, the menu features new permutations stuffed with things like fava bean fritters, beef tongue, and chicken *escabeche*. Also on the menu are flatbread pizzas called "coca," a pozole-ramen hybrid called "bäzole," and nearly two dozen small plates constructed in the same seasonal spirit as those at Lazy Ox. To drink there are beers, spirits, and wines from around the world, as well as tart and tangy sodas made from scratch using vinegars infused with fruits and herbs.

FURTHER EXPLORATION: BAR AMÁ

Chef Centeno opened **Bar Amá** (118 W. 4th St., Los Angeles, CA 90013; 213-687-8002; bar-ama.com) in Downtown Los Angeles in late 2012. While the Tex-Mex menu draws inspiration from family recipes, the beverage program celebrates tequila, mescal, and Mexican beers.

The Bazaar by José Andrés, 465 La Cienega Blvd., Los Angeles, CA 90048; (310) 246-5551; thebazaar.com; Spanish; $$$. Chef José Andrés, an unofficial ambassador for Spanish cuisine, takes diners on a wondrous tour of traditional and modern small plates at The Bazaar. Set in a Philippe Starck–designed space, the restaurant spans two tapas bars (Blanca and Rojo), a frilly pink Patisserie, and a cocktailian paradise (Bar Centro). The rooms dazzle diners at every turn and prove to be the perfect setting for this kind of cutting-edge cookery. From the Traditional Tapas menu, the *jamón Ibérico de bellota Fermín* (acorn-fed, free-range Ibérico ham) is splurge-worthy, while the *pa'amb tomaquet* (toasted bread with Manchego and tomato) captures the spirit of Catalonia on a slice of toasted bread. While the traditional tapas are solid all around, it's the Modern Tapas that really wow. The Not Your Everyday Caprésé has emerged as one of The Bazaar's signature dishes. Perfectly ripe cherry tomatoes are served with "liquid mozzarella" spheres. The moment when the smooth mozzarella orbs give in to the pressure of one's teeth is quite spectacular. The standout Philly Cheesesteak pipes "air bread" full of oozy cheddar cheese and tops it all off with slices of Wagyu beef. The Bazaar puts its best foot forward at Saam, the "Chef's Tasting Room," which requires advance reservations. Here, Chef Andrés curates a multicourse tasting menu highlighting The Bazaar's greatest bites.

Bernie's Teriyaki, 318 Glendale Blvd., Los Angeles, CA 90026; (213) 250-8413; Filipino; $. Prices are low and plates are piled high at Bernie Cruz's namesake teriyaki hut in Historic Filipinotown. The specialty here is Filipino barbecue with a nod to Hawaiian plate lunches. In place of scoops of mac salad and steamed white rice is a fluffy bed of garlicky fried rice served with Thousand Island–dressed iceberg and charbroiled proteins. Whether it's chicken, pork, beef, or a combination of the three that moves your spirit, you'll be treated to an impressive char and moist, juicy meat. The loose teriyaki sauce that coats every meaty crevice brightens just about everything it touches, so reach for one of the squeeze bottles filled with the sticky soy sauce–based stuff if a little extra somethin' somethin' is needed on your Styrofoam plate. A platter here rings in at well under $10 and provides enough provisions for two well-portioned meals or one really hefty feast.

Bestia, 2121 7th Place, Los Angeles CA, 90021; (213) 514-5724; bestiala.com; Italian; $$. Everything about Bestia—the food, the energy, the room, the service—is simply the best. Prior to joining forces with his wife, Pastry Chef Genevieve Gergis, and Restaurateur Bill Chait to open the southern Italian restaurant in the Arts District, Chef Ori Menashe spent the past three and a half years as executive chef at Angelini Osteria. Every dinner at Bestia should start with an order of the Ventrigli di Pollo Rosolati, also known as the tenderest chicken gizzards known to man. Pan-roasted and paired with roasted beets, Belgian endive, and aged capra sarda cheese, the *ventrigli* are like no other gizzards in town. Then, select a few pastas to share. The

Cavatelli alla Norcina, ricotta cavatelli with house-made pork sausage, black truffles, and Grana Padano, is particularly spectacular. The intense aroma released by the black truffles, a whoosh really, will send you into a tizzy. Another must is the Spaghetti Rustichella, fabulously toothsome noodles dressed with sea urchin, garlic, fermented chile, and bread crumbs. Don't leave Bestia without trying Genevieve Gergis' sweets, especially the "Coffee & Donuts," fried-to-order spiced chestnut doughnuts with softly whipped cream and coffee gelato.

The Boiling Crab, 3377 Wilshire Blvd., Los Angeles, CA 90010; (213) 389-2722; theboilingcrab.com; Seafood; $$. For a complete description, see p. 145.

Byul Gobchang, 3819 W. 6th St., Los Angeles, CA 90020; (213) 739-0321; Korean; $$. If you don't look the slightest bit Korean, chances are good that Byul Gobchang's owner Jessica Lee will give you the third degree upon entering her restaurant to make sure that you're onboard the offal train. The menu here offers standard barbecuing cuts like brisket, tongue, and pork belly, but the specialty is cow stomachs and intestines large and small. Once you've assured her that offals are indeed your rapture, a smile will creep across her face and the show will officially begin. The Star Combination pairs a large bottle of *soju* with the aforementioned beefy bits. There's a lot of care that needs to go into preparing intestines properly, so the waitresses handle all the cooking while diners look on and sip *soju*. Once the grill is properly warmed up, the stomach and intestines meet the heat, which firms up their texture almost instantly. With a pair of trusty tongs, the offals are removed from the grill, snipped into bite-size bits, and marinated in a potent puree of garlic, pineapple, pear, sesame oil, and *soju* before returning to the heat once more. Only after the exterior of each piece is evenly caramelized are diners given the okay to dig in. Two sauces, one sweet and the other spicy, are on hand for dipping, while marinated mountain garlic leaves are ready for wrapping. With all that booze and entrails swishing about, a fried rice finish is a must. This evening-only joint is poppin' until 4 a.m. nightly.

Chego, 727 N. Broadway, Unit 117, Los Angeles, CA 90012; (323) 380-8680; eatchego.com; Korean; $. After launching a nationwide gourmet food truck revolution with Kogi, Chef Roy Choi followed it up with a rice bowl venture called Chego, which roughly translates to "the best." The concept was inspired in part by the rice-bowl-hawking tenants who previously occupied the restaurant's space, as well as the Chinese oven that they left behind. When Chef Choi saw the metal box in the kitchen, he knew it would be perfect for cooking proteins slow and low. Start with the Mushroom Egg Rolls and the Ooey Gooey Fries. The former is kickin' with crispness, while the cheese-laden latter is dude food at its finest. For the main event, order the *Kimchi* Spam Bowl, a combination of fried rice, scrambled eggs, and baby bok choy with a touch of butter and toasted sesame. All mixed up and tied together, it packs an avalanche of flavor and heat. The Chubby Pork Belly is equally bold with its *gochujang* (fermented red chile paste) lacquered Kurobuta, pickled radishes, *cotija* (crumbly Mexican cheese), and peanuts. Warning: eating at Chego may be habit-forming.

The Corner Place, 2819 James M. Wood Blvd., Los Angeles, CA 90006; (213) 487-0968; cornerplacerestaurant.com; Korean; $. The Corner Place might look like a Korean barbecue restaurant and smell like one too, but the specialty here is hardly meaty at all. The *dong chi mi gook soo* is an ice-cold noodle soup that refreshes the palate at first slurp. The soul of the bowl lies in the masterfully constructed broth. Its deceptively clear appearance shows no sign of the intense concentration of flavor that's packed within. The essence of scallions, fermented green chiles, ginger, and *bae* (Korean pear), along with a spike of watery brine, packs a bright and acidic punch that is unrivaled. The thin and bouncy noodles soak up the broth's subtleties, while julienned cucumber, sliced tomatoes, and chopped scallions further perfume the bowl. When the sun's relentless rays are beating down on L.A., there's no better escape than a bowl of *dong chi mi gook soo.*

FURTHER EXPLORATION:
YU CHUN CHIC NAENG MYUN

Yu Chun Chic Naeng Myun (3185 W. Olympic Blvd., Los Angeles, CA 90006; 213-382-3815) in Koreatown makes a critically acclaimed bowl of *chic mool naeng myun,* a beefy cold noodle soup made with arrowroot noodles that can be further intensified with lashes of vinegar and mustard. This bowl's got ice, spice, and everything nice.

Daikokuya, 327 E. 1st St., Los Angeles, CA 90012; (213) 626-1680; dkramen.com; Japanese; $. Head to Daikokuya in Little Tokyo for one of the most beloved bowls of *tonkotsu ramen* in town. This branch of a local chain is notorious for having tortuously long waits, but it's possible to snag a seat either along the counter or in one of the plush red booths without too much hassle by avoiding peak hours and dining with a small group. A *ramenya* experience is incomplete without a few plates of *gyoza* (Japanese dumplings) to start. The ones served here are stuffed with pork and vegetables, wrapped in thin papers, and pan-fried in a raftlike mass. Daikokuya's signature *tonkotsu ramen* is made from Kurobuta pork bones that are carefully simmered for hours on end. Once the broth is perfectly milky and luscious, it's ladled atop curly noodles and garnished with scallion confetti. Don't forget to request extra back fat (*kotteri*) for an even porkier experience.

FURTHER EXPLORATION: SHIN SEN GUMI

Also vying for the title of Little Tokyo's best *ramenya* is **Shin Sen Gumi** (132 S. Central Ave., Los Angeles, CA 90012; 213-687-7108; shinsengumigroup.com), another local chain with additional locations in Gardena and Rosemead. Shin Sen Gumi specializes in customizable Hakata-style ramen, which is characterized by thick, pork bone–based soup (*tonkotsu*) paired with thin, straight noodles. The restaurant simmers Berkshire pork bones for 15 hours to achieve its distinctly rich broth.

Don Day, 300 S. Hobart Blvd., Los Angeles, CA 90020; (213) 380-9292; Korean; $$. The competition is fierce in the all-you-can-eat Korean barbecue arena, which means fair prices and ample choices for diners. For the best deal around, don't look to the restaurant with the lowest price tag, but rather the one offering the most value. When it comes to all you can eat, it's important to emphasize variety and quality. Don Day comes through on both fronts, with efficient service to boot. Diners can choose from several set menus that vary in price; the option just below the top tier offers the most bang for your buck. Included in the price of admission are a small army of refillable side dishes (*banchan*) like blanched broccoli with sesame oil, pickled daikon, kimchee, macaroni salad, bamboo shoots with jalapeños, and rice papers. Also on hand is a steamed egg, as well as a fresh green salad. Pair these cool and tangy morsels with the sizzling hot meat for a seriously explosive bite. To be grilled tableside are delicate slices of beef tongue, whole rib eye, shell-on shrimp, *bulgogi* (marinated beef), small and large intestines, marinated chicken, pork shoulder, pork belly, and abomasum, also known as "the fourth and final stomach." Don't sweat it if you're not handy with the grill; the women who staff Don Day have a miraculous sixth sense that allows them to know exactly when each table's meat is ready for consumption.

Further Exploration: Bud Namu Korean BBQ and Hae Jang Chon

Koreatown's **Bud Namu Korean BBQ** (809 Ardmore Ave., Los Angeles, CA 90005; 213-385-9292; budnamubbqla.com) distinguishes itself from the all-you-can-eat pack with an impressive *banchan* buffet that diners can help themselves to, as well as a standout selection of meat. **Hae Jang Chon** (3821 W. 6th St., Los Angeles, CA 90020; 213-389-8777) offers a smooth stone grilling surface in place of the more common metal grates for a unique barbecuing experience. The homey atmosphere and table settings are also quite appealing.

Drago Centro, 525 S. Flower St., Los Angeles, CA 90071; (213) 228-8998; dragocentro.com; Italian; $$$$. Drago Centro's location on the ground floor of the City National Plaza attracts a diverse crowd of suited gents, serious couples, and happy-hour revelers. While worker bees stationed in and around Downtown escape here for bar bites and expertly made cocktails, urban dwellers make reservations weeks in advance for a proper night out on the town. The menu is thoroughly Italian with an emphasis on the handmade pastas that Chef Celestino Drago is famous for. His signature *Pappardelle al Fagiano*, inch-wide egg noodles coated in a roasted pheasant and morel mushroom sauce, is wonderfully silky and possesses a most pleasant bite. Also noteworthy is the *Tagliolini Neri* with its scent of lemon verbena and perfectly cooked mussels, clams, and shrimp served over squid ink noodles. The most popular *secondi* option is the rib eye for two: 32 ounces of USDA prime prepared just as you like it. For something a little homier, try the braised oxtails over polenta.

Further Exploration: Enoteca Drago, Il Pastaio, and Osteria Drago

For a taste of Chef Drago's modern Italian fare outside Downtown visit **Enoteca Drago** (410 N. Canon Dr., Beverly Hills, CA 90210; 310-786-8236; celestinodrago.com) and **Il Pastaio** (400 N. Canon Dr., Beverly Hills, CA 90210; 310-205-5444; giacominodrago.com) in Beverly Hills or **Osteria Drago** (8741 W. Sunset Blvd., West Hollywood, CA 90069; 310-657-1182; osteriadrago.com) in West Hollywood.

Dwit Gol Mok, 3275 Wilshire Blvd., Los Angeles, CA 90010; (213) 382-8432; Korean; $$. Dwit Gol Mok, better known as DGM, is fittingly named after the Korean expression for "back alley." While its address reads Wilshire Boulevard, the entrance is actually tucked far behind the main drag. Upon locating parking near Vermont, walk down Berendo and cross the parking lot. Follow the wondrous smells of smoky barbecue and *gochujang* (fermented red chile paste) because there isn't an English sign in sight. You'll know when you've arrived by the deafening levels of K-pop blaring throughout the building. The specialty at this two-story graffiti palace is a killer combination of Korean bar food and potent *soju*. The crowd is young, mostly Korean-speaking, and always seem to be having a rowdy time. A copper pot or two of *soju* is an absolute must, but sip slowly because it tends to hide behind a curtain of sweetness and attack when one least expects. To pair with the alcohol, order a platter of marinated pork ribs coated in a sweet glaze, fried oysters, a bubbling cauldron of *budae jigae,* an "army base stew" complete with ramen noodles and hot dogs, and a serving of one of the best *bo ssam* (do-it-yourself pork belly wraps) preparations in town. If there's still room for more, the *ton dak* (spicy chicken wings) and *hamul pajun* (seafood pancake) are the way to go.

FURTHER EXPLORATION: DAN SUNG SA

Slightly less dingy than Dwit Gol Mok but equally festive is **Dan Sung Sa** (3317 W. 6th St., Los Angeles, CA 90020; 213-487-9100), located a quarter mile from DGM. The seafood pancake and spicy pork are just the things to soak up *soju* shots.

Elf Cafe, 2135 W. Sunset Blvd., Los Angeles, CA 90026; (213) 484-6829; elfcafe.com; Vegetarian; $$. Vegetarians dining out are usually stuck ordering less-than-thoughtful pastas and salads, but here at Echo Park's Elf Cafe, Chef Scott Zwiezen prepares creative meatless fare that satisfies herbivores and carnivores alike. Reservations are encouraged at this barely 450-square-foot jewel box, especially on Saturday and Sunday nights when tables are at a premium. Elf can feel admittedly tight and cramped at times, but thankfully the chill crowd keeps the mood appealing. What's unique about Chef Zwiezen's cooking is his firm commitment to using vegetables instead of meatlike wheat gluten and soy products. Perhaps the best example of his culinary style is the Cornmeal- and Herb-Dusted Buffalo Oyster Mushrooms, skillfully charred and marinated tubers served with a marinated celery salad and blue cheese cream reduction. Take a bite of all three elements together for a one-of-a-kind hot wings experience. Follow it up with the Spicy Moroccan Kale Salad, a tangy mountain of raw kale, avocado, and sheep's-milk feta that boasts a mellow spice from the house-made harissa. The Collard Green Dolma, one of the restaurant's strongest main courses, wraps collard greens around grilled mushrooms with crisp risotto croquettes and house-made goat yogurt tzatziki served on the side. To satisfy vegan diners, most everything on the menu can be prepared without animal products upon request.

FURTHER EXPLORATION: SHOJIN

Hidden on the third floor of the Little Tokyo Shopping Center in Downtown is **Shojin** (333 S. Alameda St., #310, Los Angeles, CA 90013; 213-617-0305; theshojin.com). Specializing in Japanese vegan cuisine, Shojin's candlelit space and hushed service exude Zen-like peace, while the delicately flavored food is a visual feast.

Flavors of Belize, 1271 S. La Brea Blvd., Los Angeles, CA 90019; (323) 937-7710; Belizean; $. Anywhere else in America it might seem strange that the best Belizean restaurant in town is located in a motel complex, but here in Los Angeles, no one bats an eye—culinary diamonds in the rough are our specialty. Situated near the front desk of the pretty pink Relax Inn Motel on La Brea, Flavors of Belize nourishes vagabonds and visitors with its soulful brand of Central American cooking. The appetizers section is filled with a bevy of crunchy bites like *garnaches*, Belizean tostadas slathered with refried beans, a saucy tomato and onion mixture, and powdery Parmesan. Who knew the stuff in the green can worked so well atop expertly spiced legumes? The *salbutes*, hollowed tortilla shells filled with shredded chicken, onions, peppers, and tomatoes, as well as the *panades*, meat pies stuffed with fish, chicken, or refried beans, make for solid starters as well. Ask for the house-made habanero sauce to kick up anything and everything. Choose any of the homey stews on offer for a fitting follow-up. While the oxtail and chicken varieties are sure to satisfy, it's the Pig Tail with Split Peas served with coconut rice, fried sweet plantains, and potato salad that's unforgettable. The weekend special "boil-up" comprising braised cured pig tails and starchy vegetables covered in a dumpling shroud is also not to be missed. Be sure to call ahead to confirm availability.

Ganda Siamese Cuisine, 5269 Hollywood Blvd., Los Angeles, CA 90027; (323) 466-4281; Thai; $. Heat lamps don't usually signal deliciousness, but some of the best Thai food in Los Angeles is found on the steam tables at Ganda Siamese Cuisine. Chef-Owner Sue Klinmalai rotates the selection of curries, braises, and stir-fries available each day, but expect to find two dozen or so dishes that are carefully made and intensely flavored. The array of offerings can be a bit daunting for the uninitiated, so feel free to ask the gals behind the counter for further details since most of the dishes aren't labeled. The crispy catfish (*pla duk pad ped*) is the restaurant's most popular dish, and for very good reason. The central Thai specialty, dry-braised in galangal, Kaffir lime leaves, and a plethora of spices, delivers on all fronts—crisp, sweet, savory, and spicy. The pork and green bean *prik king*, a dry curry with plenty of chiles and aromatics, packs an equally mean punch. When it comes to curries, the green one brimming with house-made fish balls is a creamy and comforting brew that's mild enough to sip straight up or to spoon over rice. The made-from-scratch sour sausages aren't included in the two- or three-item combos, but are worth the extra add-on. For just under $10, you'll be treated to one of the boldest, spiciest, and most deeply flavorful meals in town.

Genwa Korean BBQ, 5115 Wilshire Blvd., Los Angeles, CA 90036; (323) 549-0760; genwakoreanbbq.com; Korean; $$. While it's hard to resist the bargain of all-you-can-eat Korean barbecue, there are occasions when something more refined, but just as meaty, is in order. Genwa Korean BBQ is part of a pack of places that serve higher-quality beef in spiffier environs. The prices tend to be a few notches higher, but the quality of the food and service warrants the slight bump. Twenty varieties of pitch-perfect *banchan* are spread atop the table as soon as diners settle in. From there, appetizers and proteins (beef, pork, chicken, and seafood) can be ordered a la carte, or choose one of the set menus that feed anywhere from two to ten people. Start with kimchee-stuffed dumplings (*mandu*) and seafood pancakes, then move on to prime *galbi* (marinated short ribs), prime *bulgogi* (marinated beef), and best of all, *kot sal*, thinly sliced prime boneless short ribs. There's also *sam gyup sal*, pork belly marinated in a spicy miso sauce. Every protein can be cooked tableside on the miraculous "smokeless grills" or prepared in the kitchen and brought to the table while still sizzling. Rice, soups, and noodles make for the perfect ending.

FURTHER EXPLORATION:
CHOSUN GALBEE AND PARK'S BBQ

Chosun Galbee (3330 W. Olympic Blvd., Los Angeles, CA 90019; 323-734-3330; chosungalbee.com) and **Park's BBQ** (955 S. Vermont Ave., Los Angeles, CA 90006; 213-380-1717; parksbbq.com), both located in Koreatown, are also known for offering quality meats and top-notch service. See Park's BBQ's recipe for **Bulgogi** on page 306.

Gish Bac Restaurant, 4163 W. Washington Blvd., Los Angeles, CA 90018; (323) 737-5050; gishbacrestaurant.com; Mexican; $$. A meal at Gish Bac is memorable any day of the week, but especially on Saturday and Sunday when owners David Padilla and Maria Ramos fire up the barbecue pit. The Oaxacan natives churn out two types of *barbacoa*. While the *blanca* consists of lamb, the enchilada is all goat; both are perfumed with avocado leaves and roasted until exceptionally tender. Served alongside the lamb are Oaxacan black beans and a bowl of rich consommé made from the meat's drippings. The goat, on the other hand, arrives sopping in its own juices along with warm tortillas and a cabbage slaw for wrapping and garnishing. For further pizzazz, scope out the condiment bar featuring a number of worthwhile salsas. Both the *blanca* and enchilada are preceded by a platter of *pancita*, a haggislike creation of lamb offals flavored with chiles and stuffed in a whole stomach. Available every day of the week are made-from-scratch moles that glisten and shine. The *mole negro* served over chicken sings of sweet and savory spices.

FURTHER EXPLORATION: EL BORREGO DE ORO

Weekends bring Hidalgo-style *barbacoa* to Boyle Heights' **El Borrego de Oro** (2403 Whittier Blvd., Los Angeles, CA 90023; 323-780-4213; see borregodeoro.com for more locations). Mutton is covered with maguey leaves and pit-roasted for hours before being dished up with a side of tortillas and consommé. Delicious.

Guelaguetza Restaurante, 3014 W. Olympic Blvd., Los Angeles, CA 90006; (213) 427-0608; guelaguetzarestaurante.com; Mexican; $$. As you gaze around the expansive 300-seat dining room at Guelaguetza's Koreatown flagship, it's hard to imagine that the restaurant only fit three tables when Fernando Lopez Sr. opened it in 1994. Today, the temple of Oaxacan delights is outfitted with a sleek mescal bar and a central stage for mariachi and *folklorico* performances. Lopez's four children, Bricia, Paulina, Fernando Jr., and Elizabeth, grew up working at Guelaguetza and now oversee its day-to-day operations. While the restaurant has expanded and contracted over the years, the stellar cooking by matriarch Maria Monterrubio that made the place a dining destination has remained dependably delicious over time. *Tlayudas,* crisp flatbreads smeared with black beans and *asiento* (unrefined pork lard) and topped with stringy Oaxacan cheese, chorizo, *queso fresco*, lettuce, and meat, are perfect for sharing before diving into a sea of moles. The pitch-black *mole negro* is rightfully famous with its 26 ingredients and unparalleled sweet and savory depth. It's sauced over chicken, stuffed in banana leaf–wrapped tamales, ladled atop enchiladas, and even jarred to take home. There's a spicier *mole rojo* and milder *mole coloradito* for further exploration. Be sure to cap off any meal here with something sweet. The *nicuatole*, a gelatinous dessert made of ground corn and sugar with hints of cinnamon and cactus fruit flavors, is as traditional as they come. Oaxacan hot chocolate is served with *pan de yema* (sweet bread) on the side. See Guelaguetza's recipe for **Mole Negro** on page 295.

Ham Ji Park, 3407 W. 6th St., #101C, Los Angeles, CA 90020; (213) 365-8773; **Korean; $$.** The restaurants in Los Angeles' Koreatown are wonderfully specialized places where one or two dishes reign supreme. Here at Ham Ji Park, it's all about *gamjatang*, a pork bone and potato stew that bubbles its way to the table in a metal pot. Glossy grains of steamed rice and a half dozen or so *banchan* complete a feast that satisfies and comforts like few can. When ladling the stew into bowls, make sure to include pieces of pork spine; these meaty hunks of tendon, muscle, and fat are what make *gamjatang* simply spectacular, that and the spicy yet nuanced broth that tastes even better once it has thickened some from residual heat. Spine meat can be difficult to extract using chopsticks alone, so don't be shy about employing nimble fingers—it's how the pros get it done. Ham Ji Park's pork spare ribs are also worthy of gracing your table. Bone-in slabs are coated in a sticky sweet glaze and served on a sizzling platter over a bed of softened white onions. The green salad served alongside offers the perfect cooling, savory counterpoint.

Hatfield's Restaurant, 6703 Melrose Ave., Los Angeles, CA 90038; (323) 935-2977; **hatfieldsrestaurant.com; New American; $$$$.** Named after the husband-and-wife duo who run the show, Hatfield's Restaurant is a perennial favorite among locals who appreciate thoughtful food, seamless service, and an enchanting space that's swathed in natural tones and home to one of the city's most exciting open kitchens. While Quinn Hatfield focuses on savories, his wife,

Karen, is charged with sweets. Together, the two Hatfields have created a dining experience that is perfect for every occasion, from birthdays to dates to friendly gatherings. Quinn's *croque-madame* is the stuff dreams are made of. Pristine slices of yellowtail sashimi and prosciutto come smothered between two buttery rounds of grilled brioche. A sunny side up quail egg provides a delicate finish. Karen's desserts are always playful, beautifully plated, and a treat for the senses. Her fried-to-order sugar-and-spice beignets, which are served with a Venezuelan chocolate fondue and a cool shot of Mexican chocolate milk shake, are as crowd pleasing as they come.

FURTHER EXPLORATION: THE SYCAMORE KITCHEN

Hatfield's Quinn and Karen opened **The Sycamore Kitchen** (143 S. La Brea, Los Angeles, CA 90036; 323-939-0151; the sycamorekitchen.com), a bakery and cafe in Mid-City, during the summer of 2012. While the sandwiches and salads here are standard fare, the ever-changing bakery case is simply irresistible. Karen has a way with flour, butter, and sugar, especially when it comes to the sticky sweet babka roll.

Hoan Kiem, 727 N. Broadway, #130, Los Angeles, CA 90012; (213) 617-3650; Vietnamese; $. Named after Hanoi's misty and mystical Sword Lake, Hoan Kiem serves just three dishes on weekdays and four on weekends. While the kitchen's repertoire might seem limited, the menu has actually doubled in size since the Ho family first opened the restaurant in 1989. The proprietors, who hail from Halong Bay, a city more famous for its limestone karsts and isles than its cuisine, draw upon family recipes that have been passed down for several generations in executing each of their specialties. The *banh cuon* (steamed crepes filled with ground pork and wood ear mushrooms) is chewier than its Saigon and Hanoi counterparts, signaling the presence of more tapioca starch in the mostly rice flour batter. The *nuoc cham* (fish sauce vinaigrette) served alongside, as well as the slices of pork loaf, is wholly familiar. The *pho ga* (chicken noodle soup) is a soothing mix of clear broth and rice noodles. Chopped cilantro, thinly sliced onions, and a few shakes of pure fish sauce are the only garnishes this pristinely made bowl needs. The latest menu additions, the Hoan Kiem Chicken with Rice and the Hoan Kiem Beef Noodle Soup, are executed with the same care as the mainstays.

Ink, 8360 Melrose Ave., Los Angeles, CA 90069; (323) 651-5866; mvink.com; New American; $$$. Chef Michael Voltaggio, the former chef de cuisine at José Andrés' Bazaar and the winner of season six of Bravo's *Top Chef*, opened his highly anticipated first restaurant in 2011 on a stretch of Melrose more known for its fashion than for its fare. Here at Ink, in a minimally appointed space painted a shadowy shade of gray, the chef creates "modern Los Angeles cuisine" that marries inventive techniques with surprising flavor combinations and highly stylized plating. The food here is playful, beautiful, thoughtful, and almost always delicious. Order family style from the a la carte menu (three to four dishes per person is recommended) or indulge in a four-course tasting plus dessert orchestrated by the kitchen. While the former allows for freedom, the latter features unique dishes not available on the a la carte menu. For those ordering plate-by-plate, the duck rillettes served with savory waffle crisps, griddled pear, and a ribbon of jellified mustard are familiar yet innovative. The corn porridge, a marvelously mushy mash of sweet kernels and nori (dried seaweed), is topped with house-made "doritos" reminiscent of Vietnamese shrimp chips. The brussels sprouts, halved and draped in house-cured *lardo*, are accented with a tangle of fried pig ears and a tart green applesauce. The sweets here are as exciting as the savories. The Burnt Wood Ice Cream, infused with applewood ashes, sings of smoke and is paired with a caramel tart, compressed green apple, and an apple juice *gelée*.

FURTHER EXPLORATION: INK SACK

Chef Voltaggio debuted **Ink Sack** (8360 Melrose Ave., #107, Los Angeles, CA 90069; 323-655-7225; mvink.com) a few months prior to opening Ink. Here at this sandwich shop located a few doors down from the flagship restaurant, classic sandwiches are elevated by premium ingredients and refined techniques. The José Andrés (aka The Spanish Godfather) includes a smattering of charcuterie and cheeses, while the Cold Fried Chicken comes slathered in house-made ranch dressing and hot sauce.

Jae Bu Do, 474 N. Western Ave., Los Angeles, CA 90004; (323) 467-2900; Korean; $$$. Gather a group of seafood-loving friends and head to Jae Bu Do for Korean-style tableside grilling that's interactive, slightly dangerous, and all the way delicious. The menu offers three different options based on the number of individuals at the table—the larger the group, the more variety you'll be treated to. Before grilling commences, small *banchan* are sent out from the kitchen. The cheese- and mayonnaise-laden corn served on a skillet is strangely addicting, while the fish and shrimp Korean ceviche is mildly spicy with a strong sesame kick. When it's time to fire up the grill, a bevy of raw seafood arrives on an impressive wooden vessel. From clams to abalone to mussels to shrimp to octopus to oysters to scallops, every fruit of the sea eventually meets its fate on the grill. Best of all are the knife-cut noodles served at the very end of the meal. You'll likely be filled to the brim at this point, but make room for a slurp or two because this comforting soup is worth it.

Jeon Ju, 2716 W. Olympic Blvd., #101, Los Angeles, CA 90006; (213) 386-5678; Korean; $$. Sizzling stone bowls heaped with steamed rice and a rainbow of vegetables and topped with a wobbly egg are the specialty at this Koreatown stalwart. Just before digging in, combine all of the ingredients together along with a few squirts of *gochujang* (fermented red chile paste) and a drizzle of sesame oil. This process of mixing and mingling the components earned this dish its name, *bibimbap,* which means "mixed meal" or "mixed rice" in Korean. While there are a couple of *bibimbap* varieties listed on the menu, the one with *kalbi* (marinated beef) is the most flavorful. When the *bibimbap* first arrives at the table, hissing and searing like it means business, leave it be so that a nice, crisp crust can form. Only stir after the sound effects have subsided. Also delightful on the menu is the *doenjang chigae* (soybean paste stew) that's served with purple rice. It arrives steaming and bubbling aggressively in a clay pot with cubes of silken tofu and stalks of virtuous greens floating about. The stew's flavors are mild, but intriguing, and provide a great contrast to the spicy sizzling *bibimbap* sharing table real estate. Try the fermented soybean paste stew for a funkier stew experience.

Jitlada, 5233 Sunset Blvd., Los Angeles, CA 90027; (323) 667-9809; jitladala.com; Thai; $$. Chef Suthiporn Tui Sungkamee re-creates the recipes from his native southern Thailand, the district of Pak Phanang to be exact, at this Thaitown gem. Jitlada's unique menu highlighting sour, spicy, funky, and fermented flavors has not only set it apart from neighboring restaurants serving the typical pad thai and *tom yum* but has also attracted critical acclaim both locally and nationally. Plenty of good press and buzz from foodies near and far means a seat can be tough to snag, especially on weekend evenings, but persevere because the food is worth it. Jitlada is a family affair at its heart. While Chef

Tui manages the kitchen, his sister Sarintip "Jazz" Singsanong makes sure that every diner is well taken care of. First-timers must order the Crispy Morning Glory Salad to start, where stalks of water spinach are battered, fried, and topped with fresh shrimp and a tangy dressing. Another must-order is the green-lipped New Zealand mussels that are steamed with lemongrass, chiles, garlic, basil, and Kaffir lime. Be sure to slurp the fragrant broth once the mussels have disappeared. If a curry's in the cards, try the green one with fish balls stuffed with salted duck eggs or the eye-wateringly spicy jungle curry.

Jun Won, 3100 W. 8th St. #101, Los Angeles, CA 90005; (213) 383-8855; Korean; $$. Jun Won makes the kind of everyday fare that Korean moms and grandmas prepare for their brood. Opened in 1994 by Jung Ye Jun, the restaurant can be difficult to find. Park and enter through the back, following the signs that read KOREAN RESTAURANT, of course. The seafood-centric bill of fare is printed onto place mats, but before getting down to deciding what to order, take a moment to relish the *banchan* scattered about the table. Jun Won's regulars swing by three to four times each week, so Jun makes sure to change up these little nibbles every day. Fermented squid, several varieties of kimchee, wilted sprouts, marinated cucumbers, and fish cakes are constantly rotated in and out. The portions here are quite large, and the prices reflect the bounty. The pan-fried fish is particularly excellent. Whether it's yellow corvine, mackerel, belt fish, or seasonal trout, the expert cooking assures that the flesh is dependably moist, while the skin crisps up like a dream. A squeeze of fresh lemon juice is the only accent needed. Another simple yet spectacularly well-executed dish is the "steamed" mackerel, cod, or pollock that is slowly simmered in a chile-garlic sauce with daikon and heaps of onions and scallions. Accompanying every dish is a house-special rice blend made with a trio of grains (barley, sweet brown rice, and white rice) and even more legumes (black beans, peas, kidney beans, and white beans). Moving beyond fishes are seafood pancakes and sautéed octopus, squid, pork, and beef.

> ## FURTHER EXPLORATION: SOBAN
>
> Turn to **Soban** (4001 W. Olympic Blvd., Los Angeles, CA 90019; 323-936-9106; sobanusa.com) in Koreatown for slightly fancier, but still quite homey, Korean cooking. The spicy *galbi jjim* (short rib stew) and the *ganjang gaejang* (raw crabs marinated in soy sauce) are the two signature dishes.

Kagaya, 418 E. 2nd St., Los Angeles, CA 90012; (213) 617-1016; Japanese; $$$$. There are plenty of places to swish-swish around town, but no restaurant does it better than Masato Kagaya's nearly two-decade-old Kagaya in Little Tokyo. Small groups of friends and family gather here for soul-warming *shabu-shabu*, a festive meal centered on a communal hot pot served with various meats and vegetables for dipping. For those dining solo, the seats along the counter offer individual burners with a terrific view of the chefs at work. What sets Kagaya apart from other hot pot spots is the quality of meat offered—Japanese Wagyu (Grade A5) and USDA prime rib. While the former is mesmerizingly marbled, the latter boasts a beefier profile. Additionally, there's a purely seafood hot pot selection, as well as a meat and seafood combination. Tofu, glass noodles, and an assortment of vegetables including Napa cabbage, shiitake mushrooms, and chrysanthemum are also on hand for swishing. Two sauces, a citrusy *ponzu* and an aromatic sesame seed one, are served alongside for flavoring as one sees fit. Once the meat and vegetables have disappeared, the remaining broth is whisked away to the kitchen and transformed into a soothing *udon* noodle soup or *zosui*, a tart rice porridge made with pickled plums. Both choices make for a mighty fine finish.

Kobawoo House, 698 S. Vermont Ave., #109, Los Angeles, CA 90005; (213) 389-7300; Korean; $$. Mention Kobawoo House to anyone who regularly dines in Koreatown and chances are good that their eyes will light up and their mouths will water. This porky palace has been around since 1983, and the crowds haven't let up one bit in the past 30 years. The star here is the *bossam*, a platter of pork belly that's wrapped in slices of radish or salted Napa cabbage and accented with marinated radishes, kimchee, or jalapeños. There's also a soy-based dipping sauce served on the side for additional zing. It's a do-it-yourself affair that's as fun to construct as it is to eat. Kobawoo's *bossam* brings a landslide of flavors and textures with every bite. The pork belly strikes a swell balance between meaty and fatty, while the thinly sliced vegetables wrap each parcel tidily. Since pork belly alone does not make a meal, add on a *haemul pajun*, a seafood-stuffed pancake that's packed with chives and octopus, crisp on the outside, and tender within. The *jang ban guk su*, a dish of clear acorn noodles tossed with herbs, julienned vegetables, and a spicy-sweet dressing, plays well with others.

Kyochon Chicken, 3833 W. 6th St., Los Angeles, CA 90020; (213) 739-9292; Korean; $. Twice-fried sweet-spicy chicken has long been a favorite in Korean homes and eateries. Nineteen years ago in a small shop in Gumi, South Korea, a restaurant owner named Kwon Won Kang added his own savory garlic-soy dressing to double-fried wings and drumsticks, and the specialty known as *yangnyeom dak* (Korean fried chicken) took off as a fast-food phenomenon. Today, the business Kwon founded, called Kyochon, has more than 1,000 outlets worldwide and four branches in Los Angeles. The restaurant's popularity is no surprise. Its wings and drumsticks, served on platters in the brightly lit shop, are unfailingly juicy inside, crunchy on the outside, and glazed with one of two delicious house sauces: hot-sweet or garlic-soy. The heat from the hot-sweet glazed ones has a way of lingering on the palate, so be sure to purchase pickled daikon radishes to quell the burning.

FURTHER EXPLORATION: CHICKEN DAY

The Korean fried clucks at Koreatown's **Chicken Day** (301 S. Western Ave., Los Angeles, CA 90020; 213-387-9933; 2383 Foothill Blvd., La Crescenta, CA 91214; 818-957-9933) come coated in a unique 27-ingredient sauce that includes cinnamon, cloves, and Chinese five-spice.

La Caridad, 2619 W. Sunset Blvd., Los Angeles, CA 90026; (213) 484-0099; Cuban; $$. La Caridad stood at the intersection of Temple and Alvarado for nearly a quarter century before owner Orestes Garcia moved it to grander digs in 2012. Newly perched on a sunny stretch of Sunset Boulevard, the dining room, awash in natural light and adorned with colorful painted murals, is finally fitting of the kitchen's standout

FURTHER EXPLORATION: VERSAILLES

Versailles has been synonymous with Cuban food in Los Angeles ever since Orlando Garcia and his son William opened the first location in West Los Angeles in 1981 (1415 S. La Cienega, Los Angeles, CA 90034; 310-289-0392; versaillescuban.com). The *lechon asado* (Cuban-style roasted pork) and the *Famoso Pollo Versailles* (roasted garlic chicken) are as popular as ever. The father-son duo has since opened three additional locations. 10319 Venice Blvd., Los Angeles, CA 90034; (310) 558-3168 17410 Ventura Blvd., Encino, CA 91316; (818) 906-0756 1000 N. Sepulveda Blvd., Manhattan Beach, CA 90266; (310) 937-6829.

cooking. While one would be happy enough ordering a well-constructed *Cubano* or a *media noche* sandwich here, it's the daily specials that shine brightest. If you happen to dine when the *rabo encendido* is on offer, snatch up these oxtails on the double. Served with rice and black beans, or *moro*, a combination of both, the oxtails are meaty yet gelatinous and tender throughout. The spicing isn't the least bit incendiary, despite what the name implies. Another special worth looking out for is the *pierna de puerco asada*, a roasted leg of pork complete with crispy skin and fork-tender meat. While the slow-cooked specials are really something, the standard menu isn't a slouch. The *arroz con calamares* (rice with squid) is dyed a wicked shade of black courtesy of the squid's ink. Every platter comes with the choice of caramelized sweet plantains or garlicky yucca—both are well executed.

La Cevicheria, 3809 W. Pico Blvd., Los Angeles, CA 90019; (323) 732-1253; Guatemalan; $$. If seafood swimming in citrus and herbs is your kind of thing, then you'll be happy as a bloody clam at Julio and Carolina Orellana's La Cevicheria. The Guatemalan duo opened the restaurant in 2002, serving an array of pan-Latin seafood preparations including tacos, stews, *cocteles*, and of course, ceviches. The midnight brew atop every table is the *concha negra*, a murky mix of bloody clams, tomatoes, onions, avocado, mint, lime juice, and Worcestershire sauce. Add shrimp, octopus, or both to your goblet for no extra cost. The bloody clams, which are delivered to the restaurant twice a week from Baja and points south, are snappy little things that aren't as gory as their name implies. The tangy marinade makes this dish the one to try. For those who suffer from hemophobia, dig into the *chapin*, a Guatemalan-style ceviche with shrimp, imitation crab, octopus, tomatoes, onions, avocado, mint, lime juice, and Worcestershire sauce, or any of the *Tostadas de Ceviche* (shrimp, fish, crab, and octopus). Make sure to request a squeeze bottle of the house-made yellow mustard and habanero chile sauce—it pairs magnificently with the barely rare fruits of the sea. The *Mariscada Caribeña*, a Caribbean-style coconut milk-based seafood stew served warm over rice, offers a comforting contrast to the sea of ceviches.

La 27th Restaurante Familiar Nicaraguense, 1830 W. Pico Blvd., Los Angeles, CA 90006; (213) 387-2467; Nicaraguan; $. Yolanda and Hernaldo Gutierrez opened La 27th Restaurante in 2001 after operating an informal eatery from their home for six years. The restaurant's name is a nod to their previous location on 27th Street where it all began. The boisterous crowds that frequented the old spot have made their way to the new location for the Gutierrezes' unrivaled Nicaraguan fare. The Chunk Squash, a hollowed-out zucchini stuffed with ricotta's saltier and grittier cousin and blanketed with a fluffy omelet, makes for a wonderful appetizer. To keep the cheesiness from becoming monotonous, spoon on some of the *cebollita*, a lightly pickled and spiced diced onion condiment—there's a jar on every table. The plantain leaf–wrapped *nacatamal*, a Nicaraguan-style tamale delicately textured and stuffed with spice-rubbed chicken and bell peppers, is hefty enough to make a meal or to share as a starter. The latter is recommended because room needs to be saved for the Fritanga a la 27th, a monstrously portioned platter composed of three different proteins (steak, pork, and chorizo), sweet plantains, plantain chips, rice and beans, fried cheese, and a cabbage slaw. The snappy, well-seasoned chorizo, as well as the squeaky squares of cheese, is nothing short of glorious. The weekends-only *mondongo*, a vegetable and beef tripe soup, brings all the hungover Nicaraguans to the 27th.

Little Next Door, 8164 W. 3rd St., Los Angeles, CA 90048; (323) 951-1210; thelittledoor.com; French; $$. Little Next Door, a charming Parisian brasserie, wine bar, and marketplace on 3rd Street, attracts a steady crowd of Francophiles, French expats, and pretty peo- ple shopping in the neighborhood. Some swing in briefly for a baguette or pastries, while others linger over cafe au lait and flaky croissants smothered in house-made jams and preserves. And then there are those who come ready to indulge in heartier fare, French classics prepared extraordinarily

Gourmet Food Trucks

Street-side delights have always been a part of the Los Angeles dining landscape, but with the launch of the Kogi truck by Chef Roy Choi, the mobile dining game's been forever changed. From "slutty" breakfast sandwiches to Maine lobster rolls, gourmet food trucks continue to offer Angelenos on the go something to really sink their teeth into.

Buttermilk Truck, follow @ButtermilkTruck on Twitter for location updates; Breakfast; $. Aboard the Buttermilk Truck, founder and chef Gigi Pascua serves inventive breakfast delights at all hours of the day. The Morning Menu brings french toast sticks made from sweet and soft Hawaiian bread, made-from-scratch Powdered Cake Donuts with a cinnamon vanilla glaze, and best of all, red velvet chocolate chip pancakes. The highlight of the Late Night Menu is the fried chicken with cinnamon waffles.

Egg Slut, follow @EggSlutLA on Twitter for location updates; Breakfast; $. While most gourmet food trucks land someplace new every day, the folks at Egg Slut can be found on weekdays 7 to 10 a.m. at Coffee Commissary on Fairfax and on weekends 9 a.m. to 1 p.m. at Handsome Coffee Roasters Downtown. The truck's signature dish is "The Slut," a soft-boiled egg layered with potato puree, topped with gray salt and chives, and served in a glass jar with crostini alongside for dipping.

well: terrines, country-style pâté, and rillettes to start, steak frites to follow, and a lemon tart to finish. Bordeaux-born brothers Frederic and Nicolas Meschin opened the casual spot in 2006 following the success of their more intimate restaurant The Little Door located a few paces away. Little Next Door captures a piece of Parisian cafe life like few French restaurants in town can.

The Gastrobus, follow @TheGastrobus on Twitter for location updates; New American; $. Catch The Gastrobus on Organic Sundays at the Los Feliz Farmers Market, where J. Antonio Medina, a former Wolfgang Puck chef, and his wife, Lana, prepare reasonably priced food using market produce. Depending on the day's haul, expect to find delightful bites like ricotta doughnut holes with strawberry sauce, tomato confit omelets, and barbecue ribs with corn flapjacks, citrus coleslaw, and pickled watermelon.

Grill 'Em All, follow @GrillEmAllTruck on Twitter for location updates; American; $. Heavy metal and gourmet burgers collide aboard chefs Ryan Harkins and Matthew Chernus' Grill 'Em All truck. As the winners of Food Network's *The Great Food Truck Race*, these guys know a thing or two about constructing memorable and delicious burgers, like the Dee Snider with peanut butter, jelly, bacon, and Sriracha, and the Molly Hatchet with seared fennel sausage gravy, bacon, and maple syrup.

Grilled Cheese Truck, follow @grlldcheesetruk on Twitter for location updates; American; $. There's always a formidable line snaking away from Dave Dahni's Grilled Cheese Truck, where comfort food is at its best. The truck's signature sandwiches come either plain and simple with just butter, bread (white or wheat), and cheese (American, cheddar, gruyère, brie, or habanero jack) or gussied up with things like barbecued pork, caramelized onions, and even smothered pork chops. A cup or "shot" of tomato soup and tater tots with sea salt serve as fitting foils to the cheesy menu.

Lotería! Grill, Stall #322 at the Original Farmers Market; (323) 930-2211; loteriagrill.com; Mexican; $$. After devoting nearly two decades to an advertising and film production career, Jimmy Shaw left the Hollywood scene behind to open Lotería! Grill at the Original Farmers Market on 3rd and Fairfax in 2002. His aim from the start was to share the regional dishes of his native Mexico in a modern and

Gourmet Food Trucks Continued

India Jones Chow Truck, follow @IndiaJonesCT on Twitter for location updates; Indian; $. Chef Sumant Pardal, a native of Jaipur, India, launched the India Jones Chow Truck to share Punjabi specialties like butter chicken and lamb *biryani* with food lovers across the city. The menu also features *frankies* (roti wraps with cilantro and tamarind chutneys and chopped onions), *parathas* (spicy stuffed roti served with yogurt), and curries.

Jogasaki Truck, follow @JogasakiBurrito on Twitter for location updates; Japanese; $. A sombrero-donning samurai is a fitting mascot for Jogasaki, a sushi burrito slangin' truck. Here, jumbo sushi rolls are constructed from flour tortillas or soy paper and stuffed with a hodgepodge of fixings including spicy tuna, crabmeat, eel, shrimp tempura, avocado, cucumber, and lobster. In addition to sushi burritos, there are funky dishes like Spicy Tuna Nachos ($5), Dorritos topped with spicy tuna, avocado, and eel sauce.

Kogi, follow @kogibbq on Twitter for location updates; Korean; $. Chef Roy Choi sparked a nationwide gourmet food truck trend when he fused Korean and Mexican cuisines aboard the Kogi truck. Here, tacos, quesadillas, and burritos come stuffed with Korean marinated proteins like short ribs and pork and garnished with a

comfortable setting. With Lotería! Grill locations now in Santa Monica, Studio City, Downtown, Westlake Village, and Hollywood, in addition to the taqueria stand that started it all, it is clear that his vision has resonated with Angelenos in a big way. Located smack-dab in the center of the eternally lively market, Lotería! Grill looks and feels as playful as the Mexican game of chance that it's named after. Breakfast is served all day here, including the *huevos divorciados*, two fried eggs served on fried corn tortillas with a Christmassy splash of *salsa ranchera* and *salsa* light and bright slaw tossed in a chile-soy vinaigrette, sesame oil, and fresh lime juice. This is what Los Angeles tastes like. See Chef Choi's recipe for **Kimchi Quesadillas** on page 320.

Lobsta Truck, follow @lobstatruck on Twitter for location updates; Seafood; $. Inspired by a lobster roll bender through Maine, Justin Mi launched the Lobsta Truck to bring the simple, clean, and satisfying flavors of New England seafood to Los Angeles. In addition to its signature lobster rolls served on toasted, split-top buns, the truck also offers crab rolls, clam chowder, whoopie pies, and fresh-squeezed lemonade.

Ludo Truck, follow @LudoTruck on Twitter for location updates; French; $. It takes three full days to prepare Chef Ludo Lefebvre's rosemary and herbes de Provence–infused fried chicken, the Ludo Truck's signature item. Composed of boneless dark meat magically bound together by a crisp and golden batter, the fried chicken balls are juicy as all get out. Also memorable onboard are the Honey-Glazed Garlic Wings with a sweet and savory glaze that penetrates straight through to the meat. The honey lavender biscuits never fail to sell out, so show up early to avoid disappointment.

verde. There are also three versions of *chilaquiles*, smothered tortilla chips garnished with *queso fresco* and *crema*. The one sautéed in the complex and earthy *mole poblano* is simply irresistible. The heart of every taco is a thick, homemade corn tortilla. Sample the ones stuffed with *chicharron en salsa verde* (pork rinds stewed in a spicy tomatillo sauce) and *carne deshebrada* (shredded beef, fresh guacamole, and *salsa roja de chipotle*). Visit the Hollywood, Studio City, and Santa Monica locations for larger menus featuring composed plates and free-flowing margaritas. **Additional Location:** 6627 Hollywood Blvd., Los Angeles, CA 90028; (323) 465-2500. See Jimmy Shaw's recipe for **Salsa Verde Chilaquiles** on page 297.

Lucques, 8474 Melrose Ave., Los Angeles, CA 90048; (323) 655-6277; lucques.com; New American; $$$. After refining her culinary chops at some of the world's best restaurants including Paris' L'Arpège and Berkeley's Chez Panisse, Suzanne Goin opened Lucques in 1998 with her business partner, Caroline Styne. Here in this beautifully appointed former carriage house, diners are treated to thoughtful dishes inspired by the seasons; the flavors lean toward Mediterranean with one foot firmly planted in California. The menu changes every few days depending on what's available at the market, but every meal begins with thick slices of crusty bread accompanied by butter, *fleur de sel*, and a dish of toasted almonds and Lucques olives, a variety grown primarily in Languedoc, France. To start, select one of the expertly composed salads. Fall brings bountiful kabocha squash, brussels sprouts, and carrots, while summer promises nectarines, arugula, and Medjool dates. The main

FURTHER EXPLORATION: A.O.C. AND TAVERN

Following the tremendous success of Lucques, Suzanne Goin and Caroline Styne joined forces again to open **A.O.C.** (8700 W. 3rd St., Los Angeles, CA 90048; 310-859-9859; aocwine bar.com), a small plates and wine-driven concept in Mid-City, and **Tavern** (11648 San Vicente Blvd., Los Angeles, CA 90049; 310-806-6464; tavernla.com), a casual neighborhood restaurant in Brentwood with a full retail market, Tavern Larder.

courses are a study in seasonality as well, with apricots served along-side harissa-grilled lamb sirloin in the summer and veal cheeks with winter squash and chanterelles during colder months. Available year-round are Lucques classics like the braised beef short ribs with Swiss chard, roasted cippolinis, and horseradish cream, and the Grilled Club Steak for Two.

Ma Dang Gook Soo, 869 S. Western Ave., #1, Los Angeles, CA 90005; Korean; $. Comfort cuisine reigns supreme at Ma Dang Gook Soo, a charming den of Korean home cooking. Ladies donning red-striped aprons are quick to pour glasses of iced barley tea as menus are perused and considered. The food photographs plastered overhead are helpful in narrowing down the array of options. The Korean dumplings (*mandu*) stuffed with minced pork, tofu, and scallions are particularly good here, especially with a dab of vinegar and soy sauce. *Kimbap*, a Korean sushi roll of sorts studded with egg, fish cakes, vegetables, pickled radish, and ham, is a kaleidoscope of colors and flavors. The most alluring dish on the menu is the namesake *kal gook soo*, steaming bowls of knife-cut noodles served in a chicken, clam, anchovy, or kim-chee (fermented cabbage) broth. The soup's subdued flavors allow for the irregularly edged and toothsome noodles to soak up the spotlight. A garnet-tinged condiment made from scallions, garlic, and chiles is on hand to add some zip to the soup if need be. The Cold Soy Bean Noodles are a subtle but satisfying choice for those who can warm up to a frothy and frosty bowl of noodle soup.

Mapo Kkak Doo Gee, 3611 W. 6th St., Los Angeles, CA 90020; (213) 736-6668; Korean; $$. One of the perks of dining in Koreatown is the free and refillable *banchan* served alongside every meal. While it's always nice to receive something for nothing, it is rarely the case that these pickled and marinated nibbles are as memorable as the main course. Here at Mapo Kkak Doo Gee, the *banchan* are so remark-ably good that chopsticks can't help but reach for more. There are several varieties of kimchee, of course, as well as macaroni salad, acorn jellies topped with soy sauce and scallions, pickled seaweed, boiled cabbage with *gochujang* (fermented red chile paste), and scallion pancakes. Seconds and thirds are all but guaranteed, but try to hold off because the restaurant's braised cod and *sujebi*, a soul-soothing "dough flake soup," are just as good as the *banchan*. While the former spices and dazzles, the latter satisfies with subtlety. Order both for a harmonious balance.

Meals by Genet, 1053 S. Fairfax Ave., Los Angeles, CA 90019; (323) 938-9304; mealsbygenet.com; Ethiopian; $$. The block of Fairfax Avenue south of Olympic Boulevard is lined with Ethiopian restaurants serving spiced-out stews atop *injera*, spongy and sour flatbreads made from teff flour that are used as both platters and utensils. Here at Meals by Genet, Chef-Owner Genet Agonafer sets herself apart from neighboring establishments by preparing these specialties in a refined and romantic room with a mighty fine wine list to boot. Choose from 20 different vegetarian and meat-based stews to build your communal Ethiopian feast; one dish per person ought to be enough. Meatless options include delicately and distinctly seasoned *alitcha kik* (yellow split peas), *gomen* (collard greens), *tikil gomen* (cabbage and carrot), and *azifa* (green lentils with Ethiopian mustard). Complementing the legumes and greens are *doro wat*, the national dish of Ethiopia

FURTHER EXPLORATION: MESSOB

Located a few paces away from Meals by Genet is **Messob Ethiopian Restaurant** (1041 S. Fairfax Ave., Los Angeles, CA 90019; 323-938-8827; messob.com). Order the Super Messob Exclusive for a generously portioned potpourri of the restaurant's vegetarian and meaty delights including *doro wot, kitfo,* and *yemisir-wot* (red lentil stew).

composed of stewed chicken and boiled eggs with ground red chiles, and cardamom-laced *kitfo*, raw chopped beef mixed with Ethiopian spiced butter and served slightly warm. The *yebeg siga alitcha,* a positively musty lamb stew, is also lovely. To eat, tear off a piece of *injera*, balance it between your fingertips, and use it to scoop up whatever your hungry heart desires.

Mexicali Taco & Co., **702 N. Figueroa St., Los Angeles, CA 90012; (213) 613-0416; mexicalitaco.com; Mexican; $.** It used to be that one had to wait for the sun to set and the streetlights to flick o n for a taste of Esdras Ochoa and Javier Fregoso's Baja-style *carne asada* tacos, *vampiros*, and *cachetadas*. Fortunately, the street-side operation formerly stationed at First and Beaudry landed a permanent home in Downtown Los Angeles in 2011; now their peerless menu is available for lunch and dinner 6 days a week. Both Esdras and Javier grew up along the Mexicali/Calexico border, and the menu at Mexicali Taco & Co. is a reflection of the region's culinary traditions, as well as family recipes. The *vampiro*, a flour tortilla folded over chorizo, chicken, or *carne asada* along with loads of melted cheese, earned its name from the potent garlic sauce that's drizzled into every crevice. From the crunch of the tortilla to the pull of the cheese to the punch of the garlic, this could very well be the most perfect package. The *cachetada,* a tostada topped with chorizo, chicken, or *carne asada* and melted Mexican cheese and finished with an aioli chipotle sauce, might not have as much bite as the *vampiro,* but it certainly holds its own. While most *taqueros* around town prepare *carne asada* on a flattop, Esdras and Javier take pride in preparing theirs the proper way, on a grill over open flames. The char on the meat adds a smokiness that can't be beat. Visit the extensive salsa bar tucked into the corner for fresh radishes, limes, salsas, and a loose guacamole that tastes superb with all of the above.

Mirak, 1134 S. Western Ave., #A2, Los Angeles, CA 90006; (323) 732-7577; **Korean; $$.** If you research Mirak on the Internet, a temple of goat delicacies in Koreatown, you'll likely encounter mixed messages. While some claim that goat meat has properties beneficial to women's health, others allude that it has a Viagra-like effect on men. Once you've had your fill of the meat in question, I'm sure you'll agree that both health claims are dubious at best and beside the point really. One ought to eat goat because it is delicious. Here at Mirak, goat comes grilled, roasted, and stewed. The latter is the most popular, even though it barely drops below 50 degrees in Los Angeles. Before the main attraction arrives, bunches of *banchan* are scattered across the table. The tastiest morsel is the *amja jorim*, glazed potatoes imbued with soy sauce and sugar. Feel free to ask for seconds or thirds of any of these small bites. The stew lands on the table soon after, gurgling and boiling upon a burner. The steaming hot broth has a distinct gamey flavor from the meat and a slight kick from the chiles. Don't slurp too fast or the spice will cling to your throat, burning on its way down. For extra oomph, dip the goat in the mixture of mustard seeds, hot mustard, chili sauce, and scallions. As you make your way to the bottom of the stew, one of the lovely waitresses will prepare a nori (dried seaweed) and kimchee (fermented cabbage) fried rice in its dredges. Save room for this unbeatable final course.

Mo-Chica, 514 W. 7th St., Los Angeles, CA 90014; (213) 622-3744; **mo-chica.com; Peruvian; $$.** Chef Ricardo Zarate relocated Mo-Chica to swanky Downtown digs after courting legions of admirers with his contemporary Peruvian cooking at the Mercado La Paloma. At Mo-Chica 2.0, the room is as vibrant as the chef's flavors, while the menu has more than doubled in size. Many of the original dishes have carried over to 7th Street. The *causas*, layers of *aji amarillo* (Peruvian yellow chile pepper) mashed potatoes stacked with fresh seafood and avocado, as well as the ceviches, seafood marinated in citrus and chile peppers, remain menu mainstays and are absolute musts for those experiencing

FURTHER EXPLORATION: EL ROCOTO

Expect to find polished Peruvian fare served in an equally refined setting as Mo-Chica at Jorge and Javier Chan's **El Rocoto** in Cerritos (11433 South St., Cerritos, CA 90703; 562-924-1919; elrocoto.com) and Gardena (1356 W. Artesia Blvd., Gardena, CA 90248; 310-768-8768; elrocoto.com). The menu features creative plates like the Passion Tiradito, tender cuts of halibut garnished with crispy quinoa, red chiles, cilantro, and a passion fruit sauce, as well as homier fare like the *fettuccine a la huancaina*, cheesy fettuccine served with stir-fried beef tenderloin and mushrooms.

Chef Zarate's cooking for the first time. The *ceviche mixto* offers the most variety, with halibut, prawns, scallops, and squid swimming in a tangy *rocoto leche de tigre* sauce. The *arroz con mariscos* (Peruvian seafood paella) and the *Quinotto* (quinoa risotto with wild mushrooms) have been around the block as well and epitomize the kind of deliciously comforting dishes that Mo-Chica excels at. While the *Estofado De Alpaca* is the new kid in town, one slurp of the alpaca stew—coated tagliatelle and it's clear that it's an instant classic. The Pan Con Tuna, grilled bread piled with spicy tuna and drizzled with *rocoto* (red chile pepper) sauce and *yuzu* mayo, achieves the same effect. While it's difficult not to fill up on savories here, save room for the *picarones*, sticky sweet Peruvian doughnuts made from sweet potato and *kabocha* (Japanese winter squash), and the chocolate and *dulce de leche*–filled *alfajores*. See Chef Zarate's recipe for **Ceviche Mixto** on page 307.

Natraliart Jamaican Restaurant and Market, 3426 W. Washington Blvd., Los Angeles, CA 90018; (323) 732-8865; natraliart .com; Jamaican; $$. Natraliart might not look like much from the outside, or even from the inside for that matter, but the fantastic Jamaican cooking found here makes up for any aesthetic shortcomings. Enter through the small and tidy market and make your way to the front counter, where Owner Charles Forrester is at your service. Start with one of his signature fruit juices; the man's nickname is "Jucy" after all. There's ginger beer, an old-fashioned Jamaican brew of fresh ginger and pineapple sweetened with honey, as well as soursop, mango, and carrot juices. Anything containing cucumber is seriously refreshing. While the black and peppery jerk chicken is certainly popular, the menu offers much more in the way of island specialties. The goat is especially fabulous with its mild heat and curried rub. It's a bone-in affair, which guarantees an avalanche of flavors and just a little fuss. The *ackee* and cod, Jamaica's national dish, combines imported *ackees* (a type of starchy fruit) with cod and spices in delicious fashion. The *ackees* are mostly flavorless, while the salt cod brings a distinct savoriness. All of the main courses are served with rice and "peas" (red kidney beans) cooked in coconut milk, fried sweet plantains, and a cooked cabbage slaw. Also of note is the *ital* stew, a meatless dish of the Rastafarians, a vegetarian Jamaican religious sect; it is composed of vegetables, dumplings, and red kidney beans in spicy coconut milk.

Night + Market, 9041 Sunset Blvd., West Hollywood, CA 90069; (310) 275-9724; nightmarketla.com; Thai; $$. Chef Kris Yenbamroong opened Night + Market after spending years behind the stove at his parents' decade-old restaurant Talésai on the Sunset Strip. Preparing the same dishes every day for a crowd of longtime patrons limited his creativity in the kitchen, so when the space next door became vacant, he quickly snatched it up and transformed it into a dining room more fitting of his style. Here, in this pleasingly minimalist space, a spotlight is shone on the gritty street foods of Thailand's night markets. Start with the fried pigtails, which are dressed in a tangy, chile-laced vinaigrette. There isn't much meat on the bone, just a mouthful of deliciously fatty, beautifully caramelized bits. Meat on a stick is the quintessential Thai street food, and here pork satay skewers are bathed in condensed milk and grilled over open flames. Moving on to larger plates, the five-spice pork hock (*kar moo parlow*) is braised for days, yielding ridiculously tender meat and skin that practically melts in one's mouth. The border beef (*kua gling*) simmered in a Southern chili paste is also fantastic, as is the *kao kluk gapi*, a rice dish composed of shrimp paste–seasoned rice, candied pork, egg ribbons, dried shrimps, green mangoes, and bird's-eye chiles. Chef Yenbamroong's approach to Thai food is bold, different, and seriously delicious. He's got a way with pork.

OB Bear, 3002 W. 7th St., Los Angeles, CA 90005; (213) 480-4910; Korean; $$. Named after a Seoul-based professional baseball team that was once sponsored by Oriental Brewery (OB), OB Bear is a festive pub that's perfect for big groups with even bigger appetites. A soft spot for Korean grub paired with light beer is also a requirement. After ordering a pitcher or two of OB or Hite, settle into a platter of spicy chicken wings. Twice-fried and lacquered in a sweet chili sauce, the

FURTHER EXPLORATION: HITE KWANG-JANG

The K-Town tradition of cold beers and spicy food served in a hunting lodge atmosphere continues at **Hite Kwang-Jang** (3839 Wilshire Blvd., Los Angeles, CA 90010; 213-384-7999). The *yangnyeom dak* (Korean fried chicken), with its hefty coating and sticky sweetness, is a favorite among the local set.

wings bring on a sensational and addictive burn. Pickled daikon cubes and a Thousand Island–dressed cabbage slaw are both effective in neutralizing the heat. If hot wings just ain't your thing, the Cornish hens with paper-thin skins are extraordinarily juicy. Not to be missed are the "pork feets" ($20.99), a massive platter of trotters thinly sliced and a touch chilled. Extracted from about half a dozen "feets," each slice has a bit of chewy skin, a thin strip of fat, and of course, pink meat—a trifecta of deliciousness. A pub grub feast would not be complete without a plate of *dukboki*, Korean rice cakes with zucchini, onions, and fried fish cakes in a wildly spicy sauce.

Olio Pizzeria & Cafe, 8075 W. 3rd St., #100, Los Angeles, CA 90048; (323) 930-9490; pizzeriaolio.com; Pizza; $$. Most Neapolitan-style pizzas suffer from unfortunately soggy centers, but here at Olio the pies hold their paper-thin heads up high. While working as a private chef onboard a motor yacht cruising through the Americas in 2003, Chef Bradford Kent began developing a recipe for the mother dough. His careful research and stellar results led to launching Farmers Market Pizza, a mobile catering business that prepared made-to-order wood-fired pizzas at farmers' markets around the city. All of the pieces finally came together in 2010 with Olio Pizzeria & Cafe, a casual spot serving pizzas and small plates for lunch and dinner, and inspired bialys during weekend brunch. Nearly every dish on the menu is toasted and blistered in the California olive wood-burning oven for a hot minute. Grab a seat along the counter that wraps around the hearth for the best view in the house. The aptly named Margherita Plus brings together crushed tomatoes, burrata, Grana Padano, fresh basil, and basil-infused olive oil on a crisp yet chewy crust. The pristine ingredients simply shine, while the charring isn't overwhelming. The gooey fresh mozzarella makes this simple production memorable. The Veggie Bianco with Burrata, seasoned ricotta, burrata, pesto, fresh spinach, roasted tomatoes, and fire-roasted seasonal vegetables celebrates summer's bounty on a pie. Wood-fired baked cookies are a must for dessert.

Ondal 2, 4566 W. Washington Blvd., Los Angeles, CA 90016; (323) 933-3228; Korean; $$. Begin by tying on the neatly folded apron placed at your table. Made of polyester and half the usual length, it's there to protect clothing from any soupy splashes that might occur during your impending spicy crab feast. For roughly $20 a person, you'll be treated to four different crab preparations, each made tableside. A meal at Ondal 2 is a supremely satisfying affair that highlights the kind of showmanship that's king in Korean restaurants around town. Each course is centered on the bubbling cauldron of as-spicy-as-you-wish crab soup. The first consists of a crab shell filled with rice and bean sprouts—be sure to scrape the shell for the tasty bits of roe. The second entails dirtying one's fingers to extract sweet meat from the crabs' claws. Thirdly, nubs of dough are tossed into the bubbling soup to create a simple but effective noodle soup. Finally, white rice meets crab soup dredges for a memorable fried rice. This meal gets better and better with each course.

Osteria Mozza, 6602 Melrose Ave., Los Angeles, CA 90038; (323) 297-0100; osteriamozza.com; Italian; $$$$. More elegant and a touch moodier than **Pizzeria Mozza** (p. 57) next door, Osteria Mozza serves an upscale Italian menu featuring excellent pastas and hearty mains, as well as beautiful cheeses from Chef Nancy Silverton's beloved Mozzarella Bar. Start with a selection from the Mozzarella Bar—the runnier, gooier, and stringier the better. The burrata with leeks and mustard bread crumbs is simple and delicious, while the burricotta with braised artichokes, pine nuts, currants, and mint pesto is ideal for more adventuresome palates. Among the pasta selections, the cool Squid Ink Chitarra Freddi with Dungeness crab, sea urchin, and jalapeño is as exciting as they come. For a study in richness, go with the Ricotta and Egg Raviolo coated in browned butter. All of the desserts are solid, but the freshly fried *bombolini* served with huckle-berry marmellata and lemon mascarpone take doughnuts to a whole new level. Snag a seat at the Amaro Bar Sunday through Thursday for a three-course dinner and a glass of wine priced just under market value.

Pailin Thai Cuisine, 5621 Hollywood Blvd., Los Angeles, CA 90028; (323) 467-6775; Thai; $. Northern Thai cuisine, which is heavily influenced by neighboring Myanmar, Laos, and China and generally regarded as milder than its central and northeastern counterparts, is the specialty at this Thaitown restaurant. The deep-fried *larb* balls make an excellent starter and embody the distinct sourness that Isaan cuisine is famous for. Each ground pork nugget is marinated in an abundance of lime juice and fried to a crisp. Don't pass up trying the *khao soi* noodles, a Burmese-influenced dish composed of curly egg noodles in a curry and coconut cream sauce. It's an extraordinarily rich and intensely comforting bowl that's brightened by sparks of galangal and Kaffir lime. If boat noodles are your thing, then the murky noodle soup *kway chap* is right up your alley. The broth, which has an awesomely musty way about it, is filled with odds and ends like deep-fried tofu, congealed blood, hard-boiled egg, livery bits, pork rinds, scallions, and fried shallots. Best of all are the tightly coiled rice sheets tying everything together.

FURTHER EXPLORATION: KRUA SIRI

Don't let the orange chicken on **Krua Siri's** (5103 Hollywood Blvd., Los Angeles, CA 90027; 323-660-6196; originalkruasiri .com) menu fool you; Chef-Owner Sam Borasan's Isaan-style cooking is roaringly legit. The Garlic Bird (fried quail), *som tam* (green papaya salad), and duck *laab* (ground duck with toasted rice and duck skin) are absolute musts at this temple of Northern Thai cooking.

Pa Ord, 5301 Sunset Blvd., Los Angeles, CA 90027; (323) 461-3945; **Thai; $.** There are plenty of *kwaytiao reua* (boat noodles) to be had in Thaitown, but Lawan Bhanduram makes the best bowl around. Boat noodles, which are traditionally sold from small boats along Bangkok's canals and rivers, are intensely flavorful noodle soups not fit for the faint of heart. The broth, dark and murky from pig's blood and fragrant of cinnamon and cloves, has a distinct funk to it, while the noodles can vary from simple rice sticks to short and wide strands depending on diners' preferences. Thin slices of beef, squeaky meatballs, and tender tripe round out each bowl. When the waitress inquires as to how spicy you'd like your boat noodles, it is best to play it safe and go with mild. Here in Thaitown, the spice rubric is calibrated to local tastes, so proceed cautiously because the Thai people's tolerance for fiery foods is legendary. Also of note on Pa Ord's menu is the *khao kanah mu grob*, crispy pork and Chinese broccoli slicked in a sweet marinade and served over steamed rice along with a fried egg.

FURTHER EXPLORATION: SAPP COFFEE SHOP

Prior to Bhanduram opening Pa Ord, **Sapp Coffee Shop** (5183 Hollywood Blvd., Los Angeles, CA 90027; 323-665-1035; sapp .menutoeat.com) ruled the boat noodle roost. Since the two restaurants are less than a half mile apart, a Thaitown throw-down would be most appropriate.

Pizzeria Mozza, 641 N. Highland Ave., Los Angeles, CA 90036; (323) 297-0101; pizzeriamozza.com; Pizza; $$$. Los Angeles' culinary darling Nancy Silverton teamed up with celebrity Chef Mario Batali and restaurateur Joseph Bastianich to open Pizzeria Mozza and its sister restaurant **Osteria Mozza** (p. 55) in 2006. Even though it's been years since the first perfectly blistered pie was served, reservations at a decent hour are still hard to come by. The good news is that some of the best seats in the house, along the wine bar and in front of the wood-fired pizza oven, are available to walk-ins. The bruschette with chicken livers, capers, and *guanciale* (unsmoked Italian bacon prepared with pig's cheeks) are one of the strongest starters on the menu. Even those who generally shy away from liver due to its metallic undertones have been seduced by this preparation. Pizza-goers in the know order the Bianca with fontina, mozzarella, sottocenere, and sage and request an additional topping of Mozza's house-made fennel sausage. Regardless of what's atop your pie, Silverton's puffy crust—crisp, chewy, and airy in all the right places—is legendary. After nibbling on bruschette and digging into a pie, order the butterscotch budino to finish. Silky smooth butterscotch pudding garnished with whipped cream, a layer of caramel, and just enough Maldon salt to drive your taste buds wild— what could be better?

FURTHER EXPLORATION: MOZZA2GO

Around the corner from Pizzeria Mozza is **Mozza2Go** (6610 Melrose Ave., Los Angeles, CA 90038; 323-297-1130; mozza 2go.com), a takeout and delivery operation offering the pizzeria's signature menu items including Nancy's Chopped Salad, as well as the aforementioned chicken livers and butterscotch pudding. Additionally, the petite shop stocks fresh burrata, dried pastas, and other Italian specialties.

Providence, 5955 Melrose Ave., Los Angeles, CA 90038; (323) 460-4170; providencela.com; Seafood; $$$$. Providence, one of the final bastions of fine dining in Los Angeles, orchestrates one of the most pleasurable gastronomical experiences in the city. Chef Michael Cimarusti's exceptional cooking is perfectly matched with Donato Poto's warm and efficient service. A meal here is worth the splurge whether it's to honor a milestone, meet with colleagues, or celebrate an anniversary. Providence offers a five-course Market Tasting Menu as well as a la carte options at lunch and dinner. Only available at dinner, however, are the Chef's Menu and the multicourse dessert extravaganza. The highlight of the a la carte menu is the salt-roasted Santa Barbara spot prawns, which are elegantly served tableside. The prawns arrive on a rolling cart submerged under a heap of hot salt and rosemary sprigs. To serve, the prawns are sliced in half with their heads intact and drizzled with olive oil and lemon juice. The tasting menus are masterfully executed affairs that change with the seasons and usually begin with spherical cocktails held together by the thinnest of membranes. Seafood is Chef Cimarusti's forte, so be prepared for dazzlingly fresh fish, scallop, and sea urchin preparations sustainably sourced from near and far.

FURTHER EXPLORATION: CONNIE & TED'S

Named after Chef Cimarusti's grandparents, **Connie & Ted's** (8171 Santa Monica Blvd., West Hollywood, CA 90046; 323-848-CRAB) is a casual New England–style seafood restaurant in West Hollywood serving three kinds of clam chowder, clam cakes, steamers, and best of all, butter-drenched lobster rolls.

Ramen Jinya, 5174 Wilshire Blvd., Los Angeles, CA 90036; (323) 549-0188; jinya-ramenbar.com; Japanese; $. For a complete description, see p. 133.

Ricky's Fish Tacos, follow **@RickysFishTacos on Twitter for location updates; Mexican; $.** For a genuine taste of Baja without traveling across the border, look no further than Ricky's Fish Tacos. What started as a weekends-only, one-man stand just off Sunset Junction has grown into a full-fledged food truck operation. Ricky Piña, the grandmaster of fish tacos in Los Angeles, makes 'em just like they do down in Ensenada. Tender slabs of basa, a type of catfish from Vietnam, are battered and deep-fried in a *comal* (a thick-lipped frying vessel) before meeting a warm, griddled corn tortilla. Ricky tops the entire package off with shredded cabbage, *pico de gallo*, and *crema*, a thin sauce of mayonnaise and milk, before delivering it to diners. The batter, which is made from Mexican wheat flour with a touch of mustard, is crisp and golden with nary a trace of oil, while the fish flakes off gently with each bite. To supplement his signature fish tacos, Ricky also prepares shrimp and lobster varieties, as well as a few *aguas frescas* to wash everything down.

FURTHER EXPLORATION: TACOS BAJA

To enjoy fish tacos with a roof over your head, head to decade-old **Tacos Baja** in the heart of East L.A. (5385 Whittier Blvd., Los Angeles, CA 90022; 323-887-1980; tacosbaja.com), where fried catfish tacos are dressed in house-made *crema*, diced tomatoes, salsa, and shredded cabbage.

Rinconcito Guatemalteco, 501 N. Western Ave., Los Angeles, CA 90004; (323) 463-6602; Guatemalan; $. The hum of the evening news coupled with rusty jukebox tunes fills the dining room at Rinconcito Guatemalteco, a 30-year-old restaurant run by Aura Castaldi. Guatemalan-style enchiladas are heaped tall with fluorescent beets, stewed pork, crumbly cheese, and hard-boiled eggs on a fried tortilla base. The heavy proteins push, while the tangy beets pull, creating a harmonious balance like no other. Chiles rellenos marry sweet red bell peppers with stewed pork, carrots, chayote, green beans, and potatoes under a saucy tomato blanket. These rellenos are sweeter and milder than their Mexican counterparts but really just as satisfying. The Especial Chapin, a sampler platter that includes a chile relleno as well as cuts of *asada* (grilled steak), *adobada* (grilled pork), and *longaniza* (Guatemalan sausage), offers a crash course in Guatemala's greatest hits. The homemade tortillas served alongside are thick and fluffy things that wrap and roll splendidly with the proteins on hand. The *moyetes y torrejas*, spongy rolls filled with pudding and soaked in warm caramel syrup, are a must for dessert.

FURTHER EXPLORATION: AMALIA'S

Amalia Zuleta takes a refined approach to traditional Guatemalan fare at **Amalia's** (751 N. Virgil Ave., Los Angeles, CA 90029; 323-644-1515; amaliasrestaurant.com), her namesake Silver Lake restaurant. The *kak-kik de pavo*, a soulful turkey soup that is Guatemala's national dish, is especially noteworthy.

Rivera, 1050 S. Flower St., #102, Los Angeles, CA 90015; (213) 749-1460; riverarestaurant.com; Modern Latin; $$$$. Celebrated Chef John Rivera Sedlar pays homage to 3,000 years of Latin cuisine in all its enchanting forms at Downtown's Rivera. With three distinct rooms each serving a unique menu, diners are taken on a tequila and mescal–fueled gastronomical tour across three continents and countless regions. In the Playa Room, Chef Sedlar serves a Mexican and Southwest–inspired menu including his famous *tortillas florales,* which are adorned with wildly colorful flowers and best smothered in "Indian butter." The Samba Room focuses on South American cuisine, like the Argentine mushroom carpaccio made with king oyster, blue foot, and chanterelle varieties, which have a fittingly meaty way about them. Chef Sedlar explores the culinary traditions of Spain in the Sangre Room. The *caracoles,* a beautiful arrangement of snails and *jamón Ibérico,* instantly transport one's taste buds to somewhere between Valencia and Barcelona. Diners wanting to delve deeper into each plate are encouraged to call a hotline (310-464-6884) to learn about the dishes from the chef himself. Don't you dare leave the premises without trying one of Julian Cox's well-crafted and intriguing cocktails. The *Barbacoa,* a smoky and spicy mescal concoction plied with chipotle, bell pepper, and ginger and cleverly garnished with a piece of jerky, is irresistible. See Chef Sedlar's recipe for **Tortillas Florales and Indian Butter** on page 309.

Ruen Pair, **257 Hollywood Blvd., Los Angeles, CA 90027; (323) 466-0153; Thai; $.** Rowdy crowds reveling on Hollywood Boulevard have been heading to Ruen Pair for the past 20 years for a filling, unfussy, and economical fourth meal. The sobering effects of spicy green curry, ladled over steaming hot rice, have been well documented. While night owls flock to Ruen Pair well past midnight, it's groups of friends, families, and couples that keep the dining room packed when the sun is still out. The restaurant's bold spicing, fast service, and good value offer wide appeal across the board. A papaya salad with raw crab legs makes for an exciting starter with its pleasant snap and well-balanced lime and fish sauce vinaigrette. Tomatoes, peanuts, and dried shrimp mingle harmoniously amongst the greenery. Go ahead and slurp the crab claws. A Thai meal wouldn't be complete without a helping of curry. The roasted duck red curry with pineapples, tomatoes, and loads of fresh Thai basil teeters deliciously between spicy and creamy, with pockets of tanginess in between. Don't hesitate to order the ever-popular pad thai, which is executed with precision. The noodles are al dente, while the spicing is sweet rather than funky. Nearly every dish on the menu is priced under $10, so be bold and explore.

Sabor Colombiano, 847 S. Union Ave., Los Angeles, CA 90017; (213) 388-0150; saborcolombianola.com; Colombian; $. Rosario Hernandez, a native of Palmira, Colombia, opened Sabor Colombiano in 2010 to introduce Angelenos to her grandmother's recipes. The space isn't much to look at, just a windowless room with an exposed brick wall, but the cooking, oh the cooking, makes up for the lack of ambiance in spades. Begin with one of the *antojitos*—a small nibble to get thing started. The freshly baked Colombian cheese bread, *pan de bono*, is otherworldly just out of the oven. The cassava starch in the dough makes for some seriously stretchy innards. The *arepas*, corn cakes stuffed with beef, chicken, or cheese, are also made with care. Under the "Desayunos" section of the menu is the terrific *tamal Tolimense*, a one-pound Colombian rice flour tamale stuffed with carrots, green peas, chicken, and pork and cooked in banana leaves. Its immense heft, along with its puddinglike texture, sets it apart from the firm, masa-made parcels of the world. One *tamal* is enough for a meal. The most comforting dish on the menu is the *ajiaco santafereno,* a soulful chicken soup served with rice, avocado, sweet plantains, cream, and capers on the side. Add a spoonful of the *aji* chile condiment for some heat. The weekends-only *lechona* is not to be missed—a whole pig is stuffed with rice, peas, potatoes, and spices and roasted for the better part of a day. Due to its unpredictability and popularity, call ahead to confirm the *lechona*'s availability.

Salt's Cure, 7494 Santa Monica Blvd., West Hollywood, CA 90046; (323) 850-7258; saltscure.com; New American; $$$. There's a lot to love about Salt's Cure. For starters, the kitchen makes everything from scratch. From the ketchup to the bagels to the charcuterie, nearly every edible is sourced from within. Additionally, all of the produce, meat, cheese, wine, and beer are produced in California. Salt's Cure is committed to keeping food miles in check and highlighting the very best of the Golden State. Owned and operated by chefs Christopher Phelps, Zachary Walters, and Naomi Shim, the restaurant offers a concise and ever-changing menu that's scrawled on a blackboard overlooking the dining room. The brunch here is one of the city's best, featuring fresh-from-the-oven breakfast rolls and smoked black cod on a bagel with cream cheese and pickled red onions. The "2x2x2"—two sausage patties, two sunny eggs, and two slices of bacon—has a legion of devoted followers. Dinnertime is similarly satisfying. Everything from the smoked, cured, and pickled meat, fish, and vegetables to the braised beef cheeks to the pork chops is worth a shot.

So Kong Dong, 2716 W. Olympic Blvd., Los Angeles, CA 90006; (213) 380-3737; Korean; $. Wintertime in Los Angeles is synonymous with *soondubu jjigae,* a spicy Korean stew that never fails to curb the chills when temperatures dip below 70 degrees. Even before the main event arrives, the specialists at So Kong Dong keep diners smiling with an array of complimentary *banchan*. Marinated bean sprouts, fish cakes, spice-rubbed zucchini, and best of all, "spicy raw crabs" make the perfect snack before diving headfirst into the *soondubu jjigae*. The stew arrives bubbling and sputtering in a black stone pot that masterfully holds in heat long after it has left the stove. The broth, tinged red from copious amounts of *gochujang* (fermented red chile paste) and garlic, is brimming with silken tofu, shrimp, clams, oysters, and beef and topped with a raw egg. Give the stew a good whirl to incorporate all of the components before digging in with plenty of rice. So Kong Dong offers four levels of spice to fit everyone's tastes: "very hot," "regular hot," "mild hot," and "plain." A side order of boiled dumplings is the perfect antidote to the heat.

FURTHER EXPLORATION: BEVERLY SOON TOFU HOUSE

Beverly Soon Tofu House (2717 W. Olympic Blvd., Los Angeles, CA 90006; 213-380-1113), which is located across the street from So Kong Dong, offers a little more in the way of ambiance and prepares a comparably robust *soondubu jjigae*.

The Spice Table, 114 S. Central Ave., Los Angeles, CA 90012; thespicetable.com; (213) 620-1840; Singaporean; $$. Owned by Chef Bryant Ng and his wife, Kim, The Spice Table in Little Tokyo offers a breath of fresh air from the usual sushi and ramen offerings that dominate the landscape. While the lunchtime menu features Southeast Asian–inspired sandwiches served in a casual atmosphere, dinner is a full-service affair showcasing the traditional cuisines of Malaysia, Singapore, and Vietnam. The space is moody and cool, just like the urbane crowd that the restaurant attracts. The "Satays" portion of the menu serves up a slew of meat-on-a-stick starters. The beef tripe is impressively tender and surprisingly sweet with its marinade of soy, garlic, and palm sugar. The lamb belly skewers seasoned with cumin, galangal, and turmeric highlight the meat's distinct flavor. The *kaya* toast from the "Snacks" portion of the menu is easy on the taste buds, with coconut jam slathered on buttered toast served with a slow-cooked egg, soy sauce, and white pepper. Moving on to main courses, the short rib beef *rendang* served on a bed of jasmine rice with an addictive peanut and anchovy garnish is bold with a tinge of funk. Also great is the curry *laksa*, slippery rice noodles swimming in a spicy coconut-seafood gravy. Save room at the end for some house-made soft serve in unique flavors like milk tea and spiced cognac.

Sugarfish by Sushi Nozawa, 600 W. 7th St., Los Angeles, CA 90017; (213) 627-3000; sugarfishsushi.com; Japanese; $$$. Chef Kazunori Nozawa's "Trust Me" style of sushi has made him a notorious character in the L.A. sushi scene. In Chef Nozawa's book, there is no greater offense than serving mayo-

laden rolls heavy with bells and whistles. Instead, he prepares pristine fishes, minimally fussed and buttery on the tongue. With his Studio City flagship shuttering in 2012, Sugarfish, an ever-expanding local chain, is keeping the Nozawa tradition alive. The restaurant's three "Trust Me" menus are priced markedly lower than a meal at his original sushi bar. Sugarfish is able to keep prices in check by taking advantage of the chef's personal contacts with fish vendors, preparing the fish more efficiently in a kitchen rather than behind a sushi bar, streamlining the menu to reduce waste, and serving diners at breakneck speed. Pricing and pacing aside, the quality of food at Sugarfish is truly unparalleled. Every cut of fish served in the restaurant is handpicked by Chef Nozawa, fresh rice is made every 30 minutes, and all the sauces are prepared from scratch. Each of the set menus begins with a plate of lightly salted organic edamame (soy beans), followed by a supple stack of tuna sashimi resting in a pool of house-made *ponzu* sauce. Next up is a parade of *nigiri*, tender slices of fish draped over warm, loosely packed rice. The albacore belly, salmon, and yellowtail never fail to please. The final bite is always a hand roll or two. Eat this one as soon as it lands on the table to maximize the seaweed's crunch.

Sushi Gen, 422 E. 2nd St., Los Angeles, CA 90012; (213) 617-0552; Japanese; $$$. It's 10:45 in the morning and already the crowds are lining up outside Little Tokyo's Sushi Gen. As soon as the doors swing open at 11 on the nose, the diehards file in for the sashimi lunch special. Here, a platter of gorgeous and generously portioned tuna, yellowtail, salmon, and even the illustrious *toro* (tuna belly) is priced at just $15. Also included are miso soup, *sunomono* (cucumber salad), steamed rice, and soft tofu in a mild broth. While dinner at Sushi Gen isn't as savvy a steal as the lunchtime special, it remains the best option in the area with regards to quality and service. A seat at the bar is a must for those serious about sushi, while the dining room is fit for the teriyaki and tempura crowd. While at the bar, choose your own adventure, or let the chef prepare an *omakase* composed of the freshest cuts. It's impossible to go wrong with either choice.

FURTHER EXPLORATION: HAMA SUSHI

For those who believe that there is little better than pristine fishes, served fresh and unadorned, head to **Hama Sushi** in Little Tokyo (347 E. 2nd St., Los Angeles, CA 90012; 213-680-3454). Grab a seat at the horseshoe-shaped bar and proceed to order *nigiri*, sashimi, and hand rolls to your heart's content.

Tacos Leo, Corner of Venice Blvd. and La Brea Blvd., Los Angeles, CA 90019; Mexican; $. When the sun sets over Los Angeles, the *taqueros* come out in full force from all corners of the city. The 76 gas station on the corner of Venice and La Brea in Mid-City plays host to the city's finest *al pastor* operation, literally "shepherd-style" tacos prepared on a *trompo* (rotating spit), which was influenced by Lebanese immigrants in Mexico. The pork, colored a fetching shade of red from dried red chiles and *achiote* paste (a blend of annatto, oregano, cumin, cloves, cinnamon, black pepper, allspice, garlic, and salt), is loaded onto the *trompo* with precision and left to roast until perfectly tender and glossy. As orders roll in, the cashier scribbles tickets for the *taquero,* who lops off the perfect porky portion straight into a griddled corn tortilla with a few swift flicks of his wrist. Tacos are topped with a sliver of roasted pineapple and delivered on paper plates, ready to be dressed at the condiments bar with chile-laced *salsa roja*, tomatillo-tinged *salsa verde*, loose guacamole, onions, cilantro, radishes, and pickled vegetables. Really though, the *al pastor* needs no accompaniments; it's strong enough to stand alone. Tacos Leo operates Mon through Thur 5 p.m. to 3 a.m., and until 4 a.m. on Fri and Sat.

Trois Mec, 716 North Highland Ave., Los Angeles, CA 90038; troismec.com; French; $$$$. After training in France at Restaurant Pierre Gagnaire and l'Arpege and making his mark in Los Angeles at L'Orangerie, Bastide, and most famously, LudoBites, Chef Ludovic "Ludo" Lefebvre finally has a restaurant to call home. A collaboration between Chef Ludo and "two dudes," Jon Shook and Vinny Dotolo, Trois Mec (loosely "three guys") serves an inspired five-course pre-fixe menu loosely fashioned after the Paris bistronomy movement. Each meal begins with a smattering of small bites, followed by more substantial vegetable, protein, and dessert offerings. Each course is as delicious as it is beautiful. Reservations are released on every other Friday at 8 a.m. on the restaurant's website. For those who want to see the action up close, note that parties of two are seated at the counter.

Umami Burger, 738 E. 3rd St., Los Angeles, CA 90013; (323) 263-8626; umami.com; American; $$. In the span of less than five years, restaurateur Adam Fleischman has expanded his "fine-dining fast food" burger concept across Los Angeles and into San Francisco and New York City. Umami's blissful burgers are built upon the concept of umami, or the fifth flavor. Every creation begins with a loosely packed beef patty griddled a perfect medium-rare and nestled on a cleverly branded Portuguese-style bun. The signature Umami Burger piles on caramelized onions, roasted tomatoes, house-made ketchup, and a Parmesan crisp, while the fittingly named Manly Burger brings beer-cheddar cheese, smoked salt-onion strings, and bacon lardons. The strongest burger of the bunch is the Truffle Burger. From the unfailingly juicy patty to the house-made truffle cheese to the ever-so-soft bun, everything about this burger is intensely satisfying. Vegetarian diners are treated to the awesomely punchy Earth Burger, a mushroom and edamame patty adorned with a white soy aioli, truffle ricotta, cipollini onions, lettuce, and roasted tomatoes. A side order of the Smushed Potatoes, double-fried Dutch Yellow Creamers served with a chive-flecked garlic aioli, and Cheesy Tots is a must with any burger. Dessert comes in the form of ice creams courtesy of L.A. Creamery and confections from Cake Monkey. **Additional Locations:** 1520 N. Cahuenga Blvd., Los Angeles, CA 90028; (323) 469-3100; 4655 Hollywood Blvd., Los Angeles, CA 90027; (323) 669-3922.

Umamicatessen, 852 S. Broadway, Los Angeles, CA 90015; (213) 413-8626; umami.com; New American; $$. Umamicatessen is the genius creation of restaurateur Adam Fleischman (**Umami Burger** [p. 68], **Red Medicine** [p. 260], **800 Degrees,** [p. 251]) and is widely referred to as a "food emporium." Really though, it's just a regular restaurant with a menu that is more varied than most. The soul of Umamicatessen is the Umami Burger, a winning burger concept with locations in Los Angeles, San Francisco, and New York City. Also on the bill of fare are traditional deli dishes under the heading "The Cure." The consulting chef is Micah Wexler formerly of Mezze. San Francisco–based Chef Chris Cosentino is the chief curator of the charcuterie and offal offerings under the P!GG portion of the menu.

Wood Spoon, 107 W. 9th St., Los Angeles, CA 90015; (213) 629-1765; woodspoonla.com; Brazilian; $$. A chilled carafe of cinnamon-scented water lands on the table along with the menus at this cozy Brazilian luncheonette. Little touches like this, along with the wonderful cooking and amiable service, keep the crowds coming back for more at Downtown's Wood Spoon. Here, Chef-Owner Natalia Pereira shares her mother's treasured recipes and homey cooking with an urbane crowd. A few deep-fried small plates make for an ideal starter. There's *coxinha de galinha*, tear drop–shaped morsels made from shredded chicken that are fried until crisp-golden. The *kibe*, a mash-up of bulgur wheat, mint, and ground beef, are nuanced and juicy. Better yet, order the Mix Plate, which includes two *coxinha* and a *kibe,* as well as a potato croquette, a Portuguese croquette (potato with salted cod), and a pastel Portuguese (shrimp and coconut sauce dumpling). The pale green sauce of chiles, basil, and mayonnaise served alongside brightens and spices everything it touches. The Brazilian-style chicken potpie, one of Chef Pereira's childhood favorites that her mother constructed from leftovers, has a cultlike following. While the crust sings a flaky and buttery tune, the filling is a hearty mix of chicken, hearts of palm, and roasted corn. Also popular is the pork burger served with braised cabbage and onions on a toasted potato bun.

Xoia, 1801 W. Sunset Blvd., Los Angeles, CA 90026; (213) 413-3232; xoiaeats.com; Vietnamese; $. Vietnamese and Mexican food collide at Xoia, a neighborhood treasure in Echo Park. The menu was inspired by owners Jose Sarinana and Thien Ho's daughter, who as a toddler insisted on dipping her shrimp chips in salsa. Bright red chairs and original artwork fill the space, echoing the menu's creative and carefree spirit. The two cuisines mash up most successfully under the tacos section of the menu. The *pho* tacos, anise and cinnamon–spiced beef tucked into a warm corn tortilla, have been a hit with crowds from the start. Under the radar but still of note are the *mi Quang* tacos filled with tender pork richly spiced with paprika and shallots. In the great tradition of Mexican tacos, the ones served here are topped with fresh cilantro and diced red onions. Served on the side are lime wedges, sliced radishes, and a house-made *salsa roja*. The Vietnamese sandwiches (*banh mi*) are filled mostly with traditional proteins like grilled pork and meatballs, but the slow-cooked lemongrass pork *carnitas* are totally original. Another fabulous fusion effort is the chicken curry *tostadas* with potatoes and carrots garnished with Vietnamese coriander and a drizzle of Oaxacan cream. Any one of the house-made ice creams, in flavors like hoisin peanut and Mexican chocolate, makes for a fine finish, especially the Vietnamese-coffee float made with either condensed milk ice cream or vegan coconut ice cream.

L.A. Landmarks

Border Grill, 445 S. Figueroa St., Los Angeles, CA 90071; (213) 486-5171; bordergrill.com; Modern Mexican; $$$. For a complete description, see p. 215.

Dino's Chicken and Burgers, 2575 W. Pico Blvd., Los Angeles, CA 90006; (213) 380-3554; dinoschickenandburgers.com; Greek/Mexican; $. The Byzantine-Latino Quarter of Los Angeles is a vibrant synergy of Greek, Mexican, and Central American cultures. This unique "BLQ" spirit is captured best at Dino's Chicken and Burgers, a 40-year-old fast-food joint with roots in Patras and a Latino soul. Crowds queue up here at all hours of the day for the grilled *pollo maniaco*, an impressively moist bird that's crisp and charred and caramelized in all the right places. The signature marinade, a fluorescent blend of garlic, spices, and vinegar, comes from an old family recipe that Dino Pantazis brought with him from Greece. The formula has been tweaked over the years to fit the tastes of the neighborhood's largely Latino population; the warm corn tortillas that accompany every order serve as another nod to the clientele. Perhaps the best part of the Dino's experience is the nest of house-made shoestrings that each chicken is delivered upon. The crisp fries sponge up the poultry's tang and spice like a champ, usurping the famed chicken in the process. The burgers here don't command the room quite like the chicken does, but the double-meat-and-cheese situation is satisfying nevertheless. The patty is cooked on the same flattop as the chicken, imparting the beef with an unbeatable garlicky essence.

Fisherman's Outlet, 529 S. Central Ave., Los Angeles, CA 90013; (213) 627-7231; fishermansoutlet.net; Seafood; $. Set in landlocked Downtown in the heart of the wholesale fish district, Fisherman's Outlet has been serving Angelenos some of the area's freshest and most reasonably priced seafood since 1961. The weekday lunch rush means a complete madhouse inside the vintage redbrick building and its adjacent patio, but don't fret one bit. The snappy veterans manning the counter keep the chaos in check; it won't be long until your moment with a mountain of deep-fried shrimp is realized. In addition to the aforementioned shrimp, fish, crab cakes, calamari, scallops, and whole tilapia are also given the lightly breaded and golden, deep-fried treatment. The industrial-grade tartar sauce and cocktail sauce served alongside fit right in with the scene. A selection of charbroiled

fish (salmon, halibut, mahimahi, swordfish, tuna, sea bass, orange roughy, and pacific snapper), lobster, and giant shrimp and scallops provides a less weighty option for those who haven't penciled in a post-lunch snooze. Garlic butter, a Cajun sauce, and teriyaki sauce are on hand to dip and smother to your heart's content. Comparably fresh seafood is available for purchase at the counter for cooks looking to re-create the magic at home. Lunch is served 10 a.m. to 3:30 p.m. Mon through Sat.

La Brea Bakery, 460 S. La Brea Ave., Los Angeles, CA 90036; (323) 939-6813; labreabakery.com; Bakery; $. La Brea Bakery's founder Chef Nancy Silverton developed her very own starter from scratch back in 1988 using flour, water, and wild yeasts from the skin of organic grapes. Over a quarter century later, the original starter remains the signature ingredient in every single loaf of La Brea Bakery bread; it's an edible legacy that now spans far beyond its Los Angeles roots. Long before Chef Silverton's crusty loaves were found in places like Disneyland, LAX, and Costco, one had to visit the quaint flagship on La Brea Avenue for a taste. In addition to the celebrated baguettes, sourdough rounds, and olive-studded ovals, there's always an enticing selection of pastries including croissants, candies, and cookies. It's the kind of easygoing neighborhood place where it is as easy to grab a loaf to go as it is to linger over thoughtfully constructed sandwiches at an alfresco table.

Langer's Delicatessen Restaurant, 704 S. Alvarado St., Los Angeles, CA 90057; (213) 483-8050; langersdeli.com; Deli; $$. Located across from MacArthur Park on the cusp of Koreatown, Langer's has been smoking, steaming, and hand-slicing their world-famous pastrami for over 60 years. The dining room hasn't changed too much over time—same goes with the waitstaff (Joan's a complete doll)—but no one seems to notice once the pastrami hits the table. The pastrami at Langer's, which is considered to be some of the very best in the world, is made from whole beef brisket that's rubbed with spices, sliced thick, and piled neatly on double-baked rye. While purists might scoff at adding anything more than a little mustard onto a hot pastrami sandwich, the decked-out

#19 is the most popular sandwich on the menu. Tucked in between two impressively sturdy slices of rye bread are pastrami, swiss cheese, coleslaw, and Russian dressing. It's a monstrously portioned creation that's dressed to the nines and sensational from top to bottom. The restaurant is only open Mon through Sat 8 a.m. to 4 p.m., which means that crowds can be slightly unwieldy on the weekends. If you're the claustrophobic type, call in your order and pick it up curbside.

FURTHER EXPLORATION: NATE 'N AL AND CANTER'S

While the food at **Nate 'n Al** in Beverly Hills (414 N. Beverly Dr., Beverly Hills, CA 90210; 310-274-0101; natenal.com) and **Canter's** (419 N. Fairfax Ave., Los Angeles, CA 90036; 323-651-2030; cantersdeli.com) near the border of West Hollywood isn't as celebrated as Langer's, there's no denying the intrinsic appeal of both of these old-time delis. Come to the former for people-watching over a bowl of matzo ball soup and the latter to satisfy your pastrami cravings 24 hours a day.

Mario's Peruvian Seafood, 5786 Melrose Ave., Los Angeles, CA 90038; (323) 466-4181; Peruvian; $$. Whether it's the middle of the afternoon or the peak of the dinner rush, there's always a crowd waiting outside Mario's for an unfussy Peruvian fix. Even though it's been well over two decades since the restaurant first came onto the Hollywood scene, the dining room feels as vibrant and vital as ever. Quick and efficient service, coupled with dependably good food, keeps diners coming in year after year. Every meal here starts with a basket of warm rolls accompanied by a massive squeeze bottle of *aji verde*. While the bread lacks character, the lush green sauce of chiles and herbs really packs serious heat. The *lomo saltado*, which nearly everyone orders, is a robust stir-fry of beefsteak, onions, tomatoes, and french fries seasoned with soy sauce, vinegar, and chiles. The white rice served alongside soaks up the savory marinade, while the french fries wilt just so. The *arroz chaufa de pollo*, a Chinese-style fried rice that is a staple in the Peruvian culinary pantheon, is executed simply and effectively. One serving might be enough to feed a family, but it's still difficult to share when the flavors are this satisfying. Asian flavors are echoed in the *tallarin con carne* as well. This Peruvian-style chow mein with tender slices of beef sticks to your ribs and then some.

Musso and Frank Grill, 6667 Hollywood Blvd., Los Angeles, CA 90028; (323) 467-7788; mussoandfrank.com; American; $$$. Opened in 1919 by entrepreneur Frank Toulet and restaurateur Joseph Musso, Musso and Frank Grill captures a certain Hollywood mystique that few establishments in town can match. During its heyday, the stars of the industry's Golden Age including Charlie Chaplin, Greta Garbo, Humphrey Bogart, and Marilyn Monroe were fixtures at the restaurant's "Back Room," a legendary private space reserved for Hollywood's elite. Musso's, as everyone calls it, was also popular among the literati including F. Scott Fitzgerald, William Faulkner, and Nathanael West. The restaurant was sold in 1927 to Joseph Carissimi and John Mosso, who years later moved it next door to 6667 Hollywood Blvd., where it still stands today. The Golden Age of Hollywood has come and gone, but Musso's remains a Hollywood institution. Patrons come in for dependably good steaks, chops, and the best martinis in town served by waiters in red jackets. The bill of fare hasn't changed too much since the restaurant first debuted. Culinary relics like Welsh rarebit, a European-style fondue with bacon and tomato served with toast points, and Lobster Thermidor, lobster tails smothered in cream and butter, are alive and kicking. Musso's classic flannel cakes,

IN-N-OUT BURGER

An In-N-Out "Double-Double" with a side of fries and a cool milk shake is the quintessential Los Angeles meal for tourists and residents alike. While the original location in Baldwin Park that Harry and Esther Snyder founded in 1948 no longer stands due to the construction of I-10, there are nearly 300 locations across California, Nevada, Arizona, Texas, and Utah to satisfy one's craving.

The menu here is awesomely simple with just three burgers (hamburger, cheeseburger, and "Double-Double"), fries, milk shakes, and sodas. Every burger is built on toasted buns slathered in "spread" and layered with never-frozen beef patties, hand-leafed lettuce, a slice of tomato, and fresh or grilled onions. These iconic California-style burgers are served up perfect every time.

Highlights from the restaurant's secret menu include burgers prepared "Animal Style" (mustard-grilled beef patties with pickles, extra spread, and the usual fixings) and "Protein Style" (buns are swapped out for lettuce), as well as the "Flying Dutchman" (two slices of cheese melted between two burger patties). Neapolitan shakes and fizzy root beer floats are available to wash it all down. Requests for medium-rare patties and well-done fries are always honored with a smile.

a sweetened crossbreed of pancakes and crepes, are popular with the morning crowd.

The Original Pantry, 877 S. Figueroa St., Los Angeles, CA 90017; (213) 972-9279; pantrycafe.com; American; $$. For a side of nostalgia with your morning coffee and eggs, look no further than The Original Pantry in Downtown Los Angeles. "The Pantry," as it's often referred to by the local set, was little more than a 15-stool counter with a grill and a hot plate when Dewey Logan opened it in 1924. Following the restaurant's expansion in 1946, the property was acquired by the state for a freeway ramp. The Pantry moved into its current location at the corner of 9th and Figueroa Streets in 1950. The designated Los Angeles Historic-Cultural Monument is currently owned by former Los Angeles mayor Richard Riordan. Besides its rich history, this greasy spoon offers diner fare done right 24 hours a day. Breakfast items are popular at all hours, especially the combination plates that mix and match eggs, potatoes, toast, bacon, and sausage with steak, pancakes, and sourdough french toast.

Original Tommy's Hamburgers, 2575 Beverly Blvd., Los Angeles, CA 90057; (213) 389-9060; originaltommys.com; American; $. From burgers to hot dogs to tamales, everything on Tommy's menu gets a ladle of chili before leaving the kitchen. This slightly runny, somewhat beefy, and awfully messy touch put this fast-food shack on the map in 1946 when Tommy Koulax opened the very first location in Westlake on Beverly and Rampart. The winning combination of grease on grease served up quickly under fluorescent lights has suited Tommy well through the years; there are over 30 locations in California and neighboring Nevada. Peeling back the tidy wax paper that packages every burger reveals a seriously sloppy creation that never fails to get the salivary glands going. The quality of the patty is beside the point. Here, it's all about the warm chili and its brilliant contrast with the half-melted all-American cheese, pickles, onions, and thickly sliced tomato. Grab a load of flimsy napkins because it's about to get really messy.

Pacific Dining Car, 1310 W. 6th St., Los Angeles, CA 90017; (213) 483-6000; pacificdiningcar.com; Steak House; $$$. When Fred and Grace Cook left the East Coast to settle in Southern California, they brought with them the idea of opening a restaurant modeled after a railway dining car. They built the replica on a deserted Downtown lot at 7th and Westlake in 1921, serving all-American staples like vegetable soup, steaks, and apple pie. Two years after opening the restaurant, the location was snapped up by speculators, and thus the Pacific Dining Car was forced to move to its current location at 6th and Witmer— it's a good thing the restaurant was built on wheels. Today, Wes Idol III, a fourth-generation member of the original Cook clan, runs the show. The Victorian-era decor has been touched up throughout the restaurant's 90-year history, but remains true to the original spirit. In 1990, a second Pacific Dining Car was opened in Santa Monica; both outlets are open 24 hours a day, 7 days a week. Begin with an order of crisp and meaty crab cakes; fresh blue crabs are minimally fussed and served simply with fresh lemon and a house-made tartar sauce. This starter's all thriller and no filler. While the menu includes a number of seafood and poultry options, prime steaks aged in-house are most popular. T-bones, filet mignon, prime rib, and the signature "Cowboy Steak" are grilled over an open flame, searing a crust that locks in all the beefy, juicy goodness. Complimentary sauces including truffle butter, béarnaise, and bordelaise take the hefty slabs to another level. Share a chocolate soufflé to finish or, just like the good ol' days: a slice of pecan pie.

FURTHER EXPLORATION: TAYLOR'S STEAKHOUSE

In a neighborhood where the sweet and spicy scent of *gochujang* (Korean fermented red chili paste) fills the air, **Taylor's Steakhouse** (3361 W. 8th St., Los Angeles, CA 90005; 213-382-8449; taylorssteakhouse.com) has remained a bastion of classic American fare since 1953. It's hard to go wrong with the prime rib with horseradish cream or the filet mignon.

Papa Cristo's, 2771 W. Pico Blvd., Los Angeles, CA 90006; (323) 737-2970; papacristos.com; Greek; $. The heart and soul of the Byzantine-Latino Quarter is a barely-five-foot-tall man known to all as Papa Cristo. He purchased C&K Imports, a Greek market that his father Sam Chrys established two decades earlier, in 1968 and went on to expand the business to include a casual *taverna* serving homey, unfussy Greek fare. Steady crowds file into this marketplace/restaurant at all hours of the day, placing orders at the service counter, finding an open seat in the dining room, and patiently waiting for food to be delivered. The *dolmades*, grape leaves stuffed with lemony rice, are light and irresistible, while the Sizzling Feta and Tomato is rich and tangy. Both make solid starters while your gyro is being constructed. Papa Cristo's spectacular blend of lamb, beef, and spices comes wrapped in the pillowiest pita bread ever, making for an epically good sandwich. Rotisserie chickens coated in Papa Cristo's signature Red Rub are as popular eaten in as they are taken out. There's house-made baklava for dessert, of course, with shatteringly sweet layers of phyllo, nuts, and honey, as well as Greek yogurt sundaes drizzled with honey or sour cherries. The restaurant's Thursday-night dinners are notoriously festive affairs featuring live music, rowdy crowds, and an abundance of good food. Any visit to Papa Cristo's wouldn't be complete without perusing the market's shelves for European and Greek delicacies, wines, and spirits. Bechamel in a box, anyone?

Patina, 141 S. Grand Ave., Los Angeles, CA 90012; (213) 972-3331; patinarestaurant.com; French; $$$$. Fine dining might not be Los Angeles' forte, but under Chef Joachim Splichal's care Patina has thrived since 1989. Tucked inside the Frank Gehry–designed Walt Disney Concert Hall in Downtown Los Angeles, Patina delights a smartly dressed crowd night after night with seasonally driven tasting menus and a well-curated wine list. It's not just orchestra-goers who file into the cosmopolitan dining room; couples seeking a romantic night out and friends celebrating a milestone are common fixtures at this institution as well. To experience the full Patina treatment, skip the a la carte menu and give the kitchen and wine staff full rein over the evening. Both the vegetarian and carnivorous tasting menus are well-orchestrated, seven-course affairs punctuated by striking plates and harmonious flavors. The cheese cart at the end of the night is worth saving room for.

Philippe the Original, 1001 N. Alameda St., Los Angeles, CA 90012; (213) 628-3781; philippes.com; American; $. The French dip, a roast beef sandwich made on a roll briefly moistened in *jus,* may have originated at Cole's, but it was perfected down the street at Philippe the Original. As with many good things in life, the French dip came about serendipitously. Legend goes that Philippe Mathieu, who opened the restaurant in 1908, stumbled upon the sandwich's unique formula when he accidentally dropped a French roll into a roasting pan filled with hot *jus.* The diner at the receiving end was so thrilled with the mistake that he returned the following day with friends for several more. The rest, as they say, is history. Today, Philippe's famous French dip sandwiches are made with roast beef, roast pork, leg of lamb,

FURTHER EXPLORATION: COLE'S

Head to **Cole's** (118 E. 6th St., Los Angeles, CA 90014; 213-622-4090; 213nightlife.com/colesfrenchdip) for a French dip you can actually dip. The restaurant's pork, pastrami, prime beef, turkey, and lamb sandwiches are served with *au jus* and an "atomic" pickle spear on the side. Sneak away to The Varnish, located at the back of the restaurant behind a closed door, at the end of your meal for a handcrafted cocktail.

turkey, and ham and are served on freshly baked French rolls dipped, or double-dipped if you please, in the roasts' natural gravies. Swiss, American, Monterey jack, or blue cheese may be added. A careful slather of the house special hot mustard complements the sandwich to perfection. To accompany the dip are homemade potato and macaroni salads, coleslaw, and fluorescent pink hard-boiled eggs pickled in beet juice and spices.

Pink's Hot Dogs, 709 N. La Brea Ave., Los Angeles, CA 90038; (323) 931-7594; pinkshollywood.com; Hot Dogs; $. Paul Pink opened his first hot dog stand in 1939. It was a large-wheeled pushcart that he outgrew a few years later, trading it in for a small building constructed on the same site where the wagon once parked. For the past 70 years, hordes of tourists and curious locals have been queuing up, oftentimes for over an hour, for a taste of Mr. Pink's famous hot dogs. Adding to the chaos is Pink's celebrity clientele that includes Celine Dion, Nobu Matsuhisa, Gordon Ramsay, and Martha Stewart. The restaurant's walls are lined with smiling Hollywood faces because every mildly famous person that's ever walked through its doors has left an autographed photo behind. Gaudy? Yes. Fun? Absolutely. The food isn't as notable as the scene, unfortunately. The hot dogs are boiled, which means minimal snap and foggy flavors. The most popular menu item is the classic chili dog, but since you've been waiting in line for the better part of the day, go for something outrageous like the "Lord of the Rings," a 10-inch hot dog topped with onion rings and drenched in tangy barbecue sauce.

Pollos a la Brasa, 764 S. Western Ave., Los Angeles, CA 90005; (213) 387-1531; Peruvian; $$. After two decades operating in a rickety shack at the corner of 8th and Western, Pollos a la Brasa invested in new digs at the same Koreatown strip mall. Everything's shinier at the new spot, but thankfully the signature Peruvian-style rotisserie chicken has remained the same old bird that Los Angeles fell in love with years ago. The secret to Pollos a la Brasa's superior specimen lies in its wine-based marinade and wood-fired treatment. The restaurant's Okinawan-born owner rustled the rotisserie from Peru and feeds it a steady diet of oak, hickory, and eucalyptus, which results in a beautifully browned chicken with a crispy, smoky cloak for skin. A squirt of the spicy *aji verde* (Peruvian green chile sauce) takes the chicken to a perfect 10. Choose a few sides such as rice, french fries, beans, or salad and you're good to go.

Roscoe's House of Chicken and Waffles, 5006 W. Pico Blvd., Los Angeles, CA 90019; (323) 934-4405; roscoeschickenand waffles.com; Southern; $$. For a complete description, see p. 118. **Additional Location:** 1518 N. Gower St., Los Angeles, CA 90028; (323) 466-7453.

Sam Woo Barbecue, 803 N. Broadway, Los Angeles, CA 90012; (213) 687-7238; Chinese; $. With barbecued ducks and pigs glistening by the window and lightning-fast service from the kitchen, the smells, flavors, and spirit of Hong Kong are captured at Sam Woo Barbecue. The original Sam Woo was opened in Chinatown over 30 years ago, and there are now a number of additional locations across the greater Los Angeles area. Sam Woo, by the way, is not a person, but rather the romanization of the Cantonese pronunciation for "triple harmonies"— "Sam" meaning three and "Woo" meaning harmony. The three harmonies of feng shui are heaven, earth, and humanity. Philosophical roots aside, the food here is solid. The taut-skinned roasted ducks and pigs are terrific eaten in or taken out. Be prepared for crispy skin, moist meat, and plentiful pockets of fat. The sugary plum sauce served on the side is worthy of sipping alone. The Tung Kong–style salty chicken is a fragrant bird with distinct gingery and garlicky notes. A generous pour of scallion oil adds even more depth. In addition to proteins, Sam Woo executes noodle dishes superbly. The classic wonton noodles are satisfying, as are the crispy chow mein noodles served with a pork, beef, or seafood gravy. The sauce might be borderline goopy, but it soaks and softens the noodles effectively.

Soot Bull Jeep, 3136 W. 8th St., Los Angeles, CA 90005; (213) 387-3865; Korean; $$. While most Korean barbecue spots fire up neat and tidy gas or electric grills, this Koreatown institution insists on burning hardwood coals that sputter, spark, and singe. In a part of town where there's always someplace newer and shinier to get one's *galbi* fix, crowds have been descending upon Soot Bull Jeep nightly for the past two decades for a feast that is as satisfying as it is smoky. The *banchan* that arrive before the meal are mostly adequate, but save room for the marinated short ribs, several types of prime beef, and wicked cuts of eel. It's a do-it-yourself situation, but don't fret if you haven't found your inner grill master because the efficient staff is ready to swoop in at any moment to rescue meat from turning into ash. The marinated squid, paper-thin tongues, and honeycomb tripe are a bit more forgiving odds and ends. The ventilation here isn't the greatest, so be prepared to smell like a well-charred hunk of protein by meal's end.

Water Grill, 544 S. Grand Ave., Los Angeles, CA 90071; (213) 891-0900; watergrill.com; Seafood; $$$$. In the heart of Downtown Los Angeles, miles away from the ocean, you'll find some of the best seafood in town at Water Grill. The restaurant, which opened in 1991 in the historic PacMutual Building, underwent a massive renovation and thoughtful rebranding in 2012, transforming its formal white-tableclothed dining room into an urban seafood shack with an upbeat vibe and more approachable menu. The prices are still quite hefty, but the food is mostly worth it. Snag a seat at the gorgeous marble bar and start with some selections from the raw bar. The seafood towers featuring fresh-as-can-be sea urchin, clams, mussels, and lobster tails are extravagant and festive, while oysters served on the half shell are simple yet luxurious. If you're feeling particularly indulgent, the giant crab legs priced at $50 a pound are worthy of a splurge. The house-made cocktail sauce and saffron aioli pair perfectly with just about all of the raw bar offerings. For a classic taste of New England, order the lobster roll either Connecticut-style with drawn butter or Maine-style with mayonnaise; both options feature generous hunks of claw and tail meat neatly crammed into a toasted split-top bun. The steamed Whidbey Island Manila clams bathed in a bacon, vermouth, and white wine broth make for a fine appetizer or main course. **Additional Location:** 1401 Ocean Ave., Santa Monica, CA 90401; (310) 394-5669.

Yang Chow, 819 N. Broadway, Los Angeles, CA 90012; (213) 625-0811; yangchow.com; Chinese; $$. The Chinese restaurants in Chinatown might not be as inexpensive or as regionalized as those found in the San Gabriel Valley, but they certainly have their histories and charms, and they're more convenient for Westside dwellers. The Yang family opened Yang Chow upon arriving in Los Angeles from Hong Kong in 1976. Even though there are well over 100 items on the menu, every customer that comes through the doors orders the same thing: Slippery Shrimp. An ocean-dwelling cousin of General Tso, Slippery Shrimp is lightly coated in cornstarch and wok'd to perfection before being doused in a sticky sauce made of ginger, garlic, chiles, and plenty of the refined white stuff. It's sweet as all hell but also addictively crunchy. Also atop everyone's tables are the Dry Sautéed Vegetable Delights, savory spears of asparagus and green beans with a hint of heat and a dousing of oil. With longtime manager William Sung in charge of the front of the house, the service at Yang Chow is head and shoulders above the indifference that one usually encounters at Chinese restaurants.

Zankou Chicken, 5065 Sunset Blvd., Los Angeles, CA 90027; (323) 665-7845; zankouchicken.com; Lebanese; $. It's all about the addictive garlic sauce at this much-loved rotisserie chicken shack founded in Beirut in 1962 by Vartkes and Markrid Iskenderian. The couple opened the first American branch of Zankou in Hollywood in 1984 after fleeing war-torn Lebanon. Today, there are nearly a dozen locations in and around the Southland. Nothing's too formal at this fast-casual spot where orders are placed and paid for at the counter, and numbers are shouted out as food is ready for pickup. The famous white- and dark-meat chicken plates come with a side of curiously pink pickled turnips, out-of-season tomatoes, spicy peppers, pita bread, and hummus. You can count on Zankou to produce an impressively golden bird that's juicy inside and crispy outside. Even though the chicken stands on its own, a slathering of the garlic sauce that Markrid Iskenderian brought with him all the way from Beirut makes it even better. It's hard to say what's in the sauce exactly, but its consistency isn't far from Crisco, while its flavors are tangy and sharp. The sauce lingers on the tongue long after the chicken is gone, which is a good thing as far as everyone is concerned. Rounding out the menu are platters of *shawarma* (spit-roasted steak), *tarna* (marinated chicken), falafel, *shish kabob* (marinated steak), *lule kabob* (ground steak), and chicken *kabob*. **Additional Location:** 7851 W. Sunset Blvd., Los Angeles, CA 90046; (323) 882-6365.

 *Sublime Sweets*

Bhan Kanom, 5271 Hollywood Blvd., Los Angeles, CA 90027; (323) 871-8030; bhankanomthai.com; Thai; $. Sweetened beans and starches, as well as an avalanche of coconut milk and sugar, form the base of Southeast Asian desserts. Thaitown's Bhan Kanom, which literally translates as "dessert house," makes a remarkable assortment of Thai sweets beyond the usual mangoes with sticky rice and stocks an array of cookies, snacks, and candies imported straight from the Motherland. Some of the most approachable and delightful desserts are found underneath the heat lamps. Try the *panchi*, lavender-hued griddlecakes made with taro, coconut, and corn, and the banana leaf-wrapped sticky rice filled with softened bananas or taro. The "Thai tacos" will most likely catch your eye. These fragile pancakes are brushed with meringue and topped with golden strands of *foi thong* (egg custard). There's also a savory version with coconut and shrimp. Also look for the *dok jok*, an especially crispy cookie made of flour, sesame, and sugar that looks like a flower in full bloom. Beyond the sweets lining the front counter is a refrigerator case packed with even more tropical delights. The striking green pandan pudding and the *ruammit* (corn, tapioca, and fruits in sweetened coconut milk) are refreshing choices.

FURTHER EXPLORATION: RAM SONG THAI FOODS

Neighboring sweets shack **Ram Song Thai Foods** (5185 Hollywood Blvd., Los Angeles, CA 90027; 323-667-2055), also on Hollywood Boulevard, specializes in deep-fried Thai pastries including sweet and savory nuggets filled with peanuts, shrimp, or pineapple and puff pastry pockets stuffed with chicken. The taro and banana chips are deep-fried in-house.

Bottega Louie, 700 S. Grand Ave., Los Angeles, CA 90017; (213) 802-1470; bottegalouie.com; French; $. The patisserie at Bottega Louie is a thing of beauty, especially the splendid array of French macarons that greets customers as they stroll through the breezy doorway. These airy meringue sandwich cookies filled with ganache, buttercream, and jam never fail to send hearts aflutter. The rainbow of flavors includes strawberry, violet cassis, matcha, lemon, salted caramel, and espresso. Equally swoon-worthy are

FURTHER EXPLORATION:
'LETTE MACARONS

'Lette Macarons (lettemacarons.com) is a collaboration between Paulette Koumetz, a macaron enthusiast, and Christophe Michalak, a French pastry chef. They opened their first shop in Beverly Hills in 2007 and have since added another outlet in Pasadena. All of 'Lette's macarons are handmade daily. The passion fruit is awesomely tart, with a bright curd filling sandwiched by the daintiest cookie.

122 N. Larchmont Blvd., Los Angeles, CA; (323) 469-3620
9466 Charleville Blvd., Beverly Hills, CA; (310) 275-0023
14 S. Fair Oaks Ave., Pasadena, CA; (626) 793-5551

the sugar-coated doughnuts piped with a jammy raspberry filling. If you're dining in rather than just making a pit stop for sweets, save room for a chocolate soufflé. It takes a little longer than the other desserts to prepare, but when it arrives at the table, a solid inch taller than its ramekin and with a gravy boat of crème anglaise on the side, you'll see that it's worth the wait.

Bread Lounge, 700 S. Santa Fe Ave., Los Angeles, CA 90021; (213) 327-0782; Bakery; $. After years of providing dynamite loaves to some of the city's best restaurants, Israeli baker Ran Zimon finally opened a retail space on the edge of the Arts District. Now, Downtown residents requiring pastries with their morning coffee or baguettes for a dinner party have access to the goods 7 days a week. Everything at Bread Lounge, from the traditional baguettes to the oval-shaped batards in flavors like potato-rosemary, fig-walnut, and multigrain, is masterfully baked with a crusty exterior and structural integrity. It takes years of practice and dedication to produce loaves like Mr. Zimon's, and Los Angeles residents are fortunate to have access to a place like this. Come early for the ricotta Danishes, which are lightly sweetened with white chocolate and tarted up with whole cranberries. The plain, sweet, and savory croissants are Parisian perfect, especially the ones stuffed with Emmental cheese and Black Forest ham and speckled with poppy and sesame seeds. Those looking to linger can stick around for a simple prosciutto or "Il Tricalore" (mozzarella, pesto, tomato) sandwich. When the bread's this good, it's impossible to go wrong.

Cafe Dulce, 134 Japanese Village Plaza, Los Angeles, CA 90012; (213) 346-9910; cafedulce.co; Bakery, Cafe; $. Here in Los Angeles, it seems like every city block claims at least one mom-and-pop doughnut shop selling the usual French crullers and frosted maple bars. Relatively new to the dining landscape are gourmet doughnut shops thinking outside the pink bakery box. Cafe Dulce, which is tucked into the Japanese Village Plaza in Little Tokyo, is leading the charge with intriguing flavors like green tea, macadamia caramel, frosted bacon, and spirulina churro. The custard-filled, sugar-crusted green tea doughnut is the shop's bestseller. There's a precious small window after a doughnut is fried when the stars are aligned and the taste and texture are perfect. To seize the moment at Cafe Dulce, come in early, when everything is at its absolute freshest and fluffiest. And if a batch of green tea doughnuts happens to be coming out of the fryer while you're there, you'd better grab a half dozen. The shop's cold-brewed Lamill ice coffee pairs exceptionally well with any of the aforementioned deep-fried items.

Fugetsu-Do, 315 E. 1st St., Los Angeles, CA 90012; (213) 625-8595; fugetsu-do.com; Japanese; $. It's fascinating to think that Philippe the Original, Los Angeles' oldest restaurant, is a full five years younger than Fugetsu-Do, a family owned and operated confectionary in Little Tokyo. Established in 1903, this jewel box of a store continues to thrive and gain new followers with its too-pretty-to-eat Japanese *mochi* and *manju*. While the selection of flavors and fillings is mostly in line with tradition, peanut butter-filled and chocolate *mochi* have joined the lineup in recent years to meet the changing tastes of local clientele. Still, the most popular and satisfying creations are those flavored with teas, flowers, and herbs, and stuffed with whole or pureed red and white beans. The seasonal *sakuramochi,* a sweet *mochi* filled with red bean paste and delicately wrapped in a cherry blossom leaf, is one to look out for during the warmer months. The flower-shaped *kiku mochi* is unique to the shop and is composed of pink and white *mochi* with a white bean center. The pale green *manju* filled with red bean paste and dusted in rice powder is especially fetching.

Lark Cake Shop, 3337 W. Sunset Blvd., Los Angeles, CA 90026; (323) 667-2968; larkcakeshop.com; Bakery; $$. Cupcakes are cute and all, but here at James and Colleen Standish's Silver Lake bakery, it's the sky-high layer cakes that rule the sugar high roost. A dozen different creations, including Stacey's Old-Fashioned Coconut Cake (coconut cake with cream cheese icing and coconut shavings) and the Berry Shortcake (white cake layered with fresh berries, pastry cream, and whipped cream), are baked fresh every day, ready to be personalized and picked up for backyard birthdays and celebrations of all sorts. The best cake of all is barely a cake at all. The Old-Fashioned Ice Box Cake, seven layers of chocolate wafers and fluffy whipped cream, is a tall stack of dear sweet richness. With the cream softening the cookies just so, a swift flick of the fork cuts through the layers like butter.

L'Artisan du Chocolat, 3364 W. 1st St., Los Angeles, CA 90004; (213) 252-8721; lartisanduchocolat.net; Chocolate; $. When Whajung Park met Christian Alexandre at Picholine years ago, she was a recreational confectionarian while he was a recovering finance whiz.

The two bonded over their shared passion for all things French, married a year later, and launched L'Artisan du Chocolat soon after. Here at their Silver Lake storefront and kitchen, Ms. Park produces eye-poppingly gorgeous chocolates and truffles in intriguing flavors like curry kiwi, pineapple coconut, matcha, basil, cucumber vodka, and bacon. The chef's Parisian training—she studied pastry and chocolate making at L'Ecole de la rue Jean Ferrandi and worked with the master chocolatier-confiseur Alain Furet of Le Furet Tanrade—means that the chocolates are deftly made, subtly flavored, and never too sweet.

Lazy Ox Canteen, 241 S. San Pedro St., Los Angeles, CA 90012; (213) 626-5299; lazyoxcanteen.com; New American; $. Even though Chef Josef Centeno is no longer behind the stove at Little Tokyo's Lazy Ox Canteen, his culinary legacy endures through his signature rice pudding, which has remained a menu mainstay long after his departure. The rice pudding begins with tender grains of arborio rice scented with Mexican cinnamon and vanilla. Heavy cream, half-and-half, and sweetened condensed milk combine to create a thoroughly rich and creamy consistency. What takes this rice pudding straight to heaven is the freshly whipped cream that's incorporated into the pudding at the last possible moment. It creates a light, almost airy profile that rice puddings rarely boast. A sprinkling of nutty brittle brings on the crunch, while whipped cream and sticky caramel are ready to be heaped and drizzled on as you see fit. One order is plenty for two or three.

Mae Ting's Coconut Cakes, 1100 N. Main St., Los Angeles, CA 90012; (323) 632-2071; Thai; $. Mae Ting and her merry band of Thai food vendors set up their wares every Saturday and Sunday 8 a.m. to 5 p.m. outside Downtown's LAX-C, also known as the Thai Costco. There are sweetly marinated pork and chicken skewers and Isaan-style sausages on the grill, freshly fried curry puff pastries, and made-to-order green papaya salads. Mae Ting also sells a number of specialty foods made by her friends like *nam pusadee*, a kind of garlicky pig's ear and ground pork sausage that's traditionally consumed raw over beers. While the selection of savories is truly stellar, especially the plump sour sausages, it's the coconut cakes (*kanom krok*) that get top billing. Made from a simple batter of coconut milk, sugar, and salt, the *kanom krok* are cooked in dimpled cast-iron pans. As soon as the exteriors are crisp-golden and the innards are gooey with coconut cream, the bite-size *kanom krok* are scooped out with spoons and served a moment later. Each bite tastes like a sweet and fluffy dream. For those residing on the opposite side of town, Mae Ting's son Matthew runs a similar weekends-only operation in North Hollywood in a parking lot at Coldwater Canyon Avenue and Roscoe Boulevard 9 a.m. to 5 p.m.

Mikawaya, 118 Japanese Village Plaza Mall, Los Angeles, CA 90012; (213) 624-1681; mikawayausa.com; Japanese; $. Long before Mikawaya put *mochi* ice cream on the dessert map, it quietly manufactured artful Japanese pastries called *wagashi* in Little Tokyo. It wasn't until 1994, a solid 84 years after the shop first opened, that the famous *mochi* ice creams were introduced. These four-bite wonders of pounded sticky rice folded over ice cream come in flavors like mango, red bean, green tea, coffee, chocolate, strawberry, and vanilla. While the *mochi* is round, smooth, and dusted in cornstarch on the outside, the innards are cold and sweet. Even though these frozen treats are widely available in grocery stores across the Southland, sweet seekers continue to visit the original shop for a *mochi* ice cream fix at the source. Also at the Little Tokyo flagship are *mochi*-less ice creams and gelatos available by the scoop, a selection of Japanese imported snacks, and house-made *wagashi*. Mikawaya's original founder Ryuzaburo Hashimoto named the store after his hometown of Mikawa, in Aichiken, Japan. **Additional Location:** 333 S. Alameda St., Los Angeles, CA 90013; (213) 613-0611.

Milk, 7290 Beverly Blvd., Los Angeles, CA 90036; (323) 939-6455; **themilkshop.com; Ice Cream; $.** If sweet treats served up cold and creamy are your rapture, then Milk is the place for you. Think sundaes, malts, floats, shakes, and house-made ice creams dolled up every which way. Many of the shop's flavors are inspired by the seasons, like summery sweet corn and autumnal pumpkin, so swing by often to get a true taste of what's fresh. Gathering here with a group all but guarantees a giant sundae in the center of the table. There's a classic one with hot fudge or butterscotch, whipped cream, peanuts, and a cherry, as well as a highly caffeinated "Espresso a la Mode" creation served with two shots of espresso, vanilla bean ice cream, chocolate sauce, hazelnuts, whipped cream, and dark chocolate pearls. Ice cream sandwiches constructed from airy macarons are one of the shop's signature sweets. The Thai tea and minty grasshopper sandwiches benefit from this treatment. Also irresistible is Milk's version of Nestlé's timeless Drumsticks. In addition to the chocolate and peanut–coated original, there's a butterscotch variety crusted with Butterfinger crumbles. For those rare days when it's too cold for ice cream, there are plenty of baked goods to sink your teeth into. The Windex-hued blue velvet cake is a visual stunner.

Mitsuru Cafe, 117 Japanese Village Plaza Mall, Los Angeles, CA 90012; (213) 613-1028; **Dessert; $.** It's impossible to walk through the Japanese Village Plaza Mall without peering through the glass window at Mitsuru Cafe, where *imagawayaki* are made fresh throughout the day. These Japanese pancakelike pastries filled with azuki beans are handcrafted using cast aluminum grills. A neat squirt of not-too-sweet batter fills each circular mold, followed by a generous dollop of sweetened red beans. Eventually, a fitted hat is plopped atop the filling. The entire package is griddled until evenly golden and served warm.

Watching the process from start to finish never fails to mesmerize and work up an appetite.

Mr. Churro, 15 Olvera St., Los Angeles, CA 90012; (213) 680-9036; Mexican; $. Olvera Street, which is named in honor of Judge Agustín Olvera, is the oldest section of Downtown Los Angeles. In 1930, this historical stretch was converted into a colorful Mexican marketplace where music, dancing, and holiday celebrations were centered. Today, the street is as vibrant as ever, but admittedly touristy and borderline kitschy. The jewel of Olvera is Mr. Churro, a small shop specializing in Mexican-style deep-fried *churros*. Each one is fried to order, coated in granulated sugar, and piped with all sorts of wonderful fillings including *fresa* (strawberry), *cajeta* (caramel), *crema* (custard), and chocolate. The sticky caramel made from goat's milk is the most irresistible of the lot. What makes Mr. Churro's signature cruller extra special is its delightful texture; custardy innards paired with warm caramel and a crisp exterior make for a supremely satisfying specimen.

Phoenix Bakery, 969 N. Broadway, Los Angeles, CA 90012; (213) 628-4642; phoenixbakeryinc.com; Chinese; $. Strawberries and whipped cream are the lifeblood of the Chan family, the proud proprietors of Phoenix Bakery since 1938. When Fung Chow Chan and his wife, Wai Hing, first opened the shop in Chinatown, the shelves were mostly lined with traditional Chinese pastries and cookies made using family recipes. Throughout the years, the selection has evolved to include French-style desserts like éclairs, palmiers, and fruit tarts, as well as the signature fresh strawberry whipped cream cake that Chan's brother Lun introduced in the 1940s. At the height of the cake's popularity in the 1970s, as many as 1,000 slices were sold each Saturday. The handmade mooncakes are also a huge draw when the mid-autumn moon festival rolls around each September. The classic lotus paste– filled mooncake with a single salted egg yolk in the center is certainly delightful, but it's the "fruit nut" mooncake that really exemplifies what this bakery is capable of. The filling, a sticky mixture of dried meat, fruit, and seeds, charms with its rush of sweet and savory. The price of these mooncakes is three times the cost of factory-produced ones, and they are worth every dollar.

Scoops, 712 N. Heliotrope Dr., Los Angeles, CA 90004; (323) 906-2649; Ice Cream; $. Tai Kim cleverly combines unlikely ingredients to create one-of-a-kind flavors at this little ice cream shop in Hel-Mel (the intersection of Heliotrope Drive and Melrose Avenue). His unique formula creates ice cream that is thoroughly creamy, yet somehow light on the tongue. The shop's signature scoop, "brown bread" (vanilla ice cream, candied Grape Nuts cereal, caramel swirls), is the only flavor that is available every day. The ever-rotating roster includes stand-outs like black sesame banana, roasted rice cheesecake, strawberry balsamic, bacon caramel, Guinness tiramisu, orange hazelnut, and caramel chocolate toffee. The beauty of each flavor is its clarity and nuance—the black sesame banana honestly tastes like a bold collision of the two elements. Patrons are encouraged to fuel Mr. Kim's creativity by proposing any number of kooky combinations using the shop's suggestion board. Matthew Kang opened a second branch in Palms to share Scoops' exceptional product with Westside residents. A special edition "brown brown bread" made with a caramel ice cream base is this shop's signature flavor. Vanilla is just so vanilla compared to Mr. Kim's outrageously delicious creations.

Semi Sweet Bakery, 105 E. 6th St., Los Angeles, CA 90013; (213) 228-9975; semisweetbakery.com; Bakery; $. Inventive sweets that aren't too sugary are what it's all about at this Downtown bake-shop. The lovely lady behind the operation is Sharlena Fong, a one-time New York City consultant who left the corporate world to pursue her true passion: desserts. After refining her palate and techniques at Eleven Madison Park, Per Se, and Bouchon Bakery in New York City and at **Nickel Diner** (p. 95) in Los Angeles, she teamed up with

Dennis Hunter and James Gonzales to open Semi Sweet Bakery. Mornings bring maple bacon sticky buns and their savory cousins with sun-dried tomato, pesto, and goat cheese. There are also Danishes of all stripes (spinach, prosciutto goat cheese, and Chocolate Chip Monkey), coffee cakes galore (hazelnut sour cream, almond amaretto, and pumpkin), and the ever-popular Pocket Tarts filled with things like strawberries, apple cinnamon, and peanut butter and jelly. Throughout the day you'll find Ding a Lings, a gourmet spin on Hostess Ding Dongs. In addition to the classic version from childhood with chocolate cake and vanilla cream, there's also red velvet and peanut butter. Cookies are pure bliss. Try the Samoa macaroons or the ones punched up with chocolate, butterscotch, and Ruffles potato chips.

FURTHER EXPLORATION: NICKEL DINER

Prior to striking out on her own at Semi Sweet Bakery, Fong seduced Los Angeles with her maple-glazed bacon doughnut at Downtown's **Nickel Diner** (524 S. Main St., Los Angeles, CA 90013; 213-623-8301; nickeldiner.com). Even though she's no longer the head pastry chef, the doughnut remains the diner's top seller.

Shaky Alibi, 7401 Beverly Blvd., Los Angeles, CA 90036; (323) 938-5282; shakyalibi.com; Belgian; $. Shaky Alibi has been plying its neighbors with a steady stream of sugar and caffeine since its debut during the summer of 2010. The specialty at this Fairfax District cafe is Liège-style waffles that are made to order using a recipe from Owner R.J.

Milano's great-grandmother. Whereas American-style Belgian waffles are fluffy things with deep pockets, their Liège counterparts are constructed from yeast-risen dough embedded with pearl sugar. The result is a perfectly dense, flaky, and caramelized waffle that's slightly crisp all around. The Liège waffles here come in both sweet and savory forms. Skip the Monte Cristo–esque savory creations and focus on the simpler sweet ones. The best of the bunch is smeared with Speculoos, an imported spread from Belgium made from spicy gingersnaps. Be prepared for your eyeballs roll toward the back of your head.

FURTHER EXPLORATION: WAFFLES DE LIEGE

Southern California's first waffle truck, **Waffles de Liege** (twitter .com/wafflesdeliege), whips up a terrific waffle made from a dough that owners George Wu and Lawrence Tai developed after countless trials. Waffles can be ordered plain, slathered with Nutella or Speculoos, or a la mode with ice cream from **Fosselman's** (see p. 184) in Alhambra.

Short Cake, Stall #316 at the Original Farmers Market; (323) 761-7976; shortcakela.com; Bakery; $. While the late Amy Pressman and her partner Chef Nancy Silverton were working on the launch of Short Order at the Original Farmers Market, the opportunity to open a bakery alongside the burger joint presented itself. Pressman, an expert baker by trade and former owner of the Old Town Bakery in Pasadena, jumped at the chance to share her brand of wholesome American desserts with the Farmers Market crowd. Early each morning, Short Cake's team of expert bakers lines every inch of the pastry counter with an awe-inspiring collection of bars, scones, pies, tarts, muffins, croissants, cookies, and cakes. The most irresistible treats of them all are the two-tiered cakes, available by the slice. The chocolate cake with cardamom cream is a sophisticated and satisfying little number, while the spice cake with caramel cream cheese frosting is as sensational as all get-out. Short Cake's version of classic blondies, dubbed Brunettes, top a delightfully chewy brown sugar base with toasted pine nuts and fresh thyme. The adorably named Buttercup, a muffin-shaped croissant, is a touch sweet with an irresistibly caramelized bottom. A selection of savory open-face and croissant sandwiches, salads, savory bread pudding, and hand pies are also available to supplement that sugar high.

Sweet Lady Jane Bakery, 8360 Melrose Ave., Los Angeles, CA 90069; (323) 653-7145; sweetladyjane.com; Bakery; $. Special occasions call for extraordinary cakes, and Jane Lockhart comes through with bells on at Sweet Lady Jane. She opened the original location on Melrose Avenue in 1988 after growing tired of store-bought desserts that tasted "too sweet" and "too commercial." Lockhart's firm commitment to baking with only the finest imported chocolate, the freshest butter and cream, and the highest quality in-season fruits has garnered a bevy of fans. The swoon-inducing Triple Berry Shortcake is a fetching three-layer creation made of yellow butter cake filled with lightly sweetened whipped cream and a trio of fresh berries (raspberries, strawberries, and either blackberries or blueberries). The cake is frosted with whipped cream and finished with buttercream and fresh berries. For those who believe that chocolate should be its own food group, the Old-Fashioned Chocolate with dark chocolate cake, French chocolate buttercream, and Belgian chocolate ganache is essential for a well-balanced diet. In addition to the eye-poppingly beautiful layer cakes, Sweet Lady Jane works her magic with cheesecakes, cookies, cupcakes, pies, and tarts. On the savory side are simple but satisfying salads, soups, and sandwiches.

FURTHER EXPLORATION: SUSINA BAKERY

Susina Bakery (7122 Beverly Blvd., Los Angeles, CA 90036; 323-934-7900; susinabakery.com) in Mid-City makes a layered berry number that rivals Sweet Lady Jane's. The Berry Blossom is composed of three layers of vanilla sponge cake brushed with orange liqueur and filled with white chocolate mousse and fresh berries. Crumbled meringue and white chocolate shavings offer the finishing touches.

Valerie Confections, 3360 W. 1st St., Los Angeles, CA 90004; (213) 739-8149; valerieconfections.com; Candy; $. Established in 2004 by Valerie Gordon and Stan Weightman Jr., Valerie Confections is a small shop with a big reputation for its modern interpretations of classic chocolates and confections. The duo made a splash on the local candy scene with the debut of their artisanal toffee line, which included six varieties (almond, almond *fleur de sel*, ginger, orange, mint, and classic) all hand-dipped in bittersweet chocolate. From its small-scale start, Valerie Confections grew its offerings to include nougats, truffles, caramels, petits fours, and fruit preserves, building a reputation for exceptional products along the way. While most everything is available for sale online, visiting the shop is a treat for the senses. The elegant petits fours are simply irresistible, especially the rose-scented one topped with candied rose petals and the ginger one enrobed in a bittersweet chocolate glaze. Valerie Confections also bakes up an impressive line of vintage cakes inspired by California's most iconic sweets including Blum's Coffee Crunch Cake, the Brown Derby's Grapefruit Cake, and Chasen's Banana Shortcake that are available by special order. A weekends-only line of market-inspired baked goods including hand pies, galettes, and muffins goes on sale every Saturday at the Santa Monica Farmers Market and every Sunday at the Hollywood Farmers Market.

Specialty Stores, Markets & Producers

Anzen Hardware, 309 E. 1st St., Los Angeles, CA 90012; (213) 628-2068. Whether you're looking for a new pair of bonsai shears, seeds for planting, stackable bamboo steamers, or the perfect chef's knife, Anzen Hardware is the place to go. This narrow aisled and tastefully cluttered shop has been serving Little Tokyo's Japanese community since 1946. Nori Takatani, the shop's ever-so-helpful owner, has worked here since 1954 and is incredibly knowledgeable about everything from gardening to knife sharpening. In fact, many of Los Angeles' top chefs including Ludo Lefebvre and Mary Sue Milliken bring their knives here to get their edge back. Aside from the terrific selection of imported Japanese cooking and gardening supplies, Anzen stocks traditional hardware needs like hammers, nails, screws, keys, and the like.

Bar Keeper, 3910 W. Sunset Blvd., Los Angeles, CA 90029; (323) 669-1675; barkeepersilverlake.com. Cocktailians in the know swing by this barware boutique in the heart of Sunset Junction to stock up on gadgets, glassware, bars, books, and beakers, as well as obscure bottles made by smaller producers. The boozy selection changes every three days and reflects the shop owner Joe Keeper's sensibilities; he has a penchant for ryes, tequilas, and mescals. In addition to drinkables and mixables, Keeper hunts down rare and vintage shakers, punch bowls, stirrers, and the like at flea markets and thrift stores across the country. He has an eye for detail, and the selection here is unparalleled as a result. Keeper, a treasure trove of mixology know-how, can usually be found behind the bar. Feel free to pick his well-trained brain on how to pour the perfect martini or how to best incorporate rhubarb bitters.

Cookbook, 1549 Echo Park Ave., Los Angeles, CA 90026; (213) 250-1900; cookbookla.com. They say that the best things come in small packages, and at Echo Park's premier green grocer Cookbook, that is certainly the case. Chef-Owner Marta Teegan crams every inch of this 500-square-foot space with responsibly grown produce, everyday staples like meat, cheese, butter, and eggs, and artisanal products from California and around the globe including Dr. Bob's ice cream, Mast Brothers chocolate, and Creminelli salami. There are also wonderfully thoughtful and delicious prepared foods available throughout the day. The menu changes with the seasons and highlights recipes from a different cookbook each week. Breakfast brings fluffy frittatas and plain and chocolate croissants from **Proof Bakery** (p. 128) in Atwater Village. Lunchtime means simple but well-constructed sandwiches, usually one herbivorous and the other carnivorous, as well as two remarkably fresh salads. Two different and more substantial salads are prepared for the dinnertime crowd, like torn chicken with roasted potato,

---

FURTHER EXPLORATION: CORTEZ

Cookbook's Marta Teegan introduced **Cortez** (1356 Allison Ave., Los Angeles, CA 90026; 213-481-8015; restaurantcortez .com) after years of hearing from neighbors and customers that she really ought to open a restaurant. In the spirit of Cookbook, this Echo Park eatery serves an ever-changing menu featuring locally grown organic produce, sustainable seafood, pasture-raised meats, and house-made pickles and charcuterie.

---

broccoli, parsley, chives, and roasted figs, and tuna with string beans and radicchio.

Grand Central Market, 317 S. Broadway, Los Angeles, CA 90013; (213) 624-2378; grandcentralsquare.com. Located on the ground floor of the Homer Laughlin Building in Downtown Los Angeles, Grand Central Market is a bustling place where locals and visitors of all stripes gather to eat, meet, and shop. The energy here is palpable, and everything gleams with deliciousness. With over 30 merchants selling everything from steam table Chinese food to chilled *aguas frescas* to Thai street food, there's something for everyone, so long as you arrive hungry. Before picking your poison, walk around the entire market to size up the selection. There's always a substantial crowd at Sarita's Pupuseria (Stall No. E-5). Here, the Salvadoran specialty consisting of thick corn tortillas stuffed with cheeses and meats is made from scratch and griddled to order. Once your *pupusa* arrives, garnish it with tomato salsa and *curtido*, a lightly fermented cabbage slaw with red chiles and vinegar that curbs the richness with aplomb. Across the way from Sarita is the ever-popular Tacos Tumbras a Tomas (Stall No. A-5), which specializes in supersize Michoacan-style tacos and *tortas*. The goat *tortas* weigh in at well over a pound and require two-and-a-half hands to hold. Come with a friend and order modestly. Also notable is the Thai-style chicken rice at Sticky Rice (Stall No. C-5) and Valerie's (Stall No. E-3) cold fried chicken sandwich. Before departing into the warm Southern California sun, pick up some fruits and vegetables for the week at one of the produce stands.

Joan's on Third, 8350 W. 3rd St., Los Angeles, CA 90048; (323) 655-2285; joansonthird.com. Long before 3rd Street developed into the shopping and dining destination that it is today, Joan McNamara launched a small catering company on the quiet stretch east of La

Cienega. When an adjacent storefront became available in 1998, she scooped up the space to open a gourmet marketplace where locals could stop in for a baguette or meet for a cup of coffee. Today, the 3,000-square-foot emporium includes a bakery, gelato bar, olive bar, and cheese counter. There's also a small kitchen for hot breakfast and lunch items, sandwiches, salads, soups, and seasonally inspired prepared foods including grilled vegetables and roasted meats, chicken, and fish. It's impossible to go wrong at Joan's, as it is affectionately referred to by the local set, but the sandwiches are particularly noteworthy. The apricot-glazed ham and brie with mustard caper sauce hits the perfect sweet, savory, and gooey notes, while the tuna melt with aged Vermont cheddar and tomato on a baguette is unstoppable. The selection of cookies, bars, and cupcakes never fails to satiate a sweet tooth, especially the lemon bars, magic bars (caramel, pecans, and chocolate chips), and the chocolate coconut cupcakes.

Koreatown Galleria, 3250 W. Olympic Blvd., #400, Los Angeles, CA 90006; (323) 733-6000; koreatowngalleria.com. Located on the ground floor of the Koreatown Galleria is one of the most expansive and impressive Korean supermarkets in the neighborhood. In addition to carrying every Korean ingredient imaginable and a selection of stunningly fresh seafood and produce, the store offers over two dozen prepared *banchan* including seasoned garlic stalk, pickled perilla leaves, braised lotus leaf, and seasoned baby crabs. The goods are sold by weight, so feel free to buy as little or as much as needed. Hot foods like kimchee fried rice, seafood pancakes, broiled fishes, and soups (soybean paste soup and anchovy kimchee soup) are hidden underneath heat lamps. These quick bites are ideal for an easy lunch or dinner. And of course, the selection of kimchee here is stellar. The Galleria stocks a few varieties of fresh kimchee in the refrigerator case, as well as numerous jars of the deeply fermented stuff.

Mercado Olympic. On Saturday and Sunday from early morning until early evening, Olympic Boulevard just west of Central Avenue is transformed into an exciting street market. Vendors hawking regional specialties from Mexico City, Puebla, and Michoacan perfume the streets with an intoxicating blend of stewed meats, melted cheese, and blistered *chicharones* (deep-fried pork skin). It can get a little chaotic with the crowds, but grab a cold *agua fresca* and seek out a few of the more unique offerings. The *tacos de canasta* (basket tacos), softened corn tortillas filled with a little meat and a lot of flavor, are stewed in their own sweat. Look for vendors with plastic coolers or cardboard boxes covered with a damp towel. They aren't the most substantial bites, so a half dozen can be easily tucked away. Pueblan-style quesadillas stuffed with squash blossoms and *huitlacoche* (corn smut) are made to order and are a delightfully gooey treat. The ladies with the flattops and neatly lined ingredients will make it just the way you like it. If you happen to spot sausage artisans from Toluca, purchase a pound or two of the chile spiked chorizo or *longaniza*. *Chorizo verde*, a Tolucan specialty whose brilliant hue comes from a mixture of green chiles and vegetables, isn't consistently available, but it's worth investigating just in case. Aside from the parade of food, the long-standing storefronts that line Olympic Boulevard selling kitchen supplies, discounted produce, and piñatas are worth checking out.

Selam Market, 5534 W. Pico Blvd., Los Angeles, CA 90019; (323) 935-5567. Selam Market may look like your average neighborhood liquor store at first glance, but scratch beneath the surface and you'll find that there's much more lining the shelves than the usual dusty cans of Dinty Moore and overpriced produce. Neighbors have come to depend on this Ethiopian-run corner store for everyday basics like fresh meat and bananas, as well as East African staples like lentils, cracked wheat, oats, garbanzo beans, cottage cheese, and chile pastes (most of the dry goods are sold in bulk). There's also clarified butter sold in jars and a bevy of common and not-so-common spices including *berbere*,

THE ORIGINAL FARMERS MARKET

6333 W. 3rd St., Los Angeles, CA 90036; (323) 933-9211; farmersmarket la.com. The Original Farmers Market was founded in the summer of 1934 when a group of local farmers pulled their pickup trucks into an empty lot at the corner of 3rd and Fairfax and began selling freshly picked fruits, vegetables, and flowers to passersby. In the 80 years since its serendipitous inception, the dirt lot has evolved into a year-round marketplace with a dizzying selection of artisanal food stalls, restaurants, and produce vendors. The exceptional retailers and eateries that call the market home make it an essential experience for anyone hungry for a slice of history and apple pie with cheddar on top.

Bennett's Ice Cream, Stall #548; (323) 939-6786; Ice Cream; $. Founded by Scott Bennett in 1946, Bennett's Ice Cream is a family-owned operation specializing in spectacularly good ice cream that's churned on the premises daily. The selection of ice creams and sorbets includes traditional flavors like pistachio, rum raisin, and strawberry, as well as inventive ones like Cabernet Sauvignon, pumpkin, and Fancy Nancy (coffee ice cream, banana, and caramel).

Bob's Coffee & Donuts, Stall #450; (323) 933-8929; Doughnuts, $. Set sail on the deep-fried ocean of bliss with one of Bob's classic glazed rings, or if you're feeling a little decadent, a fresh-from-the-fryer apple fritter. There are no fancy glazes or innovative flavors here, just fresh and well-made doughnuts in one of L.A.'s most iconic markets.

Du-par's, Stall #210; (323) 933-8446; du-pars.com; American, Diner; $$. James Dunn and Edward Parsons, who combined their surnames to create the restaurant's name, founded this greasy spoon in 1938, making it the Farmers Market's oldest establishment. In classic L.A. fashion, Du-par's underwent a massive nip/tuck in 2006 to modernize the kitchen, add a patio, and fully restore its classic 1930s decor. The space may look spiffier than it has in decades, but the menu and 24-hour service have stayed true to its diner roots. Breakfast is served all day, of course, and features the finest stack of classic buttermilk hotcakes in town. There's also chicken potpie, steak, burgers, turkey and mashed potatoes, and fruit pies. A slice of apple pie with cheddar cheese melted on top is a must.

Littlejohn's English Toffee House, Stall #432; (323) 936-5379; littlejohnscandies.com; Candy; $. Mr. and Mrs. Littlejohn moved their two-decade old English toffee operation into the Original Farmers Market in 1946. All of the candies are made on-site in a small room with a big window where onlookers can witness the craft firsthand. The namesake English toffee is as buttery as ever with a milk chocolate coat and crushed almonds to finish.

Lotería! Grill, Stall #322; (323) 930-2211; loteriagrill.com; Mexican; $$. For a complete description, see p. 43.

Pampas Grill, Stall #618; (323) 931-1928; pampas-grill.com; Brazilian; $$. Buffets aren't usually known for careful cooking, but here at this traditional Brazilian *comida à quilo* joint, the food is fresh, flavorful, and paid for by the pound. Move down the line to select from an assortment of side dishes (vegetables, salads, and pastas) and finish at the *churrasco* station where grilled steaks, sausages, and chicken await. The top sirloin cap and bacon-wrapped chicken are favorites among the carnivorous set.

Short Cake, Stall #316; (323) 761-7976; shortcakela.com; Bakery; $. For a complete description, see p. 96.

Short Order, Stall #110; (323) 761-7970; shortorderla.com; American; $$. Classic American fare is given a gourmet makeover at Chef Nancy Silverton and the late Amy Pressman's Short Order. The strongest burger of the lot is the least beefy of them all. Amy's Turkey Burger with cheddar, melted celery, leeks, and mustardy mayo is worth giving a moo about. Pair it with an order of "spuds," deep-fried baked potato nuggets. To wash it all down there are vanilla, chocolate, and coffee malt custard shakes, cocktails designed by Julian Cox, and boozy shakes that offer the best of both worlds.

Singapore's Banana Leaf, Stall #122; (323) 933-4627; singapores bananaleaf.com; Singaporean; $. Considering Singapore's strong tradition of hawker centers, it seems appropriate that one of L.A.'s only Singaporean restaurants is at a stall inside the Original Farmers Market. The *roti paratha,* grilled bread served with vegetarian curry, is flaky and filling. The beef and chicken *satay* skewers served with peanut sauce make for a solid main course, as do any of the curries. Those in the know get the *mee goreng* (pan-fried noodles) with an egg on top.

a blend of chile peppers, garlic, fenugreek, and ginger that is essential to the cuisines of Ethiopia and Eritrea. Freshly baked *injera*, spongy, porous, and tangy flatbreads used as utensils and platters in Ethiopian and Eritrean cooking, are available here as well.

Sqirl, 720 N. Virgil Ave., #4, Los Angeles, CA 90029; (213)-394-6526; sqirlla.com. Heirloom fruits sourced from family-owned farms located no more than 350 miles from Los Angeles are transformed into beautiful jams, chutneys, fruit butters, and marmalades at Jessica Koslow's Sqirl. Here, preserves are made the old-fashioned way, cooked slow and low in copper pots using as little sugar as possible and natural pectin. This "less is more" approach means that every jar practically bursts with nature's wholesome goodness. The magic of spring and summer is captured in flavors like wild blueberry with tarragon and Santa Rosa plums with flowering thyme, while winter's blood oranges and kumquats are delicately tamed in marmalade form, sometimes with the addition of vanilla bean. Sqirl's complete line of products is available for sale at the store; those far from Los Angeles can peruse a more limited selection online. In the fall of 2012, Koslow teamed up with Ria Wilson, formerly of **Canelé** (p. 122) to open her production space to the public for breakfast and lunch. The well-edited menu celebrates toast in sweet and savory forms and features daily specials that change with the chef's bounty and whims.

Runny eggs and preserved goodies of all stripes punctuate each plate. Sqirl also offers classes once a month highlighting various preservation techniques including dehydrating, pickling, and canning.

Eastside

Boyle Heights, East Los Angeles, El Sereno

Foodie Faves

Flor Del Rio, 3201 E. 4th St., Los Angeles, CA 90063; (323) 268-0319; Mexican; $. The specialty at this charming Boyle Heights restaurant is goat, the whole goat, and nothing but the goat. Flor Del Rio prepares Zacatecas-style *birria de chivito*, where young goat is roasted, stewed, and simmered until its flesh nearly falls off the bone. It can be served dry or moistened with a tangy consommé made from the goat's drippings; either way the *birria* dazzles with its tenderness and impresses with its depth. The best cuts contain an abundance of delightful connective tissue along with the shards of meat. To get it on with your goat, wrap the *birria* in one of the thick, handmade corn tortillas served alongside and garnish with chopped white onions, minced cilantro, and a wicked red salsa. A cup full of steaming hot goat broth makes for a soothing finish following this do-it-yourself goat taco feast.

Guisados, 2100 E. Cesar E. Chavez Ave., Los Angeles, CA 90033; (323) 264-7201; guisados.com; Mexican; $. *Guisados*, an umbrella term for stews and braises slowly simmered in spices and aromatics and served with tortillas, are most often prepared by home cooks to feed large groups of families and friends. Ricardo Diaz of **Cook's Tortas** (p. 147) and his business partner Armando De La Torre bring this most comforting of foods to the fore at their Boyle Heights taqueria. The 15 or so *guisados* available each day are neatly scrawled on a floor-to-ceiling-length chalkboard. To serve, your meat or vegetable stews of choice are heaped onto thick, handmade masa tortillas and topped with a few well-chosen embellishments including avocado, pickled red onions, cheese crumbles, or toasted seeds. The *chicharon guisado* transforms shatteringly crunchy pork rinds into delicate sponges softened in the braising liquid. The sesame and pumpkin seed–topped *mole de pollo guisado* marries sweet, spicy, and bitter into one cohesive mahogany package. The *tinga* is equally essential with its stewed chicken, onions, cabbage, chorizo, and chipotle and garnish of pickled red onions and a single slice of ripe avocado. First-time visitors, as well as indecisive eaters, are encouraged to order the sampler platter, which is composed of the first six items listed on the aforementioned chalkboard menu. Grab a tall cup of one of the house-made *aguas frescas* for the perfect antidote to the bold and homey *guisados*. **Additional Location:** 1261 W. Sunset Blvd., Los Angeles, CA 90026; (213) 250-7600.

Mariscos Jalisco, 3040 E. Olympic Blvd., Los Angeles, CA 90023; (323) 528-6701; Mexican; $. *Tacos dorados de camarones*, deep-fried shrimp parcels garnished with avocado and fresh salsa, are the specialty at this seafood truck in Boyle Heights. Run by Raul Ortega and his team of friends and family, the Mariscos Jalisco truck is parked on Olympic Boulevard just south of Soto every day 9 a.m. to 6 p.m. In addition to shrimp tacos, Ortega and Co. make mean ceviches and *cocteles* using shrimp and octopus and shuck fresh oysters by the half- or full-dozen. After receiving your order, head to the table full of condiments to further spice your taco or to grab a few saltine crackers for your cocktail. A seat at the wobbly folding table or along the weathered ledge will do just fine for digging into seafood bliss.

FURTHER EXPLORATION: MARISCOS 4 VIENTOS

Parked a few feet from Mariscos Jalisco is **Mariscos 4 Vientos** (3000 E. Olympic Blvd., Los Angeles, CA 90023; 323-264-3565), another popular truck that also specializes in the seafood dishes of Jalisco. The *tostada aguachile* features barely cooked shrimp mingling in lime juice and serrano chiles heaped atop a fried corn tortilla along with slices of fresh avocado. The chiles bring a long, slow burn that will set your mouth afire.

Mariscos Los Lechugas, 5244 S. Huntington Dr., Los Angeles, CA 90032; Mexican; $. Jaime Lechuga, his wife, Virginia, and their friend Epi Osuna have been slinging Ensenada-style *cocteles*, tostadas, and tacos at Mariscos Los Lechugas for the past decade. This trailer hitched onto the back of a pickup truck can be found on a serene-enough stretch of El Sereno every day 11 a.m. until early evening; the trailer departs between 4 to 6 p.m., depending on customer demand and staff fatigue. According to Lechuga, 80 percent of customers are nursing a hangover, while the other 20 percent are seafood lovers. Regardless of which crowd you run with, the offerings here are undoubtedly satisfying. The *cocteles* are the most expensive item on the menu and worth every dollar. The *campechana*, perfectly snappy shrimp, octopus, and tuna bathing in a tangy tomato dressing, is terrific. The shrimp and fish tacos are executed just as well, as are the tostadas, especially the albacore marinated in lime juice with white onion, tomato, and cilantro. Saltines and a selection of hot sauces are lined against the trailer's metal counter. As you're crumbling crackers into your *coctel* or spicing your tostada, take a moment to admire the vintage photos of Lechuga accepting a trophy for winning a grueling 700-mile bike race from Guadalajara to Puerto Vallarta and the photos of his son Ernie riding side-by-side with Lance Armstrong. *Mariscos*, it turns out, are the fuel of choice for world-class cyclists.

L.A. Landmarks

La Mascota Bakery, 2715 Whittier Blvd., Los Angeles, CA 90023; (323) 263-5513; lamascotabakery.com; Mexican; $. When Ygnacio Salcedo arrived in East Los Angeles shortly after the Mexican Revolution, there wasn't a single bakery serving the neighborhood. He opened La Mascota in Boyle Heights in 1952 to bring freshly baked *bolillos* (savory baguettes) and *pan dulces* (sweet breads) to the Mexican community. He drew upon his prior experience as a baker's apprentice and bakery owner in Mascota, a small town in the western Mexican state of Jalisco, to provide the highest quality products to his clients. Today, the shop is run by Salcedo's daughter, Valencia, and her three brothers, Edward, Ygnacio Jr., and Victor. It has expanded into the retail space next door to include a kitchen dedicated to tamales. In recent years, the tamales have become as big of a draw as the baked goods, especially the ones stuffed with shredded pork and red chiles. Still, it's the *pan dulces* that are the heart of the operation. Over a dozen different varieties are available each day including the corn-shaped, cinnamon-sugar-dusted *elote,* the mesmerizing raspberry jelly roll *nino envuelto*, and the ever-popular soft, sweet, and cinnamon-laced *concha* rolls. The pineapple empanadas and the Cuban guava and cheese pastries aren't traditionally Mexican, but they are executed with flair by the seasoned team of bakers.

La Serenata de Garibaldi, 1842 E. 1st St., Los Angeles, CA 90033; (323) 265-2887; laserenataonline.com; Mexican; $$$. For nearly three decades, Jose "Pepe" Rodriguez and his wife, Aurora, have charmed diners with their brilliant seafood preparations at La Serenata de Garibaldi. Señor Rodriguez, who grew up in Juarez, has been called the "Maestro de Salsas," with more than 30 different sauces in his repertoire. Every meal at this Eastside institution begins with a bowl of vegetable soup, along with chips and salsa. The wedges of cheese quesadilla hidden amidst the chips never fail to elicit a smile; same goes for the awesomely smoky salsa. For the quintessential Serenata experience, select either giant prawns or one of the day's available fishes (salmon, sea bass, halibut, and mahimahi) and pair it with one of the kitchen's signature sauces. The *mojo al ajo*, an avalanche of garlic and oil, tastes divine on just about everything, while the earthy *mole poblano* is better suited for sturdier proteins. The *molcajete* sauce is pure heaven for chile heads. For those who aren't keen on fruits from the sea, there are plenty of traditional offerings like enchiladas and gorditas prepared with chicken and beef. Fresh corn tortillas served straight from the griddle, as well as desserts, are handled by Jose and Aurora's son Marco.

Manuel's Original El Tepeyac Cafe, 812 N. Evergreen Ave., Los Angeles, CA 90033; (323) 268-1960; manuelseltepeyac .com; Mexican; $. There's no use trying to pick up your burrito at El Tepeyac Cafe. It likely weighs over two pounds and is portioned larger than your noggin. Only a knife and fork will do in this situation, along with an appetite comparable to that of an Olympic swimmer. Founded in 1942 by the Rojas family, El Tepeyac Cafe in Boyle Heights is ground zero for the kind of gluttonous eating that makes for awful indigestion and great television ratings—just ask Adam Richman. Most famous is the Hollenbeck burrito, a giant flour tortilla crammed to maximum capacity with slow-cooked pork, rice, beans, and guacamole. The massive parcel is ladled with additional pork, making for a sopping and saucy creation of epic proportions. Follow in Richman's footsteps and order "Manuel's Special," a five-pounder modeled after the original Hollenbeck. While not as notorious as "Manuel's Special," the *machaca* Hollenbeck deserves recognition for its sheer deliciousness. Stuffed with shredded beef, scrambled eggs, cheddar cheese, rice, beans, guacamole, and sautéed onions, tomatoes, and jalapeños, it is the tastiest burrito of the bunch. Dine outdoors for fast-casual service or indoors for full service.

 **Sublime Sweets**

Salinas Churros, follow @salinaschurros1 on Twitter for location updates; Mexican; $. Track down the Salinas Churros truck for the finest street-style Mexican *churros* in all of Los Angeles. The Salinas family launched the operation over a decade ago with a modest pushcart equipped with a makeshift plastic wheel extruder. These days, they've upgraded to a fully decked-out truck that roams the east side of town after sunset. The secret to Salinas' superior *churros* lies in the dough, which is firm, a touch salty, and deeply ridged. The resulting *churro* is beyond crunchy, with a custardy streak running through the center. Dusted with granulated sugar as they emerge from the scalding oil, these *churros* are a perfect 10.

Specialty Stores, Markets & Producers

El Mercadito del Este Los Angeles, 3425 E. 1st St., Los Angeles, CA 90063; (323) 268-3451. It is quite common in Los Angeles to step into a restaurant, bar, or market and feel as if you've been transported to a foreign country, but no place invokes the sensation quite as profoundly as the Mercadito del Este Los Angeles. Brush up on your Spanish or be prepared to sign because English is sparsely spoken around here. Fortunately for us, food is close to a universal language. Skip the first floor altogether unless you're in the market for western wares or imported knickknacks and head straight to the second level, where edibles reign supreme. Julia's Antojitos specializes in ice creams made from native American plants and fruits in flavors like *nance, jocote,* and *arrayan.* There are also sour cream-tinged fruit salads topped with coconut flakes and granola called *bionicos.* Head to Sonia's Artesanias for a remarkable array of candies and snacks sold in bulk. The selection of nuts, seeds, and legumes coated in chiles and salt and mangoes dried, spiced, and pickled never fails to get the salivary glands going. Thick and luscious *cajeta* (cow's milk caramel) and *cajeta de leche de cabra* (goat's milk caramel) are sold by the gallon. The International Deli next door carries a mishmash of foodstuffs and ingredients including half a dozen regional Mexican moles. Whether you're in the mood for Oaxaca style, Guerrero style, *mole poblano,* or green and red *pepian,* this spot has you covered. Just add chicken broth, your protein of choice, simmer, and . . . holy mole.

La Azteca Tortilleria, 4538 E. Cesar E. Chavez Ave., Los Angeles, CA 90022; (323) 262-5977. The difference between a store-bought tortilla and the handmade wonders at La Azteca Tortilleria is like night and day. While the former cracks as it rolls and tastes like the plastic it's wrapped in, the latter is hefty yet plush and is capable of curving around copious amounts of pork, cheese, beans, or most likely, all three. When the shop's original owners, Alex Bernal and his wife, Maria Rodriguez, retired in 2010 after three decades making tortillas the old-fashioned way, from scratch and in small batches, their good friends Juan and Candalaria Villa purchased the business and continued the tradition. It's a painstaking process, to be sure, but the results are truly swoon-worthy. Head to this cramped Eastside *tortilleria* for corn and flour tortillas sold by the dozen and made-to-order burritos and quesadillas. Whether it's beef (*asada*), chicken (*pollo*), chorizo, or pork (*carnitas*) that you fancy, when the tortilla is this exemplary, the stuffing is almost an afterthought. The chile relleno burrito, a battered and fried cheese-stuffed poblano wrapped in a freshly griddled tortilla with refried beans, cheese, onions, and salsa, is the shop's sleeper hit. *Bunuelos*, deep-fried flour tortillas coated in cinnamon and sugar, make for a fabulous finish. There's also *menudo* (a traditional Mexican soup with tripe and a red chile base) to be had over the weekends.

The Harbor

Carson, Harbor City, Long Beach, San Pedro

Foodie Faves

Back Home in Lahaina, 519 E. Carson St., Carson, CA 90745; (310) 835-4014; backhomeinlahaina.com; Hawaiian; $$. For a complete description, see p. 190.

Crusty Crab Seafood Restaurant and Fish Market, 1146 Nagoya Way, San Pedro, CA 90731; (310) 519-9058; Seafood; $$. It's impossible to talk about the Crusty Crab without mentioning the word *fiesta*. This harborside restaurant at San Pedro's Ports O' Call Village feels more like an outdoor block party than a traditional dining room. The boisterous crowd downs pitchers of beer and sips frothy margaritas, while mariachi music blares throughout the alfresco space. What brings them all here is the seafood, freshly caught and sitting pretty on ice or holed up in tanks. To join in on the fiesta in progress, first choose whatever fruit you fancy. There are fish of all stripes, scallops small and large, prepared shrimp, colorful crabs, and seasonal lobster. Next, haul your loot to one of the cooking stations. It takes 40 minutes for whole fishes to be grilled, but the smoky, buttery results merit the wait. Steaming, sautéing, and deep-frying are far faster with results that are just as tasty. Finally, grab a seat at one of the communal picnic tables and dig in. In the midst of all this buying and frying are ceviche and oyster-shucking stations for your appetizing pleasure. With all this alcohol and seafood going down the gullet, make sure to purchase a toasty loaf of garlic bread to soak it all up.

Phnom Penh Noodle Restaurant, 1644 Cherry Ave., Long Beach, CA 90813; (562) 433-0032; Cambodian; $. Dining at Phnom Penh Noodle feels like sitting down for a meal at a good friend's home. It might have something to do with the converted house the restaurant is located in, but mostly it's the warm service and soulful cooking that puts diners at ease. The Tan family has been dishing up Cambodian-style noodles, porridge, and fried breads here since 1985. These days, the restaurant is mostly run by the proprietors' cheery brood, a passionate bunch poised to take over the day-to-day operations in the coming years. The Phnom Penh noodles are a must-order for first-timers and regulars alike. Each bowl is layered with springy rice noodles, tail-on shrimp, porky odds and ends, fried garlic, and fresh cilantro, and can be served ladled with scalding hot soup or "dry" with a bowl of broth on the side. The restaurant's signature dish is wholly spectacular, especially the broth-less version, which packs an extraordinary garlicky punch. The cooking is just as careful with the "rice soups," which are popular with the morning crowd. The gently flavored pork, chicken, and fish varieties are seriously soothing. Three different types of fried breads, including *cha quai* (fried cruller), *knom hing* (sesame studded doughnut), and *knom sakieu* (meat-stuffed pocket) are available to dip alongside; these are usually all snatched up well before noon. Rounding out the menu are stir-fried noodles including *mekatang*, wide rice noodles with Chinese broccoli, eggs, and various proteins prepared in an appealingly goopy gravy.

Siem Reap, 1810 E. Anaheim St., Long Beach, CA 90813; (562) 591-7414; Cambodian; $$. Khmer cuisine hasn't quite hit the mainstream like its Southeast Asian counterparts, but here in the heart of Long Beach's Cambodia Town, the country's robust cooking is celebrated on every corner. Siem Reap, a grandiose restaurant decked out with a full bar and dance floor, composes classic Khmer dishes that display as much flair as the ambiance. While the menu lists dozens of Thai and Chinese-American dishes, it's Chef Huey Be's Cambodian specialties that are really something special. The walls and windows both outside and inside the restaurant are covered with blown-up images of Khmer specialties to guide those new to the cuisine. Start with an order of fresh spring rolls and a platter of *sach ko angh*, grilled lemongrass beef skewers. Then, move on to a duo of curries. The *amok trey,* a steamed curried fish, is steeped in coconut water with bits of coconut meat throughout. The flavors are subtle, but satisfying. The *prahok ktis*, a ground pork curry made with coconut milk, is a fiery shade of orange. Spoon it over steamed rice or even better, dip the snappy cucumbers and eggplants served alongside for a wonderful contrast between cool and hot. The *trey pro ma chian*, a fluffy omelet embedded with finely

FURTHER EXPLORATION: SOPHY'S FINE THAI & CAMBODIAN CUISINE

Nearby **Sophy's Fine Thai & Cambodian Cuisine** (3240 E. Pacific Coast Hwy., Long Beach, CA 90804; 562-494-1763) is another one of the area's most successful and beloved Khmer restaurants. Here, owner Sophy Khut prepares her famous *such koh ngeat,* tubular hunks of flank steak that are oven-dried and deep-fried until jerkylike in texture. The vinegar and garlic dressing served on the side really makes the flavors sing.

minced fermented fish and garlic, is as funky as it gets in the very best way.

Tony's Barbecue and Bibingkinitan, 860 E. Carson St., Carson, CA 90745; (310) 518-7860; Filipino; $. Fans of Filipino barbecue flock to Tony Macasieb's namesake restaurant for meats and skewers grilled over charcoal, slathered in sweet teriyaki sauce, and served with classic Pinoy accoutrements. Even with three locations in town, the original in Carson and two more in Long Beach, the crowds can be relentless, especially on weekend afternoons. A sign prominently hung in between the kitchen and dining room assures the hungry hordes that "It's worth the wait!" The variety of proteins available ranges from simple pork and chicken skewers to fancier cuts like tuna collar, salmon, and pork belly. Everything is grilled to order and served simply over steamed rice or as part of a larger combination meal with egg drop soup, seasoned "Java" rice, and *atcharang gulay* (pickled vegetables). The kitchen takes extra care to make sure that everything that touches the grill is evenly charred and unfailingly juicy. Also famous here are the banana leaf-wrapped *bibingka*, sweet cakes with a puddinglike texture made from rice flour and coconut milk. Coconut and *ube* (purple yam) flavored ones are available for special orders. **Additional Locations:** 1422 W. Willow St., Long Beach, CA 90810; (562) 426-8717. 2292 E. Carson St., Long Beach, CA 90807; (562) 988-8488.

L.A. Landmarks

Roscoe's House of Chicken and Waffles, 730 E. Broadway, Long Beach, CA 90802; (562) 437-8355; roscoeschickenandwaffles.com; Southern; $$. Southern-style fried chicken paired with crisp, thin waffles has been all the rage since 1975 at Roscoe's House of Chicken and Waffles, a Long Beach–based soul food institution founded by Harlem native Herb Hudson. The ambiance tends to vary from location to location (there are five in total throughout the Southland), but expect a dinerlike atmosphere, helpful staff, and excitable crowds. Hungry birds should opt for the half chicken with two waffles, which easily feeds two. If wings are your thing, do as President Obama does and order the Country Boy, which includes three wings and a choice of a waffle, potato salad, or french fries. In honor of the restaurant's most powerful fan, the Country Boy was renamed Obama's Special in 2012. Whether you opt for wings, breast, or thigh, crispy and well-seasoned skin and splendidly moist meat are all but guaranteed. Roscoe's menu goes above and beyond the well-known chicken and waffles. Soul food staples like grits, biscuits, chicken gizzards, corn bread, and collard greens are also on the bill of fare.

 *Sublime Sweets*

Valerio's Tropical Bake Shop, 131 W. Carson St., Carson, CA 90745; (310) 830-7633; Filipino; $. For a complete description, see p. 187.

 *Specialty Stores, Markets & Producers*

La Espanola Meats, 25020 Doble Ave., Harbor City, CA 90710; (310) 539-0455; donajuana.com. Come in for the impressive selection of imported Spanish foodstuffs like olive oils, canned fish, and saffron, and stay for spectacular sausages, charcuterie, and paella handmade by Juana and Frank Faraone since 1982. Housed in an unassuming

building on a small side street in Harbor City, La Espanola Meats produces an incredible line of cured meats using recipes from Juana's native Spain. There's Catalan-style *botifarra*, Pamplona-style chorizo, *morcillas de arroz* (blood sausages), *lomo embuchado* (dry-cured pork tenderloin), Serrano-style *jamón* (dry-cured ham), and much more. Every Saturday, the Faraones serve paella for lunch on their outdoor patio. Juana, who is from Valencia, prepares her saffron-laced *bomba* rice with chicken, seafood, beans, peppers, and three kinds of sausages. Be sure to call ahead to reserve a portion—it always goes real quick.

Northeast
Los Angeles

Atwater Village, Eagle Rock, Highland Park

Foodie Faves

Cacao Mexicatessen, 1576 Colorado Blvd., Los Angeles, CA 90041; (323) 478-2791; cacaodeli.com; Mexican; $$. It takes a lot to stand out in Los Angeles' crowded sea of taco slingers, but Cacao Mexicatessen has managed to carve out a real niche with its traditional and modern interpretations of regional Mexican fare. For starters, there's the *Carnitas de Pato* taco. Succulent morsels of duck confit are tucked in a handmade tortilla along with avocado, pickled onions, radishes, and chile oil. Even better is the *Chicarron de Pato* taco made of fried duck skin, cabbage, radishes, onions, cilantro, and *salsa verde*. The bits of skin are all crunch and no grease. Also exceptional is the *Machaca de Venado*, shredded venison topped with avocado, radishes, habanero salsa, crumbly *cotija* (Mexican cheese), and cilantro. To balance out the onslaught of meaty offerings, Cacao Mexicatessen offers vegetarian tacos filled with satiating stuffings like corn truffle (*huitlacoche*), squash blossoms, and hibiscus flowers. Served alongside every taco are *cebollitas*, grilled green onion stalks marinated in lime and olive oil. The weekly specials scrawled on the chalkboard next to the cash register are always worth considering. Quesadillas stuffed with lardons and brie and *tostaditas* piled high with local halibut and sea urchin should be snatched up when available. In addition to the fast-casual restaurant, there's a working delicatessen next door selling house-made salsas, guacamole, and moles.

Canelé, 3219 Glendale Blvd., Los Angeles, CA 90039; (323) 666-7133; canele-la.com; French; $$$. Chef Corina Weibel and her business partner Jane Choi are the two forces behind Canelé, a local gem in the impossibly cool neighborhood of Atwater Village. Chef Weibel previously cooked at two of the city's most beloved restaurants, Campanile and **Lucques** (p. 46), while Choi worked the front of the house at New York City's Balthazar and Pastis. The gals joined forces to open Canelé in 2006. Weekend brunch is a bustling affair with hoards of hungry eaters eager for a taste of the restaurant's famous french toast. It's a custardy creation, monstrously portioned, and somehow even better paired with poached prunes and mascarpone. Hidden under the "Sides" section of the menu is an adorable baked pancake that arrives fresh from the oven, with a giggly center of tart Meyer lemon pudding. Classic French bistro fare takes over the menu once dinnertime rolls around. Start with the brandade with tomato confit and toast, a bubbly dip of salt cod, olive oil, and milk served in earthenware. The *confit de canard* and the *boeuf bourguignon* with buttered noodles are both as charming as their Parisian counterparts.

El Huarache Azteca, 5225 York Blvd., Los Angeles, CA 90042; (323) 478-9572; elhuaracheaztecala.com; Mexican; $. The Mexico City–style *antojitos* or "little whims" served at this Highland Park gem are perfect for *el desayuno*, *el almuerzo*, and *la cena*. The *pambazos*, potato and sausage–stuffed sandwiches dipped in a milder-than-it-appears red chile sauce, stain every finger and pair of lips in their path while satisfying even the hungriest of bellies. Equally filling are the D.F.-style quesadillas filled with your choice of animal or vegetable including squash blossoms, steak, and mushrooms. Lighter but just as satisfying are the signature *huaraches*, deep-fried "sandals" made of masa (corn) dough and topped with things like *huitlacoche* (corn smut), beef *cabeza* (head), and chorizo. Dining at El Huarache Azteca on Saturday and Sunday means that an intensely flavorful serving of *barbacoa de borrego*, pit-roasted lamb served with a consommé made from the lamb's drippings and fresh corn tortillas, is all but a given.

Good Girl Dinette, 110 N. Avenue 56, Los Angeles, CA 90042; (323) 257-8980; goodgirlfoods.com; Vietnamese; $$. American diner meets Vietnamese comfort food at this Highland Park treasure. The good girl behind the operation is Diep Tran, the former co-owner and chef of Blue Hen. It's a stylish joint complete with exposed brick walls, barely finished tables, and institutional-chic mustard yellow chairs. The dinette lights up its rough-around-the-edges neighborhood with charming service and hearty offerings. The concise menu features an array of homey stews, potpie, sandwiches, noodles, and soups that change with Chef Tran's farmers' market haul. The imperial rolls are the quintessential starter. Filled with wood ear mushrooms or chicken, carrots, and glass noodles, the rolls are fried to order and beautifully blistered. Whether eating them straight up or wrapped in lettuce leaves, make sure to dunk 'em in the accompanying vinaigrette for extra pow. Another winning starter is the deep-fried tofu slabs perched atop carefully constructed rice cakes. Drizzled in a mixture of scallions, oil, and fish sauce, the tofu is transformed into an umamified raft. Chef Diep's most popular creation is the potpies, which marry Vietnamese curries with all-American buttermilk biscuits. The deep-yellow madras broth pairs masterfully with its flaky, buttery hat. For those seeking a less stick-to-your-ribs kind of meal, the sandwiches or "rice noodle salads" are the way to go. See Diep Tran's recipe for **Chicken Curry Potpie** on page 300.

FURTHER EXPLORATION:
VIET NOODLE BAR

Chef Viet Tran takes classic Vietnamese fare to hipper and healthier pastures at his Atwater Village restaurant **Viet Noodle Bar** (3133 Glendale Blvd., Los Angeles, CA 90039; 323-906-1575). The young jackfruit salad makes for a meaty meatless starter, while the turmeric white fish noodles with dill keep the crowds coming back time and again.

Metro Balderas, 5305 N. Figueroa St., Los Angeles, CA 90042; (323) 478-8383; Mexican; $. Respects should be paid to the pork gods every day and, if you find yourself at Metro Balderas, eight times on Saturday and Sunday. Weekends here are dedicated to glorious *carnitas,* piggy parts lovingly fried in lard then slow-cooked and braised in natural juices before being tucked into a corn tortilla and garnished with diced onions and chopped cilantro. Warm up with the *maciza* (shoulder) and the *costilla* (ribs), the least adventurous cuts of the eight on offer. The former is more or less a mound of pulled pork, while the latter is lean, mean, and caramelized. The *cuerito* (skin) and *trompa* (snout) tacos are deliciously gelatinous morsels that soak up the braising liquid like a porcine sponge. The *oreja* (ear) is a textural powerhouse that's crunchy yet tender. The *nana* (uterus), *buche* (stomach), and *surtida* (combination of all cuts minus the *nana*) are absolute musts for fearless swine-hards. Don't sweat it if you miss the weekend pork service—there are still plenty of prime cuts worth eating from Monday through Friday. Nurse your pork-induced hangover with solid *tripas* (offals) and *lengua* (tongue) tacos.

The Oinkster, 2005 Colorado Blvd., Eagle Rock, CA 90041; (323) 255-6465; theoinkster.com; American; $. The Oinkster opened in 2006, and the crowds haven't let up since. A line a dozen deep snakes out the door at nearly all hours of the day, but there's no need to fret because it moves along speedily. The menu here is all-American with a "slow fast food" bent. There are burgers, roasted pork, and rotisserie chicken to be had, but everyone seems to dig the pastrami most. Chef Andre Guerrero set out to create The Oinkster's signature pastrami after learning the ropes from none other than Al Langer of **Langer's Delicatessen** (p. 73). Here, the pastrami is cured for two weeks, rubbed with a secret spice blend, and smoked with applewood. The carefully constructed meat appears on a number of sandwiches on the menu, but purists prefer it served without too many distractions on a plain white roll, where the pastrami's peppery notes and streaks of fat can shine

FURTHER EXPLORATION: MAXIMILIANO

Chef Andre Guerrero has a knack for knowing what Angelenos want to eat—classic comfort foods at moderate prices. At Highland Park's **Maximiliano** (5930 York Blvd., Los Angeles, CA 90042; 323-739-6125; maximilianohp.com), the focus is on a kind of "old school" Italian-American cooking that's familiar, no-frills, and saucy. The pizzas coming out of the wood-fired Marsal pizza oven are golden all around and sturdy enough to handle everything from runny eggs to melted cheese, while the pastas are simple yet satisfying. Visit during brunch for delightful plates of ricotta pancakes with lemon curd and Oinkster-esque pulled pork served atop an Asiago biscuit with poached eggs and hollandaise.

brightest. Make sure to get a side of Belgian fries with whatever you order; the amazingly garlicky aioli served alongside needs to be bottled and sold at finer retailers across the Southland. Salty sandwiches and greasy fries were made to be paired with thick and sweet milk shakes, so grab an *ube* (purple yam) shake with extra "whip" to hydrate. It tastes like a Filipino dream.

Rico's Mar Azul Mariscos Truck, 4702 N. Figueroa St., Highland Park, CA 90042; Mexican; $. This splashy blue truck stationed in an idyllic park off Figueroa specializes in Mexico City–style seafood preparations. The concise menu lists tostadas (fried corn tortillas topped with an array of ingredients), *cocteles* (a soupy Mexican version of shrimp cocktail), and little else. The *tostada de pulpo*, with its creamy white sauce reminiscent of *tzatziki*, abundance of avocado, and octopus chunks, can be unwieldy to eat but worth every messy bite. The *cocteles,* which are made with shrimp, abalone, octopus, or a combination of the three, swim in a sweetly tinged tomato sauce. Every dish is priced well under $10.

L.A. Landmarks

Casa Bianca Pizza, 1650 Colorado Blvd., Los Angeles, CA 90041; (323) 256-9617; casabiancapizza.com; Pizza; $$. Sam Martorana and his wife, Jennie, delved into the pizza-slinging business in 1955 when they moved from Chicago to Eagle Rock and opened Casa Bianca. Today, the couple's son and daughter, Ned and Andrea, run the day-to-day operation, carrying on the beloved business that their parents established nearly 60 years ago. Casa Bianca's tortuously long waits are as famous as their pies, so arrive as soon as doors swing open or be prepared to pace along the pavement with fellow pizza pursuers. The romantically dated dining room is all red-checkered tablecloths and dim lighting; red pepper flakes and powdery cheese sit on every tabletop. While the menu lists over a dozen pastas and sandwiches too, sticking to the house special is pretty much a given. The pie that catches everyone's eye is evenly strewn with fennel-heavy, house-made sausage and lightly battered eggplant. The signature thin crust base, painted with a tangy tomato sauce, holds up to the toppings and provides the ideal backdrop for pizza nirvana.

Sublime Sweets

Bigmista's Barbecue Catering, follow @BigmistasBBQ on Twitter for location updates; bigmista.com; Barbecue; $$. While Bigmista's ribs, pulled pork, brisket, and bacon-wrapped Moink balls are solid in their own right, none of these savory offerings can hold a candle to his beastly good Pig Candy. Wonderfully thick slices of bacon are pressed with brown sugar and spices and smoked until their edges char and caramelize. An order includes three precious slices that always seem to disappear far quicker than one intends. Smoky sweetness pervades the palate at first bite, followed by an intense heat that doesn't mess around. Small, deliberate bites are the best way to approach these blissed-out bacon strips. Neil and Phyllis Strawder, also known as Bigmista and Mrs. Mista, launched their roving barbecue operation in 2008 at the Watts farmers' market. These days, Bigmista's wares are available six days a week at farmers' markets around town. It's a good thing these outdoor affairs operate year-round, because going months without Pig Candy would surely be cruel and unusual punishment.

Caramia Gelato Tropicale, 2700 Colorado Blvd., Los Angeles, CA 90041; (323) 550-1304; Filipino; $. Full-flavored and light-bodied Italian gelato gets the full Pinoy treatment at Caramia Gelato Tropicale.

Tucked into the first floor of the sprawling Eagle Rock Plaza, this friendly shop shares real estate with fellow Filipino favorites Jollibee and Goldilocks Bakery. The *buko* gelato tastes distinctly of young coconut rather than suntan oil, while the gorgeously hued *ube* (purple yam) brings that certain something like only it can. The Sans Rival, which is inspired by a decadent layer cake of the same name, marries a cashew base with cakey crumbles. The most intriguing flavor on offer is the Maiz con Queso, an orangey-hued scoop littered with corn kernels and flavored with cheddar. It might sound a little bizarre, but don't knock it until you've rocked it.

Proof Bakery, 3156 Glendale Blvd., Los Angeles, CA 90039; (323) 664-8633; proofbakeryla.com; Bakery; $. There's never really a bad time to visit Chef Na Young Ma's Proof Bakery, which debuted in Atwater Village in late 2010. Mornings bring some of the city's best croissants made with a touch of sourdough starter. In addition to plain ones, Proof also makes croissants stuffed with Valrhona chocolate, almonds, and ham and gruyère. These flaky pastries sell out in a heartbeat, so set your alarm clock to beat the rush. The lunchtime crowd is treated to petite sandwiches that look straightforward enough but taste spectacular. The selections change from day to day, but expect to see delightful combinations like salami, Manchego, and chive butter, and cauliflower, tapenade, kale, and lemon zest. Available throughout the day is an array of stunning sweets ranging from simple to intricate. Chocolate chip cookies come crisp, caramelized, and complex with a sprinkling of coarse salt and an abundance of deep, dark chocolate discs. The triple-layered lemon meringue cake intertwines tangy with creamy in the most sophisticated of ways. The gorgeous tarts with diplomat cream and seasonal fruit, as well as the Paris-Brest, *pâte à choux* filled with praline whipped cream, never fail to take one's breath away.

Scoops, 5105 York Blvd., Los Angeles, CA 90042; Ice Cream; $. For a complete description, see p. 94.

San Fernando Valley

Burbank, Canoga Park, Encino, Northridge, Reseda, Shadow Hills, Sherman Oaks, Studio City, Sun Valley, Toluca Lake, Valley Glen, Valley Village, Van Nuys

Foodie Faves

Beba's Restaurant, 6024 Hazeltine Ave., Van Nuys, CA 91401; (818) 786-1511; bebasrestaurant.com; Bolivian; $. Beba's, a decade-old restaurant originally from Orange County, opened a second branch in Van Nuys to bring their Bolivian bites to Valley residents. A steady crowd files in daily for the signature *salteñas,* Bolivian-style empanadas so juicy that they're served with a spoon. The outer crust is golden and sweet, while the filling is seasoned and spiced with beef, chicken, hard-boiled eggs, potatoes, and raisins. The spoon served alongside comes in handy after the first bite reveals the soupy goodness within. Other satisfying starters include the sweet and savory *empanadas de queso* and the *sopa de mani,* a popular peanut soup made with beef, vegetables, potatoes, and noodles. Main dishes are mostly hearty and piled high with meat and potatoes aplenty. The *falso conejo,* i.e., "fake rabbit," is composed of a hunk of beef pounded thin, breaded, fried, and served over steamed rice with a mild tomato sauce. Equally satisfactory is the *lomo montado,* Bolivian steak and eggs served with french fries and rice. If a sweet finish is in order, Beba's offers *helado de canela,* a cinnamon sorbet that tastes uncannily of Red Hots; *alfajores,* shortbread cookies sandwiched with *dulce de leche;* and *pasteles de api,* huge hot pockets stuffed with cheese and dusted with powdered sugar.

Bombay Spiceland, 8650 Reseda Blvd., Northridge, CA 91324; (818) 701-9383; Indian; $. Bombay Spiceland, a small grocery store offering eyebrow threading and imported DVDs alongside sacks of lentils and fresh produce, has been serving the Valley's South Asian community for over 30 years. The Dua family purchased the business in 2008 and expanded it to include a vegetarian snack shop next door in 2010. In addition to a diverse array of classic *chat*-style sweets (*jalebi, barfi,* and *gulab jamun*) and savories (*samosa, pakora,* and *dosa*), Bombay Spiceland also dishes up unbeatable combos priced well under $10 that include a selection of curries, *kormas,* and *dals* from the steam table, basmati rice, bread, yogurt, and pickles. Every dish is completely vegetarian, soul-warming, and satisfying, especially the creamy *korma,* which packs a buttery punch served over rice or dipped with flaky roti.

Cemitas Don Adrian, 14902 Victory Blvd., San Fernando Valley, CA 91411; (818) 786-0328; Mexican; $. It takes a massive jaw and a serious appetite to conquer a *cemita poblana,* a beast of a sandwich constructed from a plush sesame roll jam-packed with ripe avocados, *panela* cheese, Oaxacan string cheese, salsa, onions, and meat. Here at Cemitas Don Adrian, the Pueblan specialty comes together like a dream. While the beef *milanesa,* a thinly pounded and deep-fried hunk of *carne,* is the most traditional filling, there's also house-made *queso de puerco* (pork head cheese), *pata de res* (pickled beef tendons), and even salmon to properly stuff your *cemita.* The protein that packs the biggest wallop is the *cecina*, a kind of beef jerky that the shop's proprietor Adolfo Huerta makes in-house using techniques and recipes passed down from his grandfather Don Adrian. With its distinct notes of achiote and cumin, the *cecina adobada* is absolutely irresistible.

Fab Hot Dogs, 19417 Victory Blvd., Reseda, CA 91335; (818) 344-4336; fabhotdogs.com; American; $. Joe Fabrocini was inspired to open a hot dog shop while working for Guitar Center. As the company's director of real estate, he traveled around the country often, sampling regional hot dogs at every opportunity. Here at Fab Hot Dogs, Fabrocini has curated an all-star lineup of America's best hot dogs. Representing the home team is the L.A. Street Dog, a bacon-wrapped wiener topped with grilled peppers and onions, tomato, mayonnaise, mustard, ketchup, and jalapeños. There's also a genuine Chicago Dog, complete with a steamed hot dog, neon green relish, celery salt, and a pickle spear all tucked inside a poppy seed bun. The "Manhattan Dog," also known as a dirty water dog, includes authentically New York touches like the ruddy onion sauce, sauerkraut, and brown mustard. The most famous of Fab's dogs is The Ripper, which hails from his home state of New Jersey. It's made from a specially formulated dog fit for deep-frying that is buried beneath a house-made spicy mustard relish known to all as Bald Eagle Sauce. Bullish appetites are encouraged to sample the Fairfax Burrito Dog, two all-beef dogs, pastrami, house-made chili, cheddar cheese, onions, mustard, and Fritos wrapped in a grilled flour tortilla.

Go's Mart, 22330 Sherman Way, Canoga Park, CA 91303; (818) 704-1459; Japanese; $$$$. Don't pay any mind to the racks of VHS videos or the coolers lined with hard and soft beverages as you walk into Go's Mart. Make a beeline for the eight-seat sushi bar toward the back of the room where Go-San constructs the finest sushi in the Valley. While ordering piece by piece is certainly a good option (the daily specials scrawled onto the dry-erase board are always spectacular), an even better one is indulging in a multicourse *omakase*. Go-San orchestrates a meal to remember with a series of richer dishes to start, like monkfish liver, seared *toro* (tuna belly), and cod sperm sac, followed by lighter fare like flounder sashimi and oysters with caviar. Finally, a sequence of sushi ranging from Santa Barbara abalone topped with shavings of black truffle and a shower of gold leaf to needlefish with *shiso* (perilla) and fresh wasabi makes for a startlingly delightful finish. With Go-San's reputation, limited seating, and a firm no reservations policy, arrive early or expect a wait.

FURTHER EXPLORATION: SUSHI IKI

Sushi Iki in Tarzana (18663 Ventura Blvd., Tarzana, CA 91356; 818-343-3470; sushiiki.com) is fittingly famous for its selection of live seafood. Chef-Owner "Crazy" Eddie Okamoto pursues the rarest and freshest seafood around including scallops, hairy crabs, and most enticing, live sea urchin.

Lotería! Grill, 12050 Ventura Blvd., Studio City, CA 91604; (818) 508-5300; loteriagrill.com; Mexican; $$. For a complete description, see p. 43.

Mis Raices, 7539 Reseda Blvd., Reseda, CA 91335; (818) 708-1205; Salvadoran; $. Salvadoran cuisine starts and ends with *pupusas* for many Angelenos. These thick corn tortillas filled with pork, cheese, and beans and griddled until crisp are nearly as prevalent as bacon-wrapped hot dogs on the city's streets. Served hot off the flattop and piled high with *curtido*, a lightly fermented cabbage slaw with red chiles and vinegar, *pupusas* are as satisfying as they come. For those looking to expand their Salvadoran food horizons, travel to the San Fernando Valley to dine at Mercedes Rodriguez's Mis Raices. Start with a platter of *yucca con chicharron*, a mountain of fried starch and pork accented with tomatoes, cucumbers, and a heap of *curtido*. A version made with fried baby sardines in place of pork is available on the specials menu from time to time. Also of note on the specials menu are the rice flour *pupusas* and the *flor de izote con huevo*, eggs fried with the national flower of El Salvador. Dependable on a daily basis is  the *sopa de pata*, a soulful soup popular with locals made from cow's feet, tripe, yucca, and corn. For dessert, the *chilate con nuegado*, yucca flour fritters soaked in caramel and served with a hot, unsweetened rice drink spiked with cloves and cinnamon, is a beautiful thing. Take a bite of the doughnut followed by a sip of the porridge; it makes for the perfect ending.

FURTHER EXPLORATION: SONSONATE GRILL

Ruben Laguardia's **Sonsonate Grill** (5011 S. Western Ave., Los Angeles, CA 90062; 323-296-7470) on Avalon in Southeast Los Angeles is Los Angeles' swankiest Salvadoran restaurant. The seafood dishes here are solid, but it's the *pan con gallina* (chicken and watercress sandwich on french bread) that everyone talks about.

Ramen Jinya, 11239 Ventura Blvd., Studio City, CA 91604; (818) 980-3977; jinya-ramenbar.com; Japanese; $. When Ramen Jinya first opened for business, you had to be one of the first 20 customers in line to snag a bowl of their wildly popular Hakata Tonkotsu Ramen, an intensely porky noodle soup with straight and bouncy noodles swimming in a lethally rich broth. Fortunately for ramen-goers who aren't keen on planning ahead, the highly coveted bowl has now become a menu mainstay—going out for noodles should never feel like playing the lottery. After slurping your heart out on the original Hakata Tonkotsu Ramen, sample the darker, more mysterious Tonkotsu Black. In addition to the aforementioned seriously porky broth are slices of meltingly tender pork *chashu*, spinach, bamboo, scallions, and best of all, a drizzle of pungent black garlic oil. For those who can't go a meal without a little burning action, the Spicy Tonkotsu Ramen can be ordered mild, spicy, or hot. Life's short; go with the lattermost.

FURTHER EXPLORATION: ROBATA JINYA

Since opening the first Ramen Jinya in Studio City, Japanese restaurateur Takahashi Tomonori has gone on to establish two more just like it, as well as **Robata Jinya** (8050 W. 3rd St., Los Angeles, CA 90048; 323-653-8877), an izakaya-style joint in Mid-City. The specialty here is meat and vegetable skewers prepared over a *robata* (charcoal) grill. The warm tofu made tableside is also worth trying.

Ramen Yamadaya, 15030 Ventura Blvd., Los Angeles, CA 91403; (818) 501-1115; ramen-yamadaya.com; Japanese; $. For a complete description, see p. 199.

Rocio's Mole de los Dioses, 8255 Sunland Blvd., Sun Valley, CA 91352; (818) 252-6415; moleofthegods.com; Mexican; $$. Here at Rocio's Mole de los Dioses, Oaxacan native Chef Rocio Camacho elevates mole making to an art form. After learning the ropes at **La Casita Mexicana** (p. 220) in Bell and honing her craft at Moles La Tia and La Huasteca, Chef Camacho struck out on her own, opening two branches of her namesake restaurant in Bell and Sun Valley. Made of dozens of spices, chiles, and nuts and sometimes thickened with bread, mole is a complex sauce that coats like a dream and brightens everything it touches. Perhaps the best way to experience the breadth of Chef Comacho's talents is to begin with the mole sampler. The richly colored sauces are dished out in miniature porcelain tureens and served with Nopatillas, warm tortillas made of cactus. The house-special *Mole de los Dioses* is exceedingly easy on the palate with its bewitching blend of ancho peppers, *huitlacoche* (corn smut), spices, and cheese, while the award-winning *Mole Oaxaqueno* challenges taste buds with its intriguing mix of 31 ingredients. While most moles swoop in with heat and spice, the *Mole Velo de Novia* made with white chocolate, almonds, and chili *blanco* could be drizzled atop an ice cream sundae. Any of the eight moles available each day can be spooned over filet mignon, veal, pork, salmon, chicken, shrimp, or portobello mushrooms for a complete meal. For a pretty penny and given advance notice, Chef Camacho can prepare a five-course feast of pre-Columbian Mexican cuisine. **Additional Location:** 19321 Ventura Blvd., Tarzana, CA 91356; (818) 457-4545.

Sako's Mediterranean Cuisine, 6736 Corbin Ave., Reseda, CA 91335; (818) 342-8710; sakosmediterraneancuisine.com; Turkish; $$.

Sako's Mediterranean Cuisine has been around for over two decades, but the restaurant didn't make its mark on the Los Angeles dining scene until the Panosia family took it over in 2005. Here at this cozily appointed restaurant sandwiched between a Del Taco and the Venetian Palace Banquet Hall, you'll find the city's finest Turkish cooking. Before digging into smoky grilled kebabs and juicy chops, start with a few hot and cold *mezze*. The *igara borek*, seasoned feta wrapped inside phyllo dough, is as thin as a wand and really just as magical. The *ichli kofte*, deep-fried meat and cracked wheat nuggets, are impressively nutty on the outside and beefy within. A squeeze of lemon lightens each bite just so. The Sako's Special, also known as *iskender*, makes for a tremendously satisfying main course. A heap of seasoned ground beef sirloin is thinly sliced from the spit and layered atop torn pita bread. It arrives on a sizzling platter drizzled with browned butter, tomato sauce, and a luscious yogurt sauce. Sako's Turkish desserts are as compelling as the starters and mains. The *ayva tatlisi*, a baked quince deseeded and filled with apples, comes topped with crushed walnuts and a thick dollop of unsweetened cream a few churns away from turning into butter. The *ekmek kadayifi*, a kind of Turkish bread pudding, marries syrup-soaked bread with the aforementioned cream. This family-run restaurant is one of the Valley's most precious gems.

Sugarfish by Sushi Nozawa, 11288 Ventura Blvd., Studio City, CA 91604; (818) 762-2322; sugarfishsushi.com; Japanese; $$$. For a complete description, see p. 66.

Umami Burger, 12159 Ventura Blvd., Studio City, CA 91604; (818) 286-9004; umami.com; American; $$. For a complete description, see p. 68. **Additional Location:** 4300 Riverside Dr., Burbank, CA 91505; (818) 433-3680.

L.A. Landmarks

Bill and Hiroko's, 14742 Oxnard St., Van Nuys, CA 91411; (818) 785-4086; American; $. Bill Elwell has been plugging away on the flattop grill since he started this Van Nuys burger stand in 1965. Regulars from back in the day know it as Bill's Hamburgers, while newer fans refer to it as Bill and Hiroko's. The latter addition is a nod to Hiroko Wilcox, Bill's lovely wife, who helps him run the place. Grab a seat at the L-shaped counter to watch the master at work—the best spots are the two stools closest to the grill. Patio seating away from the meat and grease is also available for those who prefer some solitude with their lunch. Bill's signature burger is a simple but immensely satisfying creation padded with iceberg lettuce, a thin slice of tomato, a couple of dill pickles, chopped onions, and mayonnaise. Commercial buns are toasted till crisped and browned, while patties are cooked all the way though. Thick slices of American cheese and crispy bacon strips, as well as additional meat patties, can and should be added to build a better burger. Bill and Hiroko's is open Mon through Fri 8:30 a.m. until 4 p.m.

FURTHER EXPLORATION: THE MUNCH BOX

It's hard to miss **The Munch Box** on Devonshire (21532 Devonshire St., Chatsworth, CA 91311; 818-998-9240). This sunshine yellow roadside hamburger stand has been around since 1956, wowing Valley residents with hickory burgers and chili cheese fries.

Brent's Deli, 19565 Parthenia St., Northridge, CA 91324; (818) 886-5679; brentsdeli.com; Jewish; $$. Since purchasing Brent's Deli in 1969, Ron Peskin and his wife, Patricia, have transformed this once-failing eatery into a world-class delicatessen. Over the years, the couple's son Brent, daughter Carie, daughter-in-law Dori, and son-in-law Marc have joined the brigade. When the crowds pile in on weekend mornings, the veteran crew runs the restaurant like a well-oiled machine. The only way to avoid an inevitable wait is to snag one of the first-come, first-served stools overlooking the open kitchen—the full view of the hustling waitresses and bustling cooks can't be beat. The thinly sliced and fat-streaked corned beef is rightfully famous. It's at its best in Reuben form, stacked 2 inches tall between slices of grilled rye bread with melted swiss cheese, hot sauerkraut, and Russian dressing. Don't forget to swap out steak fries for curly ones. Brent's solid selection of prepared fishes including a smoky whitefish salad, hand-sliced lox, barbecued cod, and baked salmon can turn any ol' toasted bagel into a breakfast event. For those digging deep into traditional Jewish fare, sample the *matzo brie*, a comforting dish of matzo fried with eggs, or the *kishke*, a kind of sausage made from meat and grain.

Katsu-Ya, 11680 Ventura Blvd., Los Angeles, CA 91604; (818) 985-6976; katsu-yagroup.com; Japanese; $$$. Long before master sushi chef Katsuya Uechi teamed up with mogul Sam Nazarian and designer Philippe Starck to launch Katsu-Ya, a sushi empire for the young and fabulously hip, he operated a modestly appointed sushi restaurant in Studio City. Opened in 1999, Katsu-Ya served as an informal testing ground for many of the dishes that have gone on to garner global fans. Even with four swanky Katsu-Ya restaurants around town in Brentwood, Hollywood, Downtown, and Glendale, the dowdier original remains as popular as ever. The restaurant's signature Crispy Rice with Spicy Tuna contrasts hot with cold and crunchy with supple, while the Baked Crab Hand Rolls tuck snow crab and rice in soy paper along with a rich and creamy sauce. Most decadent of all is the Dynamite, sautéed scallops, shrimp, mushrooms, onions, and asparagus tossed in dynamite sauce and baked till golden. Katsu-Ya may specialize in modern interpretations of Japanese fare, but there are also classic sashimi, tempura, and teriyaki preparations available for purists. **Additional Locations:** 16542 Ventura Blvd., Encino, CA 91436; (818) 788-2396. 9701 Reseda Blvd., Northridge, CA 91324; (818) 678-1700.

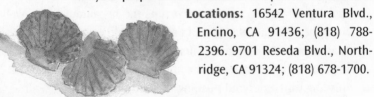

Porto's Bakery & Cafe, 3614 W. Magnolia Blvd., Burbank, CA 91504; (818) 846-9100; portosbakery.com; Cuban; $. For a complete description, see p. 240.

Sam Woo Barbecue, 6450 Sepulveda Blvd., Van Nuys, CA 91411; (818) 988-6813; Chinese; $. For a complete description, see p. 82.

Yang Chow, 6443 Topanga Canyon Blvd., Canoga Park, CA 91303; (818) 347-2610; yangchow.com; Chinese; $$. For a complete description, see p. 84.

Zankou Chicken, 1001 N. San Fernando Blvd., Burbank, CA 91504; (818) 238-0414; zankouchicken.com; Lebanese; $. For a complete description, see p. 84. **Additional Locations:** 10760 Riverside Dr., North Hollywood, CA 91602; (818) 655-0469. 5658 Sepulveda Blvd., Van Nuys, CA 91411; (818) 781-0615. 7640 Tampa Ave., Los Angeles, CA 91335; (818) 881-1151.

 *Sublime Sweets*

Crème Caramel L.A., 14849 Burbank Blvd., Sherman Oaks, CA 91411; (818) 949-8352; cremecaramella.com; Desserts; $. Kristine de la Cruz of Crème Caramel L.A. has a flair for all things decadent. What began as a weekends and nights–only side business has flourished into a full-time affair. Wider distribution at local farmers' markets and the option for home delivery and catering are a huge plus for her legion of crème caramel and bread pudding devotees and a minus for their collective waistlines. Some calories just aren't meant to be counted. The heart of the operation is the original crème caramel, a jiggly and rich French custard that's made using a treasured family recipe. Coffee- and chocolate-flavored ones are regularly available along with the original, while outside-the-box creations like Mexican hot chocolate, *ube* (purple yam), and masala chai pop up on special occasions. Also wildly popular are de la Cruz's warm bread puddings. The original version made from a combination of brioche and challah comes drizzled in salted caramel. Buttery, sweet, warm, salty, and soft, it's calculated precisely to make you crumble into little pieces. Her standard bread pudding lineup also includes caramelized bacon, and chocolate with crème anglaise.

Jerry's Soda Shoppe, 20914 Roscoe Blvd., Los Angeles, CA 91304; (818) 341-9515; Dessert; $. Jerry's Soda Shoppe, an old-fashioned lunch counter tucked into the De Soto Pharmacy, delivers dependably delicious renditions of classic frozen treats. Grab a seat at one of the seven swivel stools lining the counter and dig into luscious banana splits topped with fluffy tufts of whipped cream, crushed peanuts, and maraschino cherries; exquisite sundaes drizzled with hot fudge, marshmallow cream, and butterscotch; and shakes and malts of all stripes. The ice cream sodas are particularly decadent: as if scoops of vanilla ice cream, soda water, and chocolate syrup weren't enough, the chilled mug itself arrives coated in hardened chocolate sauce. Whipped

FURTHER EXPLORATION: FAIR OAKS PHARMACY AND SODA FOUNTAIN

South Pasadena's **Fair Oaks Pharmacy and Soda Fountain** (1526 Mission St., South Pasadena, CA 91030; 626-799-1414; fairoakspharmacy.net) has been delighting the neighborhood with old-fashioned phosphates (flavored syrup and soda water), hand-dipped malts and shakes, and egg creams since 1915.

cream, chocolate sprinkles, and a maraschino cherry add the finishing touches.

Mae Ting's Coconut Cakes, 8232 Coldwater Canyon Ave., Los Angeles, CA 91605; (818) 522-8647; Thai; $. For a complete description, see p. 90.

Martino's Bakery, 335 N. Victory Blvd., Burbank, CA 91502; (818) 842-0715; martinosbakery.com; Bakery; $. Victor and Eva Martino of Martino's Bakery may have initially launched the business in 1926 as a wholesale pie and doughnut operation, but today the Burbank bakery is most famous for its tea cakes—squat, square-shaped muffins soft enough to use as a pillow. Developed in 1945, the original tea cakes are golden hued and pleasantly sweet. The cake's crumb is somehow dense yet light, while a thin glaze sweetens the entire package. In addition to the original buttermilk flavor, there are equally winning blueberry and cranberry varieties with fruity punches and streusel topping. Pair these cakes with a mug of hot tea for a light breakfast or an effective afternoon pick-me-up.

Specialty Stores, Markets & Producers

Tashkent Produce, 5340 Laurel Canyon Blvd., Valley Village, CA 91607; (818) 752-7222. When Slava Rafailov opened Tashkent Produce nearly a decade ago, the small neighborhood market was little more than a few shelves lined with imported foods and a well-stocked meat counter. A kitchen specializing in prepared foods was added on three years later, providing a standout option for those craving a taste of Eastern European home cooking. Follow your nose to the back of the store where an army of babushkas prepares everything under the Kremlin sun, from several varieties of borscht to mushroom soup to a splendid selection of cold appetizers like pâté, cheese, mushrooms, and eggplant. There's even kimchee for Korean shoppers residing in the neighborhood. Underneath heat lamps are stuffed peppers, zucchinis, and cabbage, roasted beef tongues, grilled salmon, fried fishes, blood sausage, stuffed chicken legs with mushrooms, and perfectly pleated beef dumplings. Pastries and cakes, as well as imported German breads, round out the market's impressive take-out selection.

San Gabriel Valley

Azusa, Alhambra, Arcadia, Duarte, Glendora, Hacienda Heights, Industry, Monterey Park, Rosemead, Rowland Heights, San Gabriel, Sierra Madre, South El Monte, Temple City, West Covina

Foodie Faves

Banh Mi & Che Cali, 135 San Gabriel Blvd., San Gabriel, CA 91776; (626) 286-8728; Vietnamese; $. There's rarely an upside to colonization, but in the case of Vietnam and France, 90 years of cultural, political, and social influence led to a phenomenal fusion of cuisines. Take for instance the *banh mi,* also known as a Vietnamese sandwich. A toasty rice-flour baguette is smeared with fish sauce-laced pâté and made-from-scratch mayonnaise and stuffed with hams, headcheese, sweet pickles, chiles, cilantro, and cucumber spears. While its composition is distinctly French, its soul is all Vietnamese. Delis specializing in *banh mi* are common throughout the San Gabriel Valley, but business is most brisk at Banh Mi & Che Cali. This mini chain is headquartered in Orange County's Little Saigon and has local branches in San Gabriel, Rosemead, and Alhambra, where bargain prices and tasty fare keep customers extremely loyal. Here, *banh mi* are filled with everything under the Saigon sun including the aforementioned cold cuts (*thit* or *dac biet*), grilled lemongrass pork (*thit nuong*), and reddish-hued meatballs (*nem nuong*). The bread is baked in-house and has a buttery way about it that's quite unique. Come hungry or with friends because the shop's ongoing "buy two, get one free" deal is too good to pass up. Wash down your sandwiches with milk tea *boba* (tapioca balls); it's "buy one, get one free" after all. **Additional Locations:** 647 W. Valley Blvd., Alhambra, CA 91803; (626) 293-8396. 8450 Valley Blvd., Rosemead, CA 91770; (626) 288-5600.

FURTHER EXPLORATION:
SAIGON'S BAKERY & SANDWICHES

While the grilled pork and cold cuts at **Saigon's Bakery & Sandwiches** (718 E. Valley Blvd., San Gabriel, CA 91776; 262-288-6475) in San Gabriel lack the oomph of Banh Mi & Che Cali's, the baguettes here are spectacular—nice body, pleasant crisp, and not too much fluff. They're at their best stuffed with *bi*, a porky mixture of meat, skin, and toasted rice powder.

Banh Xeo Quan, 8742 E. Garvey Ave., Rosemead, CA 91770; (626) 288-2699; Vietnamese; $. Banh Xeo Quan, also known as Mr. Rice, specializes in Vietnamese crepes. Owner Phi Tran, who hails from Saigon, opened the restaurant over five years ago to bring this southern Vietnamese specialty to the San Gabriel Valley. *Banh xeo*, which literally means "sizzling cake," earned its name from the sound the batter makes when it hits the scorching pan. The result is a thin crepe, colored a stunning shade of yellow due to the turmeric in the batter, that's crisp and delicate throughout with lacy, caramelized edges. Stuffed inside are bunches of bean sprouts, mushrooms, shrimp, and pork. Go ahead and upgrade to the *banh xeo dac biet* for extra filling. To eat, nab a bit of the crepe and wrap it in romaine lettuce or rice paper along with some herbs, then dip the entire parcel in fish sauce. The other specialty here is *xoi ga,* sticky rice dolled up with shredded chicken, fried shallots, dried shrimp, and Chinese sausages. It's homey fare that tastes somehow better because no slaving behind the stove was required. If a noodle soup strikes your fancy, the *bun bo Hue* made here is one of the strongest bowls around. The lemongrass-inflected broth is deep, dark, and flavorful, with plenty of skin-on pork and tender beef. Don't forget to add the fresh banana flower shavings served on the side into your bowl. Wash everything down with a tall cup of freshly pressed *nuoc mia* (sugarcane juice).

Beijing Pie House, 846 E. Garvey Ave., #3A, Monterey Park, CA 91755; (626) 288-3818; Chinese; $. Don't expect slices of lemon meringue or sour cherry when you come into Beijing Pie House in Monterey Park. Here, the signature pies are *xian bing*, supersize savory hockey pucks made of flaky bread and filled with all sorts of good stuff. Each order comes with four pies that can be mixed and matched according to preference. The ones filled with lamb and the "mixed three item" (shrimp, pork, mushrooms, and egg) are the most popular. Be careful as you bite into one because these pies perform like soup dumplings, gushing hot juices that will likely scald the roof of your mouth. Still, you won't be able to resist going in for more. Maybe even better than the pies is the Homeland Meat Cake listed under the "Pancake" section of the menu, which consists of alternating layers of a rotilike bread and mildly spiced pork.

The Boiling Crab, 742 W. Valley Blvd., Alhambra, CA 91803; (626) 576-9368; theboilingcrab .com; Seafood; $$. While seafood boils were a regular part of Dada Ngo and her husband Sinh Nguyen's social lives down in Texas, Little Saigon had never before experienced such a thing before these Southern transplants opened the first Boiling Crab restaurant. From the start, the Cajun-style seafood concept caught on like wildfire, and it eventually spread north to the San Gabriel Valley and beyond. Here at the Alhambra outpost, patrons wait up to 2 hours during peak dining times to get their hands good and dirty from the restaurant's famous spice-rubbed crayfish. Before the main event arrives in a plastic sack, tables are covered in butcher paper and bibs are tied around necks. In addition to classic crayfish are king crab legs, snow crab legs, blue crab, shrimp, clams, Dungeness crab, and lobster; everything is sold by the pound. Crustaceans come spiced in original Rajun Cajun, lemon pepper, garlic butter, or The Whole Shebang, a delectable combination of all three. The Boiling Crab throws in corn on the cob, potatoes, and sausages for orders greater than 2 pounds. For those unaccustomed to eating mudbugs, just rip off their heads, suck out the juices, break the tails lengthwise, and pull out the meat. Done and done. **Additional Locations:** 33 W. Main St., Alhambra, CA 91801; (626) 300-5898. 18902 E. Gale Ave., #A, Rowland Heights, CA 91748; (626) 964-9300.

Boiling Point, 153 W. Garvey Ave., Monterey Park, CA 91755; (626) 288-9876; bpgroupusa.com; Taiwanese; $$. Individual hot pots prepared Taiwanese-style are the specialty at Boiling Point, a local chain expanding across the Southland. True to its name, each hot pot arrives from the kitchen scorching hot, bubbling well beyond the vessel's parameters. While every hot pot is prepared using the same master broth, the level of spice, as well as the individual ingredients (beef, lamb, kimchee, fish balls, vegetables, tofu, etc.) can be adjusted according to diners' preferences. For those who are as indecisive as they are gutsy, try the House Special, which includes a mélange of characters like pork intestines, meatballs, quail eggs, hot dogs, mushrooms, *kamaboko* (Japanese seafood loaf), pork, Napa cabbage, and most challenging of all, stinky tofu. The unpleasant odor emanating from the slabs of soybean is the result of marinating in fermented milk, vegetables, and meat for several months. While most find the tofu's flavor less offensive than its smell, its assertive profile certainly isn't for everyone. Plop in the tangle of noodles served on the side while the broth is still sputtering away. To jazz up the broth and its components, meander to the condiments cart for a variety of sauces— garlic soy, spicy oil, and spicy bean. The chunky and fermented spicy bean sauce adds complexity to whatever it hits. Eating the hot pot can be approached in one of two ways: either dish it out into smaller bowls, or attack the large pot directly. The latter option offers a complimentary facial steam treatment to boot. **Additional Locations:** 140 W. Valley Blvd., San Gabriel, CA 91776; (626) 300-9800. 206 S. 1st Ave., Arcadia, CA 91006; (626) 461-6688. 2020 S. Hacienda Blvd., Hacienda Heights, CA 91745; (626) 369-0928.

Cook's Tortas, 1944 S. Atlantic Blvd., Monterey Park, CA 91754; (323) 278-3536; cookstortas.com; Mexican; $. At Cook's Tortas in Monterey Park, traditional Mexican *tortas* (sandwiches) are reimagined by L.A. natives Ricardo Diaz and his in-laws Elvira and Antonio Zamora. From the traditional Milanesa with breaded steak to the out-of-the-box Salmon with capers and cream cheese to the something in between Lengua with simmered beef tongue, the flavors that the kitchen cranks out day-to-day are stunningly delicious. The crisp, chewy ciabatta that serves as the foundation for each creation is baked daily in house by Antonio, who was once the head baker at Chef Thomas Keller's Bouchon in Yountville. With bread this good and fillings this inspired, it's impossible to go wrong at Cook's. Pair your dynamite sandwich with a tall cup of *agua fresca*; the celery lime is as refreshing as it is intriguing.

Dai Ho Restaurant, 9148 Las Tunas Dr., Temple City, CA 91780; (626) 291-2295; Taiwanese; $. With its signature beef noodle soup ringing in at a whopping $9 a bowl, Dai Ho may be the most expensive noodle hawker in the San Gabriel Valley. While sticker shock might keep some penny-pinching noodle soup devotees away, those who

take a chance are handsomely rewarded with one of the best renditions of Taiwan's national dish. Each bowl is packed with bouncy egg
noodles that are the very definition of Q, a chewy texture prized by
connoisseurs. The broth is deep, dark, and unabashedly beefy, while
the chunks of stewed meat collapse with the gentlest of bites. While it's
the beef noodle soup that gets all the good press, the Minced Meat Dry
Noodles might be even better. The flavors from the heap of marinated
ground pork, tinged slightly orange from chili oil, along with fresh scallions permeate every strand. Pitch-perfect seasonings combined with
wondrously toothsome noodles send slurpers over the moon. Dai Ho
is only open for three and a half hours Tuesday through Sunday (11:30
a.m. to 3 p.m.), so plan accordingly.

FURTHER EXPLORATION: A&J AND PEARL'S

For kinder hours and slightly less Q, grab a bowl of beef noodle
soup at **A&J** in Arcadia (27 Las Tunas Dr., Arcadia, CA 91007;
626-445-7270)—it tastes just like the ones in Taipei. **Pearl's Restaurant** (p. 164) in Monterey Park prepares a homey rendition.

Daikokuya, 111 N. Atlantic Blvd., Monterey Park, CA 91754; (626)
570-1930; dkramen.com; Japanese; $. For a complete description,
see p. 22. **Additional Locations:** 1220 S. Golden West Ave., Arcadia, CA
91007; (626) 254-0127. 15827 Gale Ave., Hacienda Heights, CA 91745;
(626) 968-0810.

Dog Haus, 410 E. Main St., Alhambra, CA 91801; (626) 282-4287;
doghausdogs.com; American; $. For a complete description, see p.
232.

Dongbu Live Fish, 18785 Colima Rd., Rowland Heights, CA 91748; (626) 810-8582; Korean; $$. Angelenos seeking sashimi generally head to the South Bay or somewhere on the Westside, but they ought to consider going east instead to Rowland Heights, a predominantly Taiwanese community. Dongbu Live Fish, a Korean *hwal uh* (thinly sliced raw seafood) specialist, is reason enough to drive down the 60. A family of four runs the tiny restaurant. Dad is the chief fisherman and chef, Mom serves as his sous, and their son and daughter manage the cash register and serve customers. Together they deliver excellent service that makes both regulars and first-timers feel at ease. The bubbling and gurgling tanks full of seafood provide a fitting soundtrack to every meal. The centerpiece of the *hwal uh* experience is a gorgeous platter of freshly caught and filleted Santa Barbara halibut. The thin slices of sashimi, which absolutely shimmer with freshness, can be eaten straight up or wrapped *ssam*-style with lettuce leaves, *gochujang* (fermented red chili paste), *ssamjang* (fermented soybean paste), garlic, and jalapeños. Accompanying the halibut are seven additional dishes: a lettuce and cabbage slaw topped with roe and halibut, plates of unadorned abalone and sea squirt, cold noodles (*naengmyeon*), baked mussels, broiled mackerel, and a hot and spicy fish soup (*maeuntang*).

Duck House, 501 S. Atlantic Blvd., Monterey Park, CA 91754; (626) 284-3227; duckshouse.com; Chinese; $$$. Before dropping in at Duck House for lunch or dinner, it is essential to reserve your bird at least an hour in advance. While this might seem like a fussy thing to do in a thoroughly unfussy neighborhood, it really is very little work to guarantee a pristine Peking-style duck served in a timely fashion. Life offers few promises as satisfying as this one. If you've done your proper due diligence, a generous platter framed with crispy skin shards surrounding a heap of shredded duck meat will arrive at the table soon after you are seated. To assemble your Peking duck wrap, smear a thin wheat pancake with bean paste, followed by a shower of scallions and cucumbers; finally, add in one or two pieces of golden brown skin. Rendered almost completely of its fat, the skin is simultaneously crunchy and rich. The salty sauce and assertive onions balance out its intrinsic sumptuousness. The combination of flavors somehow gets better and better as one keeps eating. For a few dollars extra, a duck bone soup or a bean sprout stir-fry can supplement the Peking duck. The soup's milky-white broth with tofu and Napa cabbage makes for a palate-cleansing pairing.

Elite, **700 S. Atlantic Blvd., Monterey Park, CA 91754; (626) 282-9998; elitechineserestaurant.com; Chinese; $$.** Waiting for a table at Elite on a weekend morning tests one's dedication to the sport of dim sum. The bellies that gather here are a tenacious bunch; they don't seem to mind waiting an hour or even two so long as the food is tops when their number finally gets called. What's unique about the dim sum experience here is the lack of carts roaming the dining room. Diners are presented with a picture menu and an order form upon being seated. While the chaos of traditional dim sum has it charms, this approach is more civilized; dishes are steamed to order and the chore of scanning the room for the lone lady serving chicken feet is completely avoided. A simple tick mark on the form and voila,

FURTHER EXPLORATION: LUNASIA

The best part about the cart-less dim sum experience at Alhambra's **Lunasia** (500 W. Main St., Alhambra, CA 91801; 626-308-3222) is that it is available all day long, making it possible to avoid the maddening crowds on weekend mornings. Come in for a leisurely dinner of lotus leaf-wrapped sticky rice, foie gras dumplings, steamed barbecue pork buns, and turnip cakes.

steaming hot chicken feet appear at the table. Dim sum basics like *shu mai* (pork and shrimp dumplings), *har gow* (translucent shrimp dumplings), and tripe with ginger and scallions are executed very well. Fancier dishes like fried taro cakes, crispy shrimp rice noodles, and crispy snow buns have a lot of flair and flavor. From the food to the service, there's no denying that Elite is the best place to *yum cha* in the area, even though the waits can be painful. Go early. Eat up. Get out.

Golden Deli, 815 W. Las Tunas Dr., San Gabriel, CA 91776; (626) 308-0803; goldendelirestaurant.com; Vietnamese; $. Southern-style Vietnamese food is what you'll find at this perpetually busy, efficiently run, and solid-as-can-be restaurant. Come for the blistered *cha gio* stuffed with ground pork and wood ear mushrooms and served with herbs and greens for garnishing and wrapping, respectively. Then, settle into a bowl of *pho* (rare beef, brisket, and tripe are the holy trinity of beef noodle soup), a platter of broken rice (*com tam*) topped with a sunny-side egg (the one with grilled pork, shredded pork, and steamed pork loaf won't disappoint), or a bowl of cool vermicelli noodles (*bun*). The *nuoc cham* (fish sauce vinaigrette) here is top-notch, so spoon it

FURTHER EXPLORATION: VIETNAM RESTAURANT AND VIETNAM HOUSE

If the line at Golden Deli is snaking out the door and you're feeling impatient, head over to **Vietnam Restaurant** (340 W. Las Tunas Dr., San Gabriel, CA 91776; 626-281-5577) or **Vietnam House** (710 W. Las Tunas Dr., San Gabriel, CA 91776; 626-282-3630) up the street. Both are on Las Tunas Drive and crank out solid renditions of broken rice plates (*com tam*) and vermicelli noodle bowls (*bun*).

on liberally or better yet, just dump the whole thing onto your rice or noodles. No one will judge you.

Hot Pot, Hot Pot, 120 S. Atlantic Blvd., Monterey Park, CA 91754; (626) 282-1089; hotpothotpot.com; Chinese; $$. While it's usually best to leave the cooking to trained professionals when dining out, Mongolian hot pot is so drop-dead easy that even a careful, chopstick-wielding toddler could handle it. Hot Pot, Hot Pot, a brightly lit and well-serviced communal soup hall in Monterey Park, is the kind of place that's perfect for small and large groups in the mood for a tummy-warming and interactive feast. Begin by selecting a broth. There are three bases available including the mild House Original, the sweat-inducing House Spicy, and the medicinally tinged Rejuvenation Broth. The Half & Half hot pot allows for two different broths, which is perfect for variety's sake, as well as for large groups with varying tastes. Once the broths have been settled on, all manner of proteins, vegetables, dumplings, and noodles are available for the taking. The thinly sliced lamb melds beautiful with any broth, as do the intestines, maitake mushrooms, quail eggs, and handmade spinach noodles. More delicate ingredients like the oysters, enoki mushrooms, and clams were made for the House Original. There are also four sauces on hand for dipping, including a balanced chile oil and a smooth sesame number. For a diversion from the soup, try the lamb hand pies, which are impressively crisp and juicy.

Huge Tree Pastry, 423 N. Atlantic Blvd., #106, Monterey Park, CA 91754; (626) 458-8689; Chinese, Taiwanese; $. There are a handful of restaurants serving traditional Taiwanese breakfast in the San Gabriel Valley, but the one operated by the Liu family in Monterey Park rises above the rest. Tucked behind a grocery store on the far end of a strip mall, Huge Tree Pastry is the place to get your *you tiao* on. Deep-fried to order, these twisted, golden crullers shatter at first bite and are just as good dipped in a bowl of steaming soy milk. Scallion pancakes, which come with or without an eggy coating, benefit from a drizzle of soy sauce. Chile oil is nowhere to be found here. The salty soybean tofu, a combination of warm soy milk with soft tofu curds, shredded pork, and pickled mustard greens, is the very definition of comfort. Best of all are the *fan tuan*, tubular carbohydrate bombs with a *you tiao* running through the center and pork floss, scrambled eggs, and pickled mustard greens adding savory, fluffy, and tangy notes. The hodgepodge of ingredients is wrapped in either black or white sticky rice (the black rice is a touch sweeter) and a sheet of plastic wrap before landing on the table. Dig in like a burrito, peeling away the plastic wrap as you go. Order a tall glass of roasted rice milk to wash everything down.

FURTHER EXPLORATION: DOE JON STATION

While Huge Tree Pastry's fried turnip cake is solid, the dried-shrimp-studded version seasoned with loads of white pepper at **Doe Jon Station** (46 Las Tunas Dr., Arcadia, CA 91007; 626-821-2088) in Arcadia is even better. The innards are like molten lava.

Hunan Chilli King, 534 E. Valley Blvd., #2, San Gabriel, CA 91776; (626) 288-7993; Chinese; $$. The central Chinese province of Hunan is famous for its fiery cooking. Garlic, ginger, and heaps of chile peppers mix and mingle with all manner of proteins to create deadly good delights that singe tongues and unleash sweaty bouts. It might be a good idea to bring a hanky in your pocket to Hunan Chilli King, literally San Gabriel's hottest spot. The Hot and Spicy Shrimp is best enjoyed head first; the crunchy membranes go down nice and easy. The innocuous sounding Sautéed Lamb is a soulful, cumin-laced dish that balances hotness with spice in a delicious way. For those who find offal anything but awful, the Flavor Water Three—a splendid collection of kidneys, intestines, and liver—is the dish for you. To reel in the burning sensation, order a few spice-neutral dishes like the Crispy Rice Crust with Seafood and spongy Sautéed Loofah. Of course, don't feel obligated to hoover up every chile on the platter as well. Enjoy everything with plenty of steamed jasmine rice.

Itoy Sa Atin Restaurant, 1559 Amar Rd., West Covina, CA 91792; (626) 810-1883; Filipino; $. Pointing is encouraged and even considered polite when dining at a *carinderia,* a style of Filipino restaurants where diners *turo-turo,* or "point-point," to indicate which dishes they'd like to eat. West Covina's Itoy Sa Atin offers one of the city's best steam table smorgasbords. Although nothing is cooked to order, the selection of soups, stews, and stir-fries gleams with freshness. At point-point joints, it's always best to stick to dishes that are not compromised by sitting out. Stews and soups like *adobo* and *sinigang* benefit from this kind of preparation and presentation, while deep-fried items like *lechon kawali* tend to wilt over time. A combination platter at Itoy Sa Atin includes a choice of two dishes, plenty of steamed white rice, and a cup of the soup of the day. Always available is the pork *adobo,* a delectable stew redolent of garlic, soy sauce, and

FURTHER EXPLORATION: BAHAY KUBO NATIN

Closer to central Los Angeles is **Bahay Kubo Natin Restaurant** (2330 W. Temple St., Los Angeles, CA 90026; 213-413-4804) in Westlake. In addition to the usual steam table suspects, the fried chicken is made to order and worth considering.

vinegar. The hunks of meat are so tender that the plasticware provided with the platter cuts through like butter. The *kare-kare,* an oxtail and tripe stew, isn't too sweet and hits the perfect peanut-buttery note. Don't forget to dabble a bit of the awesomely salty *bagoong* (fermented shrimp paste) on each bite to really get down with your bad self.

JTYH Restaurant, 9425 Valley Blvd., Rosemead, CA 91770; (626) 442-8999; Chinese; $. Try as one might, JTYH just doesn't quite roll off the tongue. To help you remember the name of this Northern Chinese food haven, employ this genius mnemonic device: "Justin Timberlake, You're Hot." It works like a charm. Once you've committed the restaurant's name to memory, come in for knife-cut noodles made in the Shanxi tradition that are jagged edged, thick in the most pleasant of ways, and bouncy like you wouldn't believe. The noodles are served in a variety of preparations, but swimming in lamb broth is most popular. The other specialty of the house is the Mooshu Cat Ears, handmade orecchiette stir-fried with pork, mushrooms, eggs, and scallions. No felines were harmed in the making of this dish. To round out your feast, try the fried intestines with Sichuan peppercorns, which taste like crispy chicken skin, and the beef roll made with tender meat, hoisin sauce, and cucumbers snuggled inside a flaky pancake.

FURTHER EXPLORATION: KAM HONG GARDEN

For knife-cut noodles served in a more assertive mutton broth, visit **Kam Hong Garden** (848 E. Garvey Ave., Monterey Park, CA 91755; no phone) in Monterey Park. Also notable are the Shanxi sautéed pork fried noodles, a broth-less dish that highlights the noodles' unique texture.

Lucky Noodle King, 534 E. Valley Blvd., San Gabriel, CA 91776; (626) 573-5668; Chinese; $. No one executes the regional specialties of Sichuan, famous for its tongue-numbing peppercorns and mountains of dried chiles, quite like San Gabriel's Lucky Noodle King. To prepare diners for the impending burn, the restaurant's walls are painted a fiery shade of red with ornamental chiles dangling in every direction. Consider the decor fair warning of what's to come. Prior to opening Lucky Noodle King, the owners ran a place called Chuan Yu Noodle Town that was famous for its *dan dan mian*. The tradition of noodle excellence lives on within these new walls. Each bowl is mounded with fresh noodles and ground seasoned pork. A biting yet creamy sauce ties everything together, making the *dan dan* noodles here an event. Delicately wrapped and punched up with minced garlic, the wontons in chili oil are great as well, with the proportion of meat to wrapper skewed toward the latter. The Chongqing fried chicken takes boneless, skinless chicken nuggets to a whole new level with its crisp batter, fragrant with the distinct essence of Sichuan peppercorns. If you're with a group and the weather is dreary, the Fagara hot pot brewed tableside will scald your tongue and warm your soul.

FURTHER EXPLORATION: CHUNG KING

Just up the street from Lucky Noodle King in San Gabriel lies **Chung King** (1000 S. San Gabriel Blvd., San Gabriel, CA 91776; 626-286-0298), another popular spot to test one's limits for tongue-numbing cuisine. The Saliva Chicken is mouthwateringly good with its spicy sauce and supple meat. The deep-fried intestines bring a whole lot of crunch.

Luscious Dumplings, 704 W. Las Tunas Dr., San Gabriel, CA 91776; Chinese; $. In a part of town where "Engrish" reigns supreme,

San Gabriel's Luscious Dumplings scores major points for proper and provocative use of the English language. As an added bonus, the dumplings actually live up to their name. Everything is made from scratch at this mom-and-pop shop, as evidenced by the rustically formed morsels coming out of the kitchen. While all of Luscious' dumplings are quite enjoyable, the most popular are the pork pan-fried dumplings. The filling is a simple mixture of ground meat and chives, while the skins are pliable and not too thick. An intense sear crisps and caramelizes the exterior, adding some crunch to each bite. The *xiao long bao* (soup-filled dumplings) are another crowd pleaser. While not as refined as those from **Din Tai Fung** (p. 177), these taste just fine jazzed up with hot chile oil or dipped in black vinegar. Those seeking a somewhat healthier dumpling experience should try the steamed ones filled with cabbage, pork, and shrimp. The restaurant is open 11 a.m. to 2 p.m. for lunch and 5 to 8 p.m. for dinner. Due to the shop's immense popularity, several dumpling varieties often sell out well before the advertised closing time, so show up early to guarantee the most bountiful selection.

FURTHER EXPLORATION: HUI TOU XIANG NOODLE HOUSE

Hui Tou Xiang Noodle House (704 W. Las Tunas Dr., San Gabriel, CA 91776; 626-281-9888; huitouxiang.com), Luscious Dumplings' most formidable competitor, resides directly next door. The pork and crab *xiao long bao*, as well as the pork pot stickers, give the neighboring dumpling hawkers a run for their money.

Mama's Lu, 153 E. Garvey Ave., Monterey Park, CA 91755; (626) 307-5700; Chinese; $. Once you've tasted the Shanghai-style rice cakes at Mama's Lu, you'll want to revoke the name "rice cake" from those tasteless cardboard messes found in grocery breakfast aisles across America. Here, rice cakes refer to chewy, smooth discs made of rice flour that are sautéed with pork, mushrooms, and Napa cabbage in a soy-based sauce. An intense sizzle in the wok imparts a smoky quality to the entire dish. The green onion pancakes here are flaky wonders, while the *xiao long bao* (soup dumplings) unleash a flood of porky broth at first nibble. If a vegetable item is in order, the garlicky eggplant never disappoints. Come with a large group and order up a storm. If you're accustomed to Westside prices, the bill at the end of a meal here will blow your mind.

FURTHER EXPLORATION: DEAN SIN WORLD

The mother of the proprietress of Mama's Lu runs an equally notable, but smaller establishment down the street called **Dean Sin World** (306 N. Garfield Ave., Monterey Park, CA 91754; 626-571-0636), where the Lion's Head Soup and flaky pastries filled with red bean paste reign supreme. While you're there, pick up a bag of 50 frozen dumplings for $10 for a quick snack or meal at home.

Merry's House of Chicken, 2550 Amar Rd., West Covina, CA 91792; (626) 965-0123; merryshouseofchicken.com; Indonesian; $. Deep-fried birds of the Indonesian persuasion are the specialty at Merry's House of Chicken, a restaurant so genuinely homey that the proprietor's children dive into their homework alongside hungry customers. The shop's owner, Merry Istiowati-Tio, left behind a three-decade-long career running a culinary arts institution when she emigrated to the United States from Surabaya, Indonesia, in 1998. Here at her namesake house of chicken, Merry draws upon her deep-rooted culinary know-how to prepare three distinctly different styles of Indonesian fried chicken. The house special, *Aayam Goreng Kremesan*, is seasoned with garlic, turmeric, coriander, and salt and deep-fried until crisp and golden. While the chicken's flavors are harmonious and the meat is moist, it's the crunchy rice flour crumbles scattered on top that bring on the fireworks. Fresh lime wedges and a potent *sambal* made from Thai chiles and shrimp paste bring the zing. The *Ayam Kalasan*, a sweetly simmered bird that's only fried for a quick minute, strikes a completely different note. Its meat falls tenderly off the bone, while the skin is imbued with sugary and garlicky tones. Finally, there's the *Ayam Penyet*, which literally means "smashed chicken." This lovingly abused creature is marinated in turmeric and pounded with tomatoes and *sambal* on a mortar before meeting its deep-fried fate.

Nanjing Kitchen, 706 W. Las Tunas Dr., San Gabriel, CA 91776; (626) 281-8968; Chinese; $. The words "cold duck" usually don't send the salivary glands into overdrive, but here at Nanjing Kitchen it's been the bestseller for 10 years and counting. Jean Zhang and her husband, John, the endlessly affable couple behind the bare-bones eatery, take great pride in their Nanjing-style salted duck. Whole birds are carefully simmered in a deeply savory broth that cooks the meat through and renders the fat completely, leaving behind only briny meat and supple skin. The duck doesn't look like much at the get-go, but the flavor is all that matters; the freshly hacked slices disappear in an instant. Both half and whole ducks are available to be eaten in or taken out, as are individual odds and ends stowed away in the refrigerator case. Turkey wings and drumsticks are prepared in the same salty fashion. Nanjing Kitchen's regulars usually take their birds to go, but the Zhangs are happy to accommodate folks dining in. To supplement the signature foul are Giant Pork Wontons and a variety of Nanjing-style noodles. The Noodles with Ba-Bao Hot Sauce Platter slathers spaghetti-like strands with a punchy fermented bean sauce, while the Pork Shank Noodles come with a meaty hunk piled on top.

Nem Nuong Ninh Hoa, 9016 Mission Dr., Rosemead, CA 91770; (626) 286-3370; Vietnamese; $. Vietnamese meatballs are a curiously loud bunch that snap at first bite and squeak at first chew. At Nem Nuong Ninh Hoa, grilled pork meatballs and skewers are served on grand platters along with rice papers for wrapping and a forest of greens for garnishing. The parade of proteins includes the restaurant's namesake *nem nuong* (sweet pork skewers and meatballs), as well as *nem cap* (pork patties wrapped in banana leaves), *nem chua nuong* (grilled sour pork patties), and *cha ram tom* (shrimp egg rolls). In the grand tradition of Vietnamese do-it-yourself dishes, begin by moistening a sheet of rice paper and lining it with lettuce. Then, select a protein, add in some vermicelli noodles and a few herbs, wrap it up tightly, and dip in either the house-special goopy orange sauce or *nuoc cham* (fish sauce vinaigrette), which is available upon request. Repeat until thoroughly satisfied. To supplement the meatballs, share an order of *banh beo*, a Central Vietnamese specialty. An order is composed of 12 steamed rice cakes served in shallow porcelain dishes piled atop one another. Each cake is sprinkled with dried minced shrimp, smeared with scallion oil, and finished with a crisp "crouton" of rendered pork fat. To eat, spoon on a bit of sweet fish sauce and dig in. Also memorable is the *banh hoi*, woven rice noodle mats topped with various meats.

Newport Seafood, 518 W. Las Tunas Dr., San Gabriel, CA 91776; (626) 289-5998; newportseafood.com; Chinese; $$. Newport Seafood is so wildly popular that the lunch crowd files in before noon, while dinner-goers arrive at five on the dot to avoid enduring a tortuously long wait. The original Tan Cang Newport Seafood, which opened in Orange County in 1989, gained a reputation larger than its signature lobsters for expertly prepared Vietnamese-inflected Chinese fare. After selling the original location, the owner established this similarly spirited restaurant in San Gabriel in 1996. What keeps this place perpetually packed is the house-special lobster, live crustaceans fished from tanks and stir-fried with heaps of chopped chiles, scallions, roe, and garlic. The hunks of lobster are considerately cracked before landing on a platter slathered in the aromatic sauce. While there's nothing wrong with dedicating an entire meal to lobster, your wallet may appreciate a bit of diversification. Try the Catfish with Hot and Sour Soup, a superb rendition of Vietnamese *canh chua* complete with spongy upright elephant ears that soak up the tangy broth, and the *bo luc lac*, another Vietnamese classic that brings together tender cubes of filet mignon in a savory black pepper sauce. Steamed clams with Thai basil, Kung Pao chicken, and sautéed pea sprouts ought to round out a meal here just right. For the ultimate Newport experience, gather a group of friends and share a Family Meal composed of the restaurant's greatest hits. **Additional Location:** 18441 Colima Rd., Rowland Heights, CA 91748; (626) 839-1239.

Nha Trang, 311 E. Valley Blvd., San Gabriel, CA 91776; (626) 572-7638; Vietnamese; $. The menu at Nha Trang is refreshingly pared down, with only eight dishes to choose from. There's *pho*, of course, and a few *banh mi*, but the specialty here, as the restaurant's name denotes, are noodle soups from Central Vietnam. Nha Trang, by the way, is a coastal town lined with postcard-ready beaches. The *bun bo Hue*, spicy beef noodle soup with lemongrass, isn't as heady or vibrant as what you'll find in Hue, but it's one of the better bowls to be had this side of the Pacific. Mingling with the thin, slippery rice noodles are fist-size pork trotters, cubes of congealed blood, and slices of pleasantly gristly beef. The *mi Quang Nha Trang* is even better with its bright yellow noodles, slices of pork loaf, and skin-on shrimp. Whereas some cultures frown upon diners raising bowls to their mouths to scrape and slurp every last bit, this isn't the case among the Vietnamese. Make sure not to leave a single noodle or drop of broth behind—a signal that complete satisfaction was had. It's best to dine at this itty-bitty shop early to avoid being bummed out by long waits or having to endure the heartbreak of having your favorite dish run out. **Additional Location:** 742 E. Garvey Ave., Monterey Park, CA 91755; (626) 288-8825.

Noodle Boy, 8518 Valley Blvd., Rosemead, CA 91770; (626) 280-8963; Chinese; $. Hong Kong–style wonton noodle soup is dished up from morning until night at this modern and brightly lit restaurant. The chef honed his craft in Hong Kong before opening Noodle Boy in 2010. From the bounce of the noodles to the spring of the wontons, it's clear that there is an expert behind the stoves. Most everyone orders the wonton noodle soup, which comes with four wontons chock-full of shrimp and a choice of egg noodles, wide rice noodles, or thin vermicelli. You'll want to sip every last drop of the aromatic broth that's ladled on scalding hot. Add-ons include sliced beef, cuttlefish balls, meatballs, and wonderfully plump fish balls. Soup-less *lo mein* noodles served with blanched greens in oyster sauce and any of the aforementioned proteins are also available. Noodle Boy's menu is straightforward and highly specialized, just like what you'd find in Hong Kong.

FURTHER EXPLORATION: NEW DRAGON

The wonton noodle soup at **New Dragon Chinese Restaurant** (934 N. Hill St., Los Angeles, CA 90012; 213-626-6050) in Chinatown has been quietly gaining followers since it opened in 2007. The Guangzhou chef jazzes up a solid bowl of wonton noodle soup with Chinese broccoli, scallions, and beef brisket and tendon upon request.

Noodle Guy, 1257 E. Valley Blvd., Alhambra, CA 91801; (626) 284-1868; noodleguy28.com; Vietnamese; $. Noodle Guy, not to be confused with Noodle King two doors down or Noodle Boy in nearby Rosemead, serves Vietnam's greatest hits. From broken rice to spring rolls, there's enough variety here to fill a thick, spiral-bound booklet. However, glancing around the dining room, it's clear that everyone is burying their faces into a big bowl of *pho* (Vietnamese beef noodle soup). What's unique about the *pho* here is the option of having Kobe beef in place of standard rare beef. While nicer *pho* palaces have been offering filet mignon for years, Noodle Guy claims to be the first to bring American Wagyu to the fore. The petite plate of well-marbled meat will bump up the price of your noodle bowl significantly, but it's definitely worthy of a once-in-a-while splurge. You haven't had meat this tender since forever.

Omar's Xinjiang Halal Restaurant, 1718 New Ave., San Gabriel, CA 91776; (626) 570-9778; Chinese; $$.

The Islamic Uyghur cooking found at Omar's Xinjiang Halal Restaurant in San Gabriel is a touch greasy, quite musky, and always most satisfactory. The food of Northwest China, which is predominantly halal due to the Islamic population, draws influences from neighboring cuisines in every direction. Omar's *shou la mian*, ropey hand-pulled noodles that are characteristic of the genre, have an unbeatable bite—toothsome to the 10th power. A chile oil–spiked stir-fry of lamb slivers and vegetables (bell peppers, celery, and cabbage) is poured atop the platter *a la minute*. It's hard to say where these strands start and stop, so reach for the well-worn pair of kitchen shears that's served alongside to keep things neat. Reminiscent of the staples of Northern China is the Meat Pie, a deep-fried Frisbee stuffed with minced lamb and carrot that tastes even better drizzled in chile oil. The quirkily named Haggis Soup warms the belly with a bewitching brew of entrails, while the Cumin Lamb Rib comes chile-flecked and deep-fried. The Xinjiang Homemade Yogurt is listed under the beverages, but it is thick and tangy enough to make for a very fine dessert.

101 Noodle Express, 1408 E. Valley Blvd., Alhambra, CA 91801; (626) 300-8654; Chinese; $. In spite of its billing, tangled heaps of slurp-worthy strands aren't what it's all about at 101 Noodle Express. Take a glance around the dining room and it's obvious that the beef rolls are what keep crowds humming and happy. A Shandong classic, the famed beef roll is composed of a flaky wheat pancake buttered up with a hoisinlike bean paste and rolled with fresh cilantro and thin cuts of stewed beef. A single order includes two foot-long logs stuffed to the brim and neatly sliced into manageable sections. The fried pancake is warm to the touch and substantial enough to keep the fixings in line. Unadorned, the beef roll tastes something like a *carne asada* burrito, but with a bready exterior and no trace of guacamole. What really makes the beef roll shine are the two tableside condiments—a mixture of fresh chiles with cilantro and a chile-infused oil. Spoon on good amounts of each and don't be shy about asking for replenishments if either runs low. To round out your meal, try the steamed pumpkin and shrimp dumplings and cold noodles with cucumber and bean sauce. Both are fine complements to the beef roll, but showstoppers they are not. It's about time this restaurant drops the "101 Noodle" gibberish and rechristens itself Beef Rolls Express. **Additional Location:** 1025 S. Baldwin Ave., Arcadia, CA 91007; (626) 446-8855.

Pearl's Restaurant, 644 Garvey Ave., Monterey Park, CA 91754; (626) 284-2761; Taiwanese; $. Not everyone is lucky enough to have a Taiwanese grandmother, but Pearl's in Monterey Park makes a home-cooked meal available to all. While the stark white, shoebox-size room isn't particularly cozy, the cooking and prices are straight-up comforting. The boiled pork dumplings boast skins that are neither too thick nor too thin, while the filling is lean and well-seasoned. The house-made chile paste or a combination of soy sauce and vinegar make for fine accompaniments. Pork chop rice, a quint-essentially homey Taiwanese dish, is prepared with flair and care here. The platter includes fried bone-in pork cutlets served atop steamed rice and garnished with minced pork and pickled mustard greens. The chops, which have a crisp and golden panko coating, pair divinely with the fluorescent relish that's reminiscent of bread-and-butter pickles. Similarly hearty is the braised pork belly served with a soy sauce–imbued hard-boiled egg.

FURTHER EXPLORATION: OLD COUNTRY CAFE

Alhambra's **Old Country Cafe**, one of the oldest Taiwanese restaurants in the San Gabriel Valley (2 E. Valley Blvd., Alhambra, CA 91801; 626-284-4610), is a charming hole-in-the-wall tucked inside a not-so-charming office-plex. The pork chop rice, as well as the fried chicken rice, arrives airy yet crisp, seasoned simply with salt and pepper.

Pho Filet, 9463 Garvey Ave., Unit A, South El Monte, CA 91733; (626) 453-8911; Vietnamese; $. Linh Phuong Nguyen, who began her stateside culinary career at Phong Dinh Restaurant in Rosemead, makes L.A.'s best bowl of southern style *pho* (Vietnamese beef noodle soup) at this worn-in restaurant straddling the border between Rosemead and South El Monte. While the filet mignon that comes standard with every bowl is a cut above the rest, it's Nguyen's unparalleled broth that distinguishes her product from the dozens of *pho* hawkers in town. Beef bones are carefully simmered to yield a rich broth that is as clear as it is flavorful. An underlying sweetness, as well as a rush of cinnamon and anise, adds further complexity to the soup. The well-tended broth is poured over springy rice noodles to order, along with cuts of filet mignon, brisket, tripe, and a flourish of cilantro and thinly sliced onions. For an even more luxe experience, request the rare beef to be served on the side to avoid overcooking. Plenty of fresh Thai basil, bean sprouts, sawtooth herb, limes, and jalapeños are on hand for garnishing your bowl to taste. Nguyen also makes a memorable northern-style *pho bac*, a simpler beast with fewer trimmings and a subtler broth. The raft of filet mignon in the center of the bowl makes up for the lack of bells and whistles.

Pondahan Restaurant, 535 S. California Ave., West Covina, CA 91790; (626) 856-0416; pondahan.com; Filipino; $$. In the Philippines, *pondahans* are makeshift gathering places where locals catch up on news and gossip over home-cooked meals. When Lelizabeth Crisostomo opened Pondahan Restaurant in 2007, she aimed to capture the casual and comforting spirit of the *pondahan* in the community of West Covina. Pinoy classics like garlic fried rice, *pancit* (pan-fried noodles), and *lumpia* (egg rolls) are executed well, but it's the pork-heavy dishes that really shine. The *sisig*, a wonderfully gelatinous jumble of pig's head and liver seasoned with *calamansi* (Filipino citrus) and chile peppers, arrives sizzling on a cast-iron skillet. A supplemental egg yolk adds a silky dimension to an already heady mixture. The crispy *pata* (deep-fried pork hock), as well as the *lechon kawali* (deep-fried pork belly), transforms pork into a hero with bubbly, crackling skin and tender strata of fat, tendon, and meat. A sweetened pork liver sauce and dark vinegar laced with garlic are on hand for curbing the porcine richness. For dessert, the *turon* (banana-stuffed egg rolls) served with a scoop of house-made *ube* (purple yam) ice cream strikes a harmonious sweet and creamy balance. The *halo halo*, a one-of-a-kind dessert layered with ice cream, shaved ice, and boiled sweet beans and fruits, is large enough to feed a village, preferably one with a *pondahan* on every corner.

Pondok Kaki Lima, 1200 E. Huntington Dr., Duarte, CA 91010; Indonesian; $. The parking lot of the Duarte Inn plays host to some of the best Indonesian cooking in Los Angeles every Saturday 10 a.m. to 2 p.m. This outdoor "food bazaar" is composed of four different vendors, each specializing in classic Indonesian dishes. Bali Island prepares *nasi* *bungkus,* tidy banana leaf parcels filled with yellow rice and various fragrant curries. Sate Babi Manis "Heidy" serves a combination of stews and meats on a stick, while neighboring stall Satay Lenny focuses solely on the latter, also known as *satay.* The final nameless stall makes a variety of savories and sweets and sweetly tinged savories, like *siomay bandung* (steamed dumplings), *gado gado* (vegetable salad with peanut dressing), and *es cendol,* a mung bean jelly drink with coconut milk and palm sugar. Dig into your wares at one of the wobbly tables set under the lot's shaded trees.

Rika's Empanadas, 150 S. Grand Ave., Glendora, CA 91741; (626) 914-3472; rikasempanadas.com; Argentinian; $. While a pizzeria serving empanadas might seem slightly strange to American diners, in Buenos Aires it's standard fare. Carmen Rico channels the spirit of Argentina here at Rika's Empanadas in Glendora, where pizzas by the slice are sold alongside baked and fried savory hot pockets; she owned a similarly spirited joint in the capital city called Pizza al Toque prior to coming to America. While the Argentinian-style pies here possess a certain charm, it's the two dozen handmade empanadas that really satisfy. Each one is folded and pleated in a unique fashion to distinguish it from the others. The classic Salteñas is composed of a hearty mix of chopped beef, onions, bell peppers, potatoes, hard-boiled eggs, and green olives, while the Bacon and Prunes empanada pairs smoky savoriness with sticky sweetness. The open-faced baskets are made from the same flaky, golden dough as the pockets and are stuffed to the brim with things like spinach and eggplant. The latter is paired with an unbeatable combination of tomatoes, garlic, basil, black olives, and a duo of cheeses. While the blue cheese-stuffed empanada is wildly flavorful, the Arabian Fatay strikes a mellower note with ground beef, tomatoes, red peppers, onions, parsley, and fresh lemon juice.

Further Exploration: Carlitos Gardel

For an upscale Argentinian meal complete with grass-fed steaks and copious amounts of red wine, head to **Carlitos Gardel Restaurant** (7963 Melrose Ave., Los Angeles, CA 90046; 323-655-0891; carlitosgardel .com) in Mid-City. For nearly 20 years, Azniv Bozoghlian and her two sons, Max and Gerard, have been delighting diners with warm hospitality and solid cooking.

Sate House, 812 Nogales St., Walnut, CA 91789; (626) 581-7726; Indonesian; $. At Hee and Ingrid Cheung's modestly appointed Sate House in Walnut, Indonesian *satay* (seasoned and grilled meat on a stick) is simply and wonderfully executed. Pork, beef, chicken, and sometimes lamb are lightly marinated in garlic, soy sauce, sugar, and white pepper so as to let the meat's natural flavors shine through. Each skewer is grilled to order over charcoal, landing on the table mere seconds after it's been cooked through. Under the Cheungs' careful watch, the meat is evenly caramelized and charred in all the right places. Served alongside the *satay* is an awesomely nuanced sauce made of peanut butter, sugar, salt, and garlic with just a hint of heat. Nothing goes better with a feast of meaty morsels than the *nasi goreng,* Indonesian-style fried rice that's made as fiery as one desires. The classic preparation, colored an intense shade of red, is packed with pork and shrimp and topped with a sunny-side egg. Only available on Saturday and Sunday is the *nasi bungkus,* a banana leaf–wrapped parcel stuffed to maximum capacity with steamed white rice and a plethora of savory curries and stir-fries.

Shaanxi Gourmet, 8518 Valley Blvd., #102, Rosemead, CA 91770; (626) 288-9886; Chinese; $. Ten thousand miles separate Los

Angeles from Xi'an, the central Chinese city famous for its terra-cotta soldiers and Islamic cuisine, but stepping into Rosemead's Shaanxi Gourmet with its guardsmen-flanked entrance, Chinese-only menu, and relaxed service, diners are transported to the capital city, if only for one meal. Don't fret if your Chinese language skills aren't up to snuff. The restaurant's walls are helpfully plastered with photographs of the most popular dishes, and of course, there's always the fail-proof point-and-smile method. The most famous dish in Xi'an is a lamb stew served over torn bread called *yang rou pao mo*. The version served here bypasses the tradition of tearing dense bread discs tableside, but the results are still delicious. The broth is incredibly fragrant, with bits of shredded lamb, bean curd, and glass noodles swimming throughout. The doughy confetti that fills the bowl is a fine enough substitute for the hand-torn crumbles. Shaanxi Gourmet serves two versions of lamb "burgers," a popular dish found in Xi'an's Muslim Quarter, one filled with stewed shredded meat and another that's sour, spicy, and dotted with licorice root. The most soul-warming dish on the menu is the lamb soup with wide and bouncy hand-stretched noodles. The "big plate" spicy chicken with chiles, bell peppers, potatoes, and noodles lives up it its name, so dive in with a hungry group.

Shakas, 101 W. Main St., Alhambra, CA 91801; (626) 293-5520; shakas.com; Hawaiian; $. Plate lunches are the soul of Hawaiian cooking, and no one constructs a bigger, better one than Shakas in the San Gabriel Valley. In fact, the portions here are so tremendous that a mere plate cannot handle everything that's dished up—only a Styrofoam box filled to the brim will do. Take the Shaka Plate, for instance, the restaurant's signature offering; it includes teriyaki steak, sesame chicken wings, an impressive log of Spam *musubi*, Chinese chicken salad, pickles, and of course, a scoop each of rice and macaroni salad. There's plenty here to feed a family, but it's not unusual for regulars to dig in solo. One of the more unique items on the menu is the Mochiko Chicken, a special island-style bird marinated in sweetness and coated in *mochiko,* a kind of rice powder, then deep-fried to create sticky, almost sugary nuggets. **Additional Location:** 2300 S. Garfield Ave., Monterey Park, CA 91754; (323) 888-2695.

FURTHER EXPLORATION:
ALOHA FOOD FACTORY

Situated in a converted mission-style Taco Bell, Alhambra's **Aloha Food Factory** (2990 W. Valley Blvd., Alhambra, CA 91803; 626-308-0215) serves Hawaiian classics like Kalua pork, *char siu* (Chinese-style barbecued pork), *loco moco,* and macadamia nut pancakes in a warm and inviting setting.

Shin Sen Gumi Yakitori, 111 N. Atlantic Blvd., Monterey Park, CA 91754; (626) 943-7956; shinsengumigroup.com; Japanese; $$. For a complete description, see p. 202.

Shufeng Garden, 18459 Colima Rd., Rowland Heights, CA 91748; (626) 839-7589; Chinese; $. Rowland Heights is a trek from just about anywhere in Los Angeles, but one taste of Shufeng Garden's famed Sichuan cooking and it's easy to justify the extra time and mileage. With its brightly painted Kelly green walls and verdant mural of flora and fauna, the decade-old restaurant may have been a pediatrician's office in a former life. These days, it's a double dose of dried chiles and Sichuan peppercorns that heals all that ails. Zhong's Dumplings, pure pork parcels hit with red chile oil and toasted sesame seeds, are meltingly tender and fiery hot. An order of these makes for a dynamite starter along with a few cold dishes, like the Sliced Beef with Hot Oil or the Sliced Pork Ear with Red Spicy Sauce. An expertly made bowl of *dan dan* noodles will leave your tongue tingling and your heart singing, and Shufeng Garden's version comes through on both fronts.

Every chopstick-full floods the palate with an intense wave of heat, spice, and savoriness. The house special Intestine in Chili and Wild Pepper, as well as the Shufeng Spicy Chicken, perfumes deep-fried morsels with classic Sichuan flair, meaning plenty of dried chiles and Sichuan peppercorns. Served cold, the Sliced Pork with Garlic Sauce brings a touch of sweetness to the table, which can be a welcome change of pace at this chile-laden feast.

FURTHER EXPLORATION:
NO. 1 NOODLE HOUSE

Sichuan classics like *dan dan* noodles, wontons in chile oil, and cold spicy bean noodles are made with care at **No. 1 Noodle House** (18180 Colima Rd., Rowland Heights, CA 91748; 626-839-7093), down the street from Shufeng Garden. Order at the front counter and grab a table on the patio.

SinBala, 651 W. Duarte Rd., Arcadia, CA 91007; (626) 446-0886; Taiwanese; $. The night markets in Taiwan are gastronomical wonderlands where hungry bellies and food hawkers meet, greet, and gorge. Homesick Taiwanese in and around the San Gabriel Valley head to SinBala whenever a hankering for stinky tofu or oyster omelets hits; this homey restaurant whisks taste buds straight to Taipei, minus the humidity and throngs of people. Begin by selecting a cold appetizer from the front counter. The snappy celery marinated in minced garlic and sesame oil is fresh and satisfying. While SinBala executes many night market favorites well, their Taiwanese sausages are particularly outstanding. These house-made sweet and fatty links taste good straight up and even better with a well-chosen topping. There are dozens of garnishes available, including one with tangy mangoes, but the sausages served with raw garlic, basil, and Sichuan peppercorns really pack a punch. The spicy wontons smothered in chile oil, peanuts, garlic, ginger, green onions, and Sichuan peppercorns are also delightful. Make sure to take a whiff of the wonderful aromas before inhaling the entire bowl. Popcorn chicken, another night market staple, is impressively grease-less and battered in a delectable salt, pepper, and five-spice blend. The fried basil that comes along with it really takes the nuggets to another level. Perhaps the most challenging dish on the menu, especially for the uninitiated, is the oyster pancake topped with a sweet garlic chile sauce. The pancake is made with sweet potato starch, resulting in a goopy consistency that takes some getting used to.

Southern Mini Town, 833 W. Las Tunas Dr., San Gabriel, CA 91776; (626) 289-6578; Chinese; $. Shanghai cuisine might not be as splashy as its northern, western, or southern Chinese counterparts, but it certainly has its charms. The kind of hearty cooking found at Southern Mini Town in San Gabriel satisfies with subtlety rather than with a double punch of sodium and spice. A plate of Fried Seaweed Yellow Fish graces nearly every table. The fish sticks, coated in an airy, tempura-like batter flecked with green algae, are crisp-tender and completely addictive sprinkled with a bit of coarse salt. The Sautéed Finless Eel, a mountain of baby eels coated in a thick and shiny brown sauce, isn't the easiest dish on the eyes if you're the squeamish type, but persevere because the seasoning here is well-balanced enough to eat each squirmy sucker straight up. Or better yet, pair it with the Preserved Vegetable and Pork Rice Cake, chewy, ovular rice discs peppered with pickled mustard greens. An order of *xiao long bao* (soup dumplings) is essential at every Shanghainese feast. The ones served here are steamed to order with pliable skins and scalding innards. For dessert, take the fragrant and floral Osman Sesame Rice Ball with Wine Soup for a spin. The little tapioca balls filled with black sesame paste melt in your mouth.

FURTHER EXPLORATION: LAKE SPRING SHANGHAI

Lake Spring Shanghai Restaurant (219 E. Garvey Ave., Monterey Park, CA 91755; 626-280-3571) in Monterey Park has been a stronghold in the San Gabriel Valley's Shanghai restaurant scene since the 1990s. The pork pump, a whole hock simmered in soy sauce, anise, and sugar until its flesh trembles off the bone, is the quintessential Shanghainese dish at this quintessential Shanghainese restaurant.

Tasty Garden, 500 N. Atlantic Blvd., Monterey Park, CA 91754; (626) 872-0900; tastygardenusa.com; Chinese; $$. Of all the Hong Kong–style cafes lining the boulevards of the San Gabriel Valley, Tasty Garden is the undisputed king. With three spiffed-out locations in L.A. proper and a sprinkling of outlets in Orange County, this Denny's gone wild makes 3 a.m. prime rib cravings a reality for the young and the restless. Whether you're stopping in for lunch, dinner, or a post-karaoke fill, the menus, three-deep, present a universally appealing mash-up of eastern and western cuisines. To pair with your requisite milk tea are spicy fried pork chops littered with scallions and chiles, French-style filet mignon heavy on the peppercorns, and over a dozen fried rice and noodle options. Tasty Garden's menu casts a wide and varied net, with literally hundreds of items to choose from. While you might be tempted by one of the ice cream monstrosities served in a hollowed-out loaf of bread, it's the simple and so very pluckable Hong Kong–style waffle that's most satisfying. **Additional Locations:** 288 W. Valley Blvd., Alhambra, CA 91801; (626) 300-8262. 1212 S. Baldwin Ave., Arcadia, CA 91007; (626) 445-9388.

Thien An, 8837 Valley Blvd., Rosemead, CA 91770; (626) 286-6665; Vietnamese; $$. Vietnamese-style roasted catfish (*ca nuong da don*) and seven courses of beef (*bo bay mon*) are what it's all about at Thien An, a brightly lit and cavernous restaurant in Rosemead. Everything's served family style, so big groups with even bigger appetites are encouraged. Orders for the restaurant's famous crackly and caramelized catfish can be placed ahead of time; otherwise, your whiskered guest of honor will take 30 minutes to prepare. Strewn with fresh cilantro and smothered in scallion oil, the roasted catfish hits the table with a thump. While its flesh is flaky and tender, its skin is honeyed and taut. To eat, tear off generous hunks and wrap them in moistened rice papers along with vermicelli noodles, vegetables, herbs, and pickles. The fermented anchovy sauce (*mam nem*), along with a load of pickled lemongrass, makes for a perfectly pungent dip. To round out your fishin' feast, select a few beefy plates to share. The *bo la lot* (seasoned ground beef wrapped in betel leaves) are plump and deftly spiced, while the *bo mo chai* (grilled meatballs wrapped in caul fat) are rich, fatty, and all sorts of amazing. The *cha dum*, steamed meatballs made of ground beef, glass noodles, and peanuts, are served with crunchy shrimp crackers that make a fine beef delivery vehicle.

Uncle Yu's Indian Theme Restaurant, 633 S. San Gabriel Blvd., #105, San Gabriel, CA 91776; (626) 287-0688; Taiwanese; $$. It might be best to leave any sort of political correctness at the door, because Uncle Yu's Indian Theme Restaurant, also known as the Taiwanese Hooters, might get your panties in a bunch otherwise. Scantily dressed women in Pocahontas-like garb serve cold pitchers of Taiwan Beer to a mostly male crowd at this hunting lodge-cum-sports bar. While it might be difficult to focus on the food with sports on the screen and women on the scene, the pub grub here is legitimately good. The stinky tofu, which is often too foul for words at other establishments, is served hot from the fryer and somehow pleasant in all its funkiness. Also terrific with a tall glass of beer are the fried chicken with basil and any of the grilled meats on a stick.

FURTHER EXPLORATION: TOFU KING

Take another walk on the stinky side at **Tofu King** in Arcadia (713 W. Duarte Rd., Arcadia, CA 91007; 626-254-0223) and Rowland Heights (18414 Colima Rd., Rowland Heights, CA 91748; 626-964-6250). The stinky tofu made here sits in funky fermentation for only three days due to health department regulations, so it tastes more like a slap in the face than a knee to the groin.

Veggie Life Restaurant, 9324 Garvey Ave., South El Monte, CA 91733; (626) 443-8687; Vietnamese; $. The key to excellent Vietnamese vegetarian fare is a killer mock *nuoc cham* (fish sauce vinaigrette), and nobody makes it better than the folks at Veggie Life Restaurant. Ladled atop everything from salads to rice dishes, the amber-hued sauce is uncannily similar to the real thing. The *goi ngo sen*, a lotus stem salad with plenty of fresh herbs and chewy strands of agar, perks up as soon as it's doused with the vibrant vinaigrette. The same is true of the Six Delights rice platter, which includes *seitan* (wheat gluten) in various forms. There's lemongrass "beef," a "chicken" drumstick, a "pork" loaf, tofu-skin-wrapped "meat," a "fish" loaf, and thinly shredded "pork." Veggie Life also makes a standout meatless rendition of *bun bo Hue*, a spicy beef noodle soup from Central Vietnam. It can be difficult to match the robust flavors of traditional *bun bo Hue* in a vegetarian dish, but this version with an abundance of lemongrass in the broth holds its own. Like most of the Vietnamese restaurants in this part of town, Veggie Life is informal and comfortable. Don't be surprised if cooks are prepping food at the empty table next to yours and service takes some prodding.

FURTHER EXPLORATION: VINH LOI TOFU

At **Vinh Loi Tofu** in Reseda (18625 Sherman Way, #101, Reseda, CA 91335; 818-996-9779; vinhloitofu.com), Chef-Owner Kevin Tran makes fresh tofu each day for his sweet and savory Vietnamese vegetarian fare. While the mock fish sauce here isn't as strong as Veggie Life's, the warm and sweet ginger tofu "pudding" for dessert more than makes up for it.

Yunkun Garden, 301 N. Garfield Ave., #D102, Monterey Park, CA 91754; (626) 571-8387; Chinese; $. While this restaurant has had three names over the years, including Yunan Garden and Yunchuan Garden, the food has remained deliciously constant. Begin with a few cold appetizers from the selection at the front counter. The fried tofu, beef shank, and jellied headcheese are all solid choices. Yunkun Garden's spiral-bound menu is filled with specialties from both Sichuan and Yunnan provinces. While the former is famous for its tongue-numbing spice, the latter is downright mild in comparison. From the Sichuan selections, try the Water Boiled Fish, a dish composed of flaky hunks of white fish marinating in a pool of red chiles, chile oil, and Sichuan peppercorns. The flavor is more subtle and nuanced than the fiery red sauce signals, while the peppercorns leave a numbing parting gift. Also spectacular are the Yunchuan-Style Spicy Fried Shrimp—a light and crunchy batter imbued with ginger, scallions, garlic, dried chiles, and Sichuan peppercorns gives way to tender and juicy flesh. The Preserved Pork with Wild Mushrooms combines salty slices of Chinese prosciutto with toothsome mushrooms; spice comes courtesy of jalapeños and dried chiles. The most famous dish from Yunnan is the Across the Bridge Noodles, a mildly flavored chicken noodle soup from the city of Kunming. It offers a soothing diversion from the avalanche of peppercorns and chiles.

The Derby Restaurant, 233 E. Huntington Dr., Arcadia, CA 91006; (626) 447-2430; thederbyarcadia.com; American; $$$. For the longtime horse racing fans that gather at Santa Anita Park, there is no better postrace tradition than sitting down for a proper and hearty dinner at The Derby. The charming dining room, replete with stained-glass windows, plush red banquettes, and burnished wood, feels much like it did when the restaurant debuted in 1938. Most notable is the impressive collection of horse racing memorabilia provided by George Woolf, The Derby's original owner and, most famously, Seabiscuit's jockey. The aptly named Seabiscuit Room features oil paintings and faded photographs of the famed horse, while a portrait of Woolf is mounted above the fireplace in the bar. The menu, much like the space, is thoroughly classic, with dishes like French onion soup and shrimp cocktail to start and all-American mains like bacon-wrapped filet mignon, pork tenderloin, rack of lamb, and raring red steaks.

Dino's Chicken and Burgers, 843 W. Arrow Hwy., Azusa, CA 91702; (626) 812-6400; dinoschickenandburgers.com; Greek, Mexican; $. For a complete description, see p. 71.

Din Tai Fung, 1108 S. Baldwin Ave., Arcadia, CA 91007; (626) 574-7068; dintaifungusa.com; Taiwanese; $$. It's barely 10 a.m. and there's already a sizeable crowd waiting outside Din Tai Fung, a renowned Taiwanese dumpling house that opened its first and second US locations in Arcadia. As soon as the doors swing open for business, the crowds scuttle in for the first *xiao long bao* of the day. What sets Din Tai Fung's soup-filled dumplings apart from those from mainland China, namely Shanghai, is their thinner, more elastic skin and less oily filling. All of the dumplings served here are painstakingly folded by hand to exacting standards. Rumor has it that a staffer is charged with the monotonous task of making sure that each dumpling has exactly 18 pleats—no more and no less. This kind of extra care and attention translates to prices that are a touch higher than those at neighboring dumpling shacks, but it is quality you can taste. The most popular *xiao long bao* come filled with ground pork and a savory sweet broth. While there are many ways to approach consuming one, most connoisseurs slurp the soup first before eating the whole shebang with some black vinegar and fresh ginger. For dessert, sample the miniature dumplings filled with sweetened taro root.

The Donut Man, 915 E. Route 66, Glendora, CA 91740; (626) 335-9111; Doughnuts; $. Jim Nakano, along with his wife, Miyoko, purchased the 24-hour Donut Man operation shortly after they married and settled in Glendora in 1972. In addition to producing doughnut shop classics like maple bars, glazed twists, and french crullers, "The Donut Man," as Mr. Nakono is fittingly nicknamed, also makes seasonal fresh fruit doughnuts that are the talk of the town. His strawberry and peach creations, which are available from early spring through fall, have been known to inspire deep-fried dough fanatics to drive hundreds of miles for a fix. The belle of the Donut Man ball is the one stuffed with strawberries. Imagine a simple glazed doughnut, butterflied a la Pac-man, and jammed with a pint of ripe, sweet, and lightly glazed strawberries. Even those with larger-than-average mouths will find it difficult to bite from top to bottom without making a mess; the most civilized approach is to use a plastic knife and fork. Nearly as iconic as the strawberry doughnuts are The Donut Man's Tiger Tails, foot-long glazed twists with devil's food cake running through the center. The Bavarian cream with its chocolate frosting and oozy vanilla custard makes a fine addition to your daily dozen.

The Hat, 1 W. Valley Blvd., Alhambra, CA 91801; (626) 282-0140; thehat.com; American; $. The neon sign featuring a chef's toque and the words "World Famous Pastrami" has been lighting up the northwest corner of Valley and Garfield in Alhambra since 1951. The Hat's signature pastrami, intensely salted and thinly sliced, is served in mountainous heaps upon french rolls. Whether or not it is actually the world's best is up for debate, but there's no denying that The Hat churns out a product that resonates with old-timers and young guns alike. Orders are taken at the front sidewalk counter, while a back patio seats those who are dining in. The flagship location sells close to 30 tons of pastrami each year, not to mention plenty of hamburgers, hot dogs, and roast beef dips too. While the regular chili cheese fries tend to be bland, the off-menu chili cheese fries with pastrami pack a gluttonous punch. The pastrami cheeseburger strikes a similarly excessive note. **Additional Locations:** 5505 Rosemead Blvd., Temple City, CA 91780; (626) 292-1000. 2300 S. Atlantic Blvd., Monterey Park, CA 91755; (323) 721-3656. 611 W. Route 66, Glendora, CA 91740; (626) 857-0017.

FURTHER EXPLORATION: JOHNNIE'S PASTRAMI

Established in 1952, **Johnnie's Pastrami** (4017 Sepulveda Blvd., Culver City, CA 90230; 310-397-6654; johnniespastrami .com) in Culver City brings an equally nostalgic pastrami experience to Westside residents. The menu here is lengthier than the one at The Hat, but everyone sticks to the pastrami and chili cheese fries with a side of pickles.

Manuel's Original El Tepeyac Cafe, 13131 Crossroads Pkwy. South, City of Industry, CA 91746; (562) 695-2277; manuelsel tepeyac.com; Mexican; $. For a complete description, see p. 111.

Moffett's Family Restaurant and Chicken Pie Shop, 1409 S. Baldwin Ave., Arcadia, CA 91007; (626) 447-4670; moffetts chickenpies.com; American; $. Moffett's famous chicken potpies have been going heavy on the gravy and skipping out on peas and carrots since debuting in 1975. With only three simple components at play, it's essential that each one is exceptional. The chicken, a combination of white and dark cuts, is generously portioned and impressively moist. Pies made with all white meat are available for an additional but nominal fee. The golden crust tends to crumble rather than flake, but that's not really important when the flavor beams with butter. And then there's the gravy. Moffett's lifeblood runs thick and veers salty, but it ties together the chicken and crust with aplomb. Chicken potpies are available a la carte or served as a meal with a soup or salad, whipped potatoes, vegetables, and bread. Also available are beef potpies with peas and carrots, as well as fruit pies for dessert. Save a few bucks by taking your sweet and savory pies to go. Reasonably priced and dependably good pies have kept this old-fashioned diner busy through the new millennium.

Sam Woo Barbecue, 514 W. Valley Blvd., Alhambra, CA 91803; (626) 281-0038; Chinese; $. For a complete description, see p. 82. **Additional Locations:** 140 W. Valley Blvd., San Gabriel, CA 91776; (626) 572-8418. 937 E. Las Tunas Dr., San Gabriel, CA 91776; (626) 286-3118.

Savoy Kitchen, 138 E. Valley Blvd., Alhambra, CA 91801; (626) 308-9535; Singaporean; $. A traditional Hainanese dish of poached chicken and aromatic rice, "chicken rice" has been reinterpreted and adapted throughout Southeast Asia as a result of the Chinese diaspora. Here at Savoy Kitchen, chicken rice is prepared Singaporean style: the chicken is boiled in a pork and chicken stock, while the rice is cooked in chicken broth. Crushed ginger, chile sauce, and soy sauce are served on the side for sprucing up the rice and chicken as one sees fit. While the dish's components might sound quite pedestrian, hardly worthy of the crowds that gather at all hours, the flavor is truly greater than the sum of the parts. The chicken, a combination of dark and white meat (or only dark meat for a few dollars extra), is unquestionably juicy and tender, while the rice has a fluffy way about it, imbued with a distinct clucky essence. One taste of this homey dish and it's obvious why there's always a line of eager eaters at the corner of Valley and Monterey. It's been like this for the past 30 years.

FURTHER EXPLORATION: DONG NGUYEN

For a taste of Vietnamese-style chicken rice (*com ga Hai Nam*), head to **Dong Nguyen Restaurant** (1433 E. Valley Blvd., Alhambra, CA 91801; 626-300-8618), where the proprietors hail from Cho Lon in Saigon. The absolute best part of the chicken rice made here is the ginger and chile dipping sauce served on the side. Go wild and pour it over everything.

 *Sublime Sweets*

Alex Goh's Dragon Whiskers Candy, 120 E. Valley Blvd., San Gabriel, CA 91776; (919) 597-9325; facebook.com/DragonWhiskers Candy; Chinese; $. Alex Goh makes an ancient Chinese confection composed of wispy honey strands dusted in cornstarch and wrapped around crushed peanuts, sesame seeds, coconut, or a combination of all three. These poetically dubbed "Dragon Whiskers" look something like a cocoon and flutter like a butterfly. On Saturday and Sunday afternoons, Goh sets up his candy operation near the front entrance of the Hawaii Supermarket in San Gabriel, where sweet seekers can witness the process of transforming a lump of dehydrated honey into something ethereally light and most definitely hairy. First, the gooey hunk of sugar is shaped into a doughnutlike ring with an extra-large hole. Then, Mr. Goh gingerly pulls, twists, stretches, and folds the sugar over on itself up to 15 times, doubling the number of strands created after each repetition. Finally, the sugar is stretched into paper-thin "whiskers," forming the foundation of these truly unique candies. Only after witnessing the master at work can one appreciate the craft at hand.

Class 302, 1015 Nogales St., #125, Rowland Heights, CA 91748; (626) 965-5809; Dessert; $. The Taiwanese teens that flock to Class 302 might make you feel slightly old and out of place, but that's no reason to avoid this snack shack in Rowland Heights. Modeled after a Taiwanese classroom, the ambiance here is pure kitsch. Diners eat at desk clusters, waitresses don schoolgirl uniforms, and notebooks are tucked into little cubbies. Skip over the menu's savory bites and zero in on the house special shaved snow. A distant cousin of shaved ice, shaved snow has a unique ribbonlike texture that is achieved by freezing huge chunks of flavored water and milk and then shaving it using heavy-duty machinery. The resulting sheets of snow are gloriously creamy and

FURTHER EXPLORATION: PA PA WALK, FLUFF ICE, AND BLOCKHEADS

None of Class 302's competitors, namely **Pa Pa Walk** in San Gabriel (227 W. Valley Blvd., San Gabriel, CA 91776; 626-281-3889), **Fluff Ice** in Monterey Park (500 N. Atlantic Blvd., Monterey Park, CA 91754; 626-872-2123), and **Blockheads Shavery** in West L.A. (11311 Mississippi Ave., Los Angeles, CA 90025; 310-445-8725; blockheadsla.com), can match its snow's unparalleled texture. Still, when the craving for an icy treat hits, they'll do just fine.

dissolve ever so quickly on the tongue. The green tea–flavored snow topped with red beans, *mochi*, and condensed milk is perfectly balanced, while the mango snow with fresh mangoes and *mochi* is as tart and refreshing as they come. The most decadent dish is the caramel pudding shaved snow, which is doused with sweetened condensed milk and caramel syrup. Due to its immense popularity, Class 302 usually runs out of its first batch of snow sometime before 3 p.m. A fresh batch is available after 7 p.m.

85°C Bakery Cafe, 17170 Colima Rd., Hacienda Heights, CA 91745; (626) 839-7885; 85cafe.us; Bakery; $. It's a perpetually packed pastry party at 85°C Bakery Cafe, a Taiwanese import that attracts crowds at all hours due to its matchless line of baked goods and one-of-a-kind sea salt coffees. The bakery boasts over 300 stores across Taiwan; this location near the eastern limits of the San Gabriel Valley is Los Angeles' first. Pick up a plastic tray as you walk through the front door, line it neatly with a sheet of parchment paper, grab a pair of tongs, and well, the rest is up to you. The marbled taro bread, an impossibly soft and flaky bun filled with starchy sweetness, is the bakery's top seller. Fresh batches are constantly coming out of the oven, which means warm, swirly purple bread for all. The individually portioned brioche, as well as the Mochi Egg Tart, is also immensely popular and worth seeking out. The Japanese-inspired Matcha Red

FURTHER EXPLORATION: J.J. BAKERY

With nearly half a dozen locations around town, **J.J. Bakery** (Arcadia, Torrance, Hacienda Heights, Rowland Heights, and City of Industry) is the most accessible outlet for Taiwanese baked sweets and savories. The hot dog–stuffed croissants taste much better than they sound, while the pineapple buns and red bean buns come through in the sweets department.

Bean Roll combines whole red beans in a green tea sponge cake with a subtle cream filling. The most elusive pastry of the bunch is the pitch-black squid ink roll filled with melted Vermont cheddar and frosted with garlic. It is only "released" three times a day, at 9 a.m., 1 p.m., and 5:30 p.m., so plan your visit accordingly.

Fosselman's Ice Cream Co., 1824 W. Main St., Alhambra, CA 91801; (626) 282-6533; fosselmans.com; Ice Cream; $. Fosselman's Ice Cream Co. has been family owned and operated ever since it sold its first scoop back in 1919. Though the times and prices have certainly changed, the aesthetic and philosophy of this old-fashioned soda fountain remain largely the same. All of the 40-plus flavors available each day are handmade using only the best ingredients and no preservatives. In addition to standard offerings like rocky road, strawberry, and cookie dough, Fosselman's also makes a mean lychee, *horchata*, and taro. Take home a pint, quart, or half gallon for later. You'll be glad you did. For something fancier than just a scoop, try one of the shop's sundaes, banana splits, root beer floats, malts, or smoothies.

Hien Khanh, 8150 Garvey Ave., #117I, Rosemead, CA 91770; (626) 288-8128; Vietnamese; $. Hidden away in the food court of Rosemead's Square Supermarket lies Hien Khanh, a Little Saigon import that makes the very best Vietnamese desserts in town. Those unfamiliar with the genre may be a bit wary upon seeing legumes, seaweed, and root vegetables swimming in a sea of coconut milk, but there's no need to hesitate because everything tastes stupendous. The heart of the operation is *che,* a diverse collection of dessert puddings and soups. *Che dau trang* stickily combines glutinous rice with black-eyed peas; a pour of sweetened coconut cream completes the package irresistibly. Ripe baby bananas, tapioca pearls, taro, and seemingly an entire can of coconut milk come together in *che chuoi*. Best of all is *che troi nuoc*, chewy tapioca balls stuffed with mung bean paste, soaked in ginger syrup, and finished with coconut milk and a sprinkling of toasted sesame seeds. There's also freshly made *banh da lon,* which literally translates to "pig skin cake." This pork-free sweet layers pandan-infused tapioca with mung beans, forming a visually arresting little number. Come down from your sugar high with a serving of *xoi bap* and *xoi vo,* sticky rice with mung beans.

Jim's Bakery, 400 S. Atlantic Blvd., Monterey Park, CA 91754; (626) 573-5757; jimsbakery.com; Bakery; $. Oscar Jim, the founder of Jim's Bakery, was one of the first entrepreneurs to bring Hong Kong–style pastries to the San Gabriel Valley. Opened in 1991, the sweets shop slowly gained a devoted following for its matchless Hong Kong and Portuguese egg tarts. While the former is composed of a mildly sweet egg custard wrapped in a flaky crust, the latter is made from caramelized custard cradled in puff pastry that evolved from Portugal's *pastel de nata.* Both are served warm and impeccably fresh throughout the day. Jim's mango cake, which is available whole and by the slice, is sensationally celebratory with its layers of fresh mango, mango mousse, and delicate cake. The entire creation is topped with mango curd and fresh fruit. Customers in this part of town demand pastries that are "not too sweet," and Jim hits the nail on the head every time.

FURTHER EXPLORATION: KEE WAH BAKERY

Kee Wah Bakery (729 Garvey Ave., Monterey Park, 626-281-2680; 150 W. Valley Blvd., San Gabriel, 626-280-2515; 18912 E. Gale Ave., Rowland Heights, 626-913-1881; en.keewah .com), which was originally founded in Hong Kong in 1938 by Wong Yip Wing, opened its first US branch in 1985 in Monterey Park, followed by a San Gabriel outlet in 1989, and a Rowland Heights location in 1996. Hong Kong- and Portuguese-style egg tarts, as well as pineapple buns, are the shop's bestsellers.

Tea Station, 158 W. Valley Blvd., San Gabriel, CA 91776; (626) 288-3785; teastation.us; Dessert; $. Whether served scalding with dim sum or chilled with tapioca balls (*boba*), there's no denying that tea is the unofficial beverage of the San Gabriel Valley. Jimmy Huang opened the first Tea Station in the city of San Gabriel in 1995, serving a dizzying selection of hot and cold beverages as well as Taiwanese snack foods. From teens escaping the 'rents to couples enjoying a post-dinner nightcap, this thoroughly modern teahouse attracts a diverse crowd. A freshly brewed pot of hot jasmine might be the most satisfying and straightforward sip; the menu only grows sweeter and more complicated from there. Dozens of fruity infusions are on offer, not to mention extra add-ons like *boba*, puddings, jellies, and cream. The number of permutations available makes it easy to get lost, so keep it simple to avoid a saccharine mess. The Taiwanese sweet butter brick toast pairs exceedingly well with just about any beverage. **Additional Locations:** 560 W. Main St., Alhambra, CA 91804; (626) 289-7389. 9578 Las Tunas Dr., Temple City, CA 91780; (626) 291-5688. 18558 Gale Ave., Rowland Heights, CA 91748; (626) 839-2588. 1637 S. Azusa Ave., Hacienda Heights, CA 91745; (626) 913-7450.

FURTHER EXPLORATION: HALF AND HALF TEA HOUSE AND AU79

Tea Station may have been the first teahouse chainlet to sprout up in town, but others like **Half and Half Tea House** (various locations) and **AU79** (au79teahouse.com) have since followed suit. It's hard to go wrong with a black milk tea with *boba* at any of these spots.

Valerio's Tropical Bake Shop, 1509 E. Amar Rd., West Covina, CA 91792; (626) 810-8948; Filipino; $. Valerio's Tropical Bake Shop is a one-stop shop for the freshest Filipino breads and baked sweets in the Southland. The famed *pan de sal,* a lightly salted, yeast-risen roll traditionally eaten for breakfast, is so fresh that its residual heat fogs up the plastic sack. The ovens here work overtime to keep up with demand from loyal Pinoy customers. While Valerio's would do brisk business selling *pan de sal* alone, it barely scratches the surface of what the bakery has to offer. Behind the cashiers' counter are racks of *suman,* coconut milk–imbued sticky rice wrapped in banana leaves that is available plain and with cassava. The *bibingkang malagkit,* a cake made entirely of glutinous rice and topped with a *dulce de leche*–like glaze, makes for a sweet snack or a decadent breakfast. Ribbons of young coconut run through the equally sugary cassava cake. In this case, a thin slice goes a long way.

FURTHER EXPLORATION: MY MOM'S BAKE SHOP

For Filipino pastries and breads closer to the center of town, visit **My Mom's Bake Shop** in Westlake (2530 W. Temple St., Los Angeles, CA 90026; 213-380-2425; mymomsbakeshop .info). The *pan de sal* is dependably fresh, while the savories taste like Mom made 'em from scratch.

V.P. Tofu, 237 S. Garfield Ave., Monterey Park, CA 91754; (626) 572-9930; Chinese; $. Silken tofu served warm and sweet is a soothing dessert with endless appeal. While you can find this Chinese delicacy at just about any restaurant serving dim sum, V.P. Tofu in Monterey Park makes the best version around. With its smooth texture and clean, mild taste, tofu can take on flavors like few ingredients can. Try it with a syrupy ginger sauce that's as sweet as it is spicy. The root's bold flavor imbues the gentle curds beautifully. There's also a pandan version that's minty green in color and topped with creamy coconut milk. The pandan's unmistakable fragrance transports your taste buds straight to Southeast Asia. In addition to dessert tofu, this Vietnamese-run establishment also sells a selection of soy products including fresh tofu, deep-fried tofu, and plain and pandan-flavored soy milk. Vietnamese sweets like sticky rice (*xoi*) and tapioca cakes (*banh da lon*) are strewn across the counter. Seating is nonexistent inside the shop, so take your soy home to enjoy.

Specialty Stores, Markets & Producers

E. Waldo Ward & Son, 273 E. Highland Ave., Sierra Madre, CA 91024; (626) 355-1218; waldoward.com. Edwin Waldo Ward, a New York–based food salesman, didn't plan on entering the fruit preserves business when he arrived in Sierra Madre in 1891. He began experimenting with making English marmalades using Seville oranges he had imported from Spain and planted on his 30-acre property after retiring in 1915. After three years of research and development, he finally settled on a recipe that suited his fancy, and thus E. Waldo Ward was born. Today, the business is run by Richard and Jeff Ward, third- and fourth-generation preservers. The product line has grown beyond marmalades to include gourmet sauces, pickled fruits, stuffed olives, and marinades. The entire line is made on the premises in the Wards' canning facility, which sits on the now 2.5-acre ranch. The Valencia oranges, Seville oranges, blood oranges, tangerines, tangelos, and kumquats grown on the property make for some magnificent marmalades. The blood orange jam with its careful balance of sweet and sour brightens up a slice of toast like no other. The raspberry jalapeño jam made from Pacific Northwest berries sings with sweet and spice. The teriyaki marinade and Thai chile lime sauce are especially popular during the summer months, when grilling out is the way to go. Before heading down the hill, be sure to peruse the museum that Jeff Ward curated in the old barn; it includes original machinery, historic photos, and various canning paraphernalia that the family has acquired through the years.

Gioia Cheese, Inc., **1605 Potrero Ave., South El Monte, CA 91733; (626) 444-6015; gioiacheeseinc.com.** Heaven is located on an industrial stretch in South El Monte. Don't believe it? Well, then you've probably never tasted freshly made burrata from Gioia Cheese, an Italian operation established by Vito Girardi in 1992. Burrata is a fresh cheese in the mozzarella family. While the outer layer is solid mozzarella, the inside is a mixture of mozzarella and cream. With its soft, velvety texture, it's no surprise that "burrata" means "buttered" in Italian. This unassuming factory churns out 2,000 pounds of the creamiest, stringiest, most delectable burrata daily and delivers it to restaurants across the country. Gioia is one of a small number of domestic burrata producers, and fortunately for local cheese lovers, its wares are available for sale to the public.

Mitsuwa Marketplace, **515 W. Las Tunas Dr., San Gabriel, CA 91776; (626) 457-2899; mitsuwa.com/English.** For a complete description, see p. 210.

South Bay

Gardena, Inglewood, Lawndale, Lomita, Manhattan Beach, Redondo Beach, Torrance, Westchester

Foodie Faves

Back Home in Lahaina, 916 N. Sepulveda Blvd., Manhattan Beach, CA 90266; (310) 374-0111; backhomeinlahaina.com; Hawaiian; $$. Homesick Hawaiians have plenty of dining options in Los Angeles, especially of the fast-casual plate lunch variety, but full-service restaurants serving island fare can be harder to come by. Back Home in Lahaina captures the aloha spirit on the plate and in the dining room, creating a spot that's properly laid-back but nice enough to take a date. Start with an order or two of classic Spam *musubi*, a seared slab of Spam and white rice wrapped in seaweed. There's also a version made with Portuguese sausage that's a touch sweeter but just as satisfying. The lightest and brightest appetizer is the Ahi Poke, neat cubes of sashimi-grade tuna marinated in soy sauce and garnished with toasted sesame seeds, onions, green onions, and seaweed. The wasabi-tinged sauce served on the side will clear your sinuses for weeks. Moving on to mains, the kitchen prepares many of Hawaii's greatest hits including Korean-style short ribs and beef teriyaki. However, the Lahaina Fried Chicken is most famous of all. The boneless nuggets resemble Southern specimens with their golden hue and crispy crags, but their sweetish flavor is all Hawaiian. For the full island experience, order the fried chicken as part of a combination platter that includes rice, macaroni salad, fried wontons, and a cabbage slaw topped with crushed ramen noodles.

FURTHER EXPLORATION: HARRY'S CHICKEN

Hawaiian fried chicken aficionados head to **Harry's Chicken** in Gardena (1721 W. Redondo Beach Blvd., Gardena, CA 90247; 310-324-4231; harryschicken.com) for a bone-in bird that's as garlicky as it is sweet. The casual spot is also famous for its *saimin*, a noodle soup inspired by Japanese udon, Chinese *mein*, and Filipino *pancit*.

Boiling Point, 15488 S. Western Ave., #112, Gardena, CA 90247; (310) 225-5533; bpgroupusa.com; Taiwanese; $$. For a complete description, see p. 146.

Coni's Seafood, 3544½ W. Imperial Hwy., Inglewood, CA 90303; (310) 672-2339; Mexican; $$. Sergio Penuelas grills a mean *pescado zarandeado* at this Inglewood *mariscos* shack that sources its proteins straight from Mexico. A specialty of the coastal Mexican states of Sinaloa and Nayarit, *pescado zarandeado* consists of a butterflied and grilled whole fish that is redolent of lime, garlic, and spice. The flavors are damn near perfect when wrapped in a warm corn tortilla and garnished with caramelized onions. Penuelas works his magic with simple seafood preparations, too. The *camarones aguachiles,* head-on shrimp flash marinated in lime, salt, and jalapeño, have an unparalleled suppleness. The *camarones a la diabla,* or "deviled shrimp," are pleasingly spicy thanks to a blend of *chili de arbol* and California dried chiles. If you know what's good for you, don't let any of the perfectly good shrimp heads go to waste—slurp, savor, and repeat. You're welcome.

Eatalian Cafe, 15500 S. Broadway, Gardena, CA 90248; (310) 532-8880; eataliancafe.com; Italian; $$. Eatalian Cafe brings a slice of Italy to an industrial stretch of Gardena lined with manufacturers and repairmen. Owner Antonio Pellini initially planned to transform this former textile factory into a production facility for fresh cheeses, gelati, and baked goods; however, the sheer size of the space was so grand that a dining room was built into the plans. A native of Ventoso, a small village in Italy's Emilia-Romagna region, Pellini has been cooking for over two decades and has opened nearly half a dozen restaurants in the old country. Here at this cavernous temple of Italian cuisine, pastas, sauces, gelati, breads, and pastries are made fresh every morning. The heart of the menu is the brick oven-fired pizzas. There are over 30 varieties of Eatalian Pizza and Traditional Pizza available, and each one is layered with flavors on an impossibly thin, crisp, and charred crust. There's also Homestyle Fresh Eatalian Pasta, like the pillowy gnocchi served with your choice of meat sauce, butter, and Parmigiano Reggiano, a four-cheese blend, or pesto, and the Tortelli di Zucca, a butternut squash ravioli sautéed with butter and Parmigiana Reggiano or a pancetta sauce. Dessert means scoops of cool gelato in traditional flavors like *malaga* (rum raisin), *mela verde* (green apple), and *frutti di bosco* (mixed berries). Enjoy them in a cup or sandwiched inside a *focaccina*, a sweet roll embedded with golden raisins.

Flossie's Southern Cuisine, 3566 Redondo Beach Blvd., Torrance, CA 90504; (310) 352-4037; Southern; $$. For a taste of the South in the South Bay, look no further than Flossie's Southern Cuisine.

Here at this homey restaurant, Chef-Owner Sandra Miller has been preparing the kind of down-home fare that she grew up on since 1991. The restaurant, which is named after her Mississippi-born mother, is laid out a bit like a cafeteria, with Styrofoam trays and steam tables at the front. While all menu items are available a la carte, most diners choose a "meat and three" combination. There's fried chicken, baked chicken, and catfish with hush puppies available every day of the week and specialties like oxtails, turkey wings and drumsticks, and short ribs offered only on weekends. The selection of sides includes properly mushy Southern-style macaroni and cheese, three types of greens (turnip, mustard, and collard), candied yams, black-eyed peas, and corn pudding. The greens, it should be noted, are pork-free and not cooked to smithereens. All meals include a soft drink (sweet tea, unsweetened tea, or Kool-Aid) and a choice of sweet Yankee corn bread or fluffy biscuits. Under Miller's care, every dish served here is worth your while; however, leaving without sampling the restaurant's fried chicken would be tragic. The well-seasoned batter makes for a craggy crust full of golden nubs and pockets, while both white and dark meat are unfailingly juicy. A few shakes of chile-infused vinegar

FURTHER EXPLORATION: DULAN'S

Inglewood residents queue up for juicy baked chicken and smothered pork chops served with sensational sides like corn bread dressing ladled with gravy and velvety macaroni and cheese at **Dulan's** (202 E. Manchester Blvd., Inglewood, CA 90301; 310-671-3345), a cafeteria-style soul food joint named after the restaurant's owner, Adolf Dulan.

and hot sauce bring everything together. Sweet potato pie, banana pudding, and peach cobbler make for fine finishes. The nutmeg-heavy cobbler is the restaurant's bestseller.

Gaja, 2383 Lomita Blvd., #102, Lomita, CA 90717; (310) 534-0153; gajamoc.com; Japanese; $$. Upon being seated at Gaja, you'll be presented with a mountain of menus—two with aged wooden bindings and several more in plastic folders, not to mention the ones covering every inch of wall space. While you might be tempted to order noodles, rice bowls, or one of the "set menus" out of pure exhaustion, endure a little longer to locate the menu dedicated to the house specialty: *okonomiyaki* (savory Japanese pancakes). The kitchen is happy to prepare your *okonomiyaki* to order, but most everyone chooses to grill their own on the tabletop *teppan*. Playing with your food is encouraged in this format, turning an ordinary meal into a truly memorable experience. Begin by slicking the entire surface with oil. Once the grill is sizzling hot, pour on the thick batter in as round a shape as possible. In addition to the standard eggs, flour, pickled ginger, chopped scallions, shredded cabbage, and *nagaimo* (a type of Japanese yam), the batter can contain any number of add-ons including pork belly, squid, *mochi* (glutinous rice cakes), spicy cod roe, and even *yaki soba* (noodles). Use the extra-large spatula provided to flip the pancake. Once it is evenly golden on both sides and cooked all the way through, draw upon your inner *okonomiyaki* artist to add the finishing touches—*okonomiyaki*

FURTHER EXPLORATION: DOYA DOYA

Although the Osakan-style *okonomiyaki* at **Doya Doya** in Torrance (2140 Artesia Blvd., Torrance, CA 90504; 310-324-2048) are prepared in the kitchen, diners are given free rein over the toppings. No one will frown upon you if the entire surface of your pancake is inch-deep in mayonnaise.

sauce (like Worcestershire sauce but thicker and sweeter), *aonori* (sea-weed flakes), *katsuobushi* (bonito flakes), and Kewpie mayonnaise. The heat emanating from the grill and pancake never fails to make the bonito flakes dance.

Ichimi Ann Bamboo Garden, 1618 Cravens Ave., Torrance, CA 90501; (310) 328-1323; ichimiann.com; Japanese; $. While braised meats are often reserved for colder months and smoothies for warmer ones, soba slurping is a special sport that knows no meteorological bounds. At Ichimi Ann Bamboo Garden, soba noodles are made from scratch each morning using buckwheat flour shipped straight from Japan. These wonderfully firm strands with a distinctly earthy essence are served either chilled with a dipping sauce or in hot broth as a noodle soup. Hot soba may have its devotees, but here in balmy Los Angeles the cold stuff always hits the spot. Served on a sievlike bamboo tray called a *zaru*, the soba is garnished with dried seaweed (nori) and thinly sliced scallions. A dish of pickles, as well as a salty-sweet dipping sauce (*soba tsuyu*), is served on the side. To eat, finesse a small amount of soba using chopsticks and swirl it in the *tsuyu*; wasabi can be added to the broth to taste. Ichimi Ann Bamboo Garden also makes thick and slippery *udon* noodles in-house. A plethora of garnishes

Further Exploration: Otafuku Noodle House

Gardena's **Otafuku Noodle House** (16525 S. Western Ave., Gardena, CA 90247; 310-532-9348) serves notable soba in an *izakaya* setting. The house special *seiro soba*, which is made from white buckwheat flour, can be eaten cold with a dipping sauce, in a chicken soup, or in a curry.

including tempura, seaweed, raw eggs, fried bean curd, and pickled plums are on hand to top the simple noodles. Best yet is the *udon* swimming in Japanese curry. Hop on over to the beverage station for complimentary cold roasted barley tea and hot brown rice tea.

Kagura, 1652 Cabrillo Ave., Torrance, CA 90501; (310) 787-0227; littletokyorestaurant.com; Japanese; $$. The Old Torrance neighborhood in which Kagura is situated isn't much of a looker, but step into the restaurant and the mood instantly switches from gritty to Zen. Clean lines, dark woods, and cozy cubbies create a real sense of calm. Here at this convivial Japanese oasis, Tokyo native Kentaro Masuda prepares the city's best *tonkatsu*, a masterfully deep-fried pork cutlet that is evenly golden on the outside and juicy throughout. In addition to several varieties of *tonkatsu*, the kitchen also whips up chicken, eel, black cod, and salmon *katsu* (cutlet) for those who do not find swine simply divine. Every *katsu* meal begins with a bowl of *shiro goma* (white sesame seeds) and a sturdy pestle. Grind the seeds into a fine powder before pouring in the house-made *katsu* sauce from the accompanying pitcher. This salty, nutty, and thick condiment pairs exceedingly well with the rich slabs of *katsu*. While the *tonkatsu* is strong enough to stand alone, ordering it as part of a set menu is the way to go. The *gozen* includes *chawanmushi* (savory egg custard), cabbage salad, marinated edamame (soy beans), a variety of pickled vegetables, *hijiki* (sea vegetable) salad, a choice of white or "grain" rice, and a pork-based

FURTHER EXPLORATION: WAKO DONKASU

If you'd like a side of kimchee with your cutlet, then Korean-run **Wako Donkasu** in Koreatown (3377 Wilshire Blvd., Los Angeles, CA 90010; 213-381-9256; wakowilshire.com) is the spot for you. It has a tremendous reputation for stellar *katsu* preparations.

miso soup for just a few dollars more. To drink there are 30 varieties of sake and *soju*, as well as wine and Japanese beer—not to mention the complimentary *hojicha* (roasted green tea) that arrives at the close of the meal. **Additional Location:** 137 Japanese Village Plaza Mall, Los Angeles, CA 90012; (213) 680-9868.

M.B. Post, **1142 Manhattan Ave., Manhattan Beach, CA 90266; (310) 545-5405; eatmbpost.com; New American; $$$.** It's loud, fun, and unbelievably delicious at Chef David LeFevre's M.B. Post. A former industrial engineer, Chef LeFevre honed his cooking chops at Charlie Trotter's in Chicago before earning a Michelin star at **Water Grill** (p. 83) in Downtown Los Angeles. These days, he's ditched fine dining for family-style fare at this beachfront "social house," where the setting and crowd are casual and boisterous. The rustic and communal dishes coming out of the kitchen reflect the style of food that Chef LeFevre personally enjoys preparing and eating. Under the "Pass the Bread"

FURTHER EXPLORATION: FISHING WITH DYNAMITE

It's no surprise that Chef LeFevre followed up the success of M.B. Post with the seafood-centric spot **Fishing with Dynamite** (1148 Manhattan Ave., Manhattan Beach, CA 90266; 310-893-6299; eatfwd.com); after all, he earned his cheffing stripes preparing some of the finest fruits of the sea that L.A. has ever tasted. Located a stone's throw from M.B. Post, this 30-seater features a menu focusing on both East Coast tradition and West Coast innovation. Think: stellar raw bar, New England "chowdah," and a Thai-inspired shellfish and coconut soup.

section of the menu are fluffy bacon cheddar buttermilk biscuits served warm with maple butter. They're the restaurant's signature offering and can't be beat during brunch or dinner. Coming in a close second are the *fleur de sel* pretzels served with horseradish mustard. The "Seafood . . . Eat Food" section of the menu includes steamed mussels prepared in a green curry broth with Chinese sausages and a mound of rice, while the Vietnamese caramel pork from the "Meat Me Later . . ." section of the menu is a solid rendition of Vietnamese *thit kho*. A green papaya salad balances the pork's richness. The Moroccan barbecue lamb belly is a gamey hunk of flesh served with creamy semolina and Weiser Farms burgundy carrots. Come to M.B. Post with a group of adventurous eaters and order a little bit of everything; there isn't a single dud on the entire menu. See Chef LeFevre's recipe for **Green Curry Steamed Mussels with Chinese Sausage** on page 312.

Musha Izakaya, 1725 W. Carson St., Torrance, CA 90501; (310) 787-7344; musha.us; Japanese; $$. Musha Izakaya has been humming and happening since the early 1990s, when employees from nearby Japanese businesses gathered here to graze over small plates and throw back rounds of sake and beer. Today the restaurant is as boisterous as ever, with hourlong waits on the weekends for those who failed to plan ahead. Owner Tetsuro Maejima keeps crowds drinking, eating, and reveling with large communal tables and a delightful menu. The most festive dishes are those requiring tiny tableside clay braziers fueled with *binchotan* (white charcoal briquettes). Thinly sliced and lightly salted *tanshio* (beef tongues) cook through quickly and are finished with a squeeze of fresh lemon juice and a sesame sauce. The rib eye benefits superbly from this tabletop treatment as well. Even more spectacular is Musha's Cheese Risotto, a marriage of Japanese brown rice, bacon, onions, and heavy cream served tableside in a cheese wheel. It's rich and dazzling. *Takotama*, the restaurant's signature dish, layers scrambled eggs with chopped octopus, leek, and pickled ginger, while mayonnaise and a soy-based sauce tie all of the elements together. Everything tastes even better when the beers, sake, and plum wine flow like water.

FURTHER EXPLORATION: IZAKAYA BINCHO

At **Izakaya Bincho** at the Redondo Beach Wharf (112 N. International Boardwalk, Redondo Beach, CA 90277; 310-376-3889; izakayabincho.com), Chef Tomo prepares a plethora of small plates including a memorable *agedashi* tofu (deep-fried tofu steeped in a savory broth) and spicy chicken wings.

Ramen Yamadaya, 3118 W. 182nd St., Torrance, CA 90504; (310) 380-5555; ramen-yamadaya.com; Japanese; $. Not a trace of broth or a sliver of bamboo remains in the bowls that are scattered across tables after diners have departed from Ramen Yamadaya—it's the mark of absolute fulfillment when every surface is licked clean. Jin Yamada's dissatisfaction with the local ramen landscape inspired him to open his first *ramenya* in Torrance in 2010. After learning the trade and techniques from noodle experts in Japan, Yamada-san developed the recipe for the prized *tonkotsu* (pork bone) broth that takes 20 hours to prepare. The first 10 hours of cooking breaks down the bones, while the second half is devoted to coaxing out every ounce of flavor. The resulting broth is marvelously milky and sensationally well balanced. It's the kind of broth that one enthusiastically slurps even though the noodles and fixings have long since disappeared. The original *tonkotsu* ramen is served with either thin or thick noodles (thin is in) and a collection of toppings including scallions, wood ear mushrooms, bamboo, half a soy sauce egg, and several slices of tender *chashu* (braised pork). Upon request, several cloves of fresh garlic and a garlic press are made available for further enhancement. Also popular is the Tokyo-style *tonkotsu shoyu* ramen, which cuts the rich pork broth with soy sauce and black sesame paste. The *tsukemen*, thick, chewy noodles served with a side of a *tonkotsu*-based dipping sauce, is just the thing for noodle-goers looking for something lighter. The noodles are served cold while the broth is warm.

Rincon Chileno Deli, 15418 Hawthorne Blvd., Lawndale, CA 90260; (310) 349-2091; Chilean; $. Rincon Chileno Deli can be as fancy or fast as one pleases. Those short on time swing in for a quick empanada and a few sweets and hit the road soon after, while others linger over made-to-order Chilean specialties that are a rarity in this town. For the former crowd, the shop offers half a dozen different types of empanadas including varieties filled with chicken, ham and cheese, and spinach. The bestseller is the Large Beef Empanada, a beast of a pocket filled with ground beef, sautéed onions, olives, and hard-boiled eggs. The sugar-dusted and caramel-accented assortment of pastries available each day never fails to entice. There are always several varieties of *alfajores* (shortbread cookies sandwiched with *dulce de leche*), as well as *brazo de reina* (a jelly roll of sorts made with caramel rather than preserves), *ojitos* (Chilean linzer cookies), and *mil hojas* (a kind of Chilean *mille-feuille* layered with *dulce de leche*). The latter group of patrons can choose from a selection of hearty sandwiches and daily specials scrawled onto wipe boards. Expect to find homey renditions of *lomo a lo pobre* (steak and eggs with french fries), *charquican* (a thick potato and minced meat stew with pumpkin, white corn, and onions), and *longaniza a con pure* (sausages and mashed yucca).

Santouka Ramen, 21515 Western Ave., Torrance, CA 90501; (310) 212-1101; santouka.co.jp/en; Japanese; $. For a complete description, see p. 263.

Sanuki No Sato, 18206 S. Western Ave., Gardena, CA 90248; (310) 324-9184; sanukinosato.com; Japanese; $$. Named after an old Japanese province on the island of Shikoku with the same boundaries as modern Kagawa Prefecture, Sanuki No Sato is famous for its *udon*, chubby wheat-based noodles served hot or cold. The 20-year-old dining room feels as sturdy as ever, while service is swiftly executed by a team of kimono-donning waitresses. The menu here features numerous small plates and sushi, but zero in on Chef Moriaki Miyahira's spectacularly slurp-worthy *udon*. To truly appreciate the noodles' texture and nuances, insist on having them served cold. As soul-warming and comforting as noodle soups can be, hot broth tends to diminish *udon*'s impressive bite. The *Yamakake Nishin* pairs slippery strands of *udon* with even slipperier accoutrements including a raw quail egg, *tororo* (grated nagaimo yam), and a slab of sugar-cured herring. A dainty pitcher of chilled broth is served on the side. Evenly mix everything together for an awesomely goopy bowl of goodness. Toppings without the slime factor like mushrooms, radishes, tempura, and pristine cuts of seafood are also available. While hot *udon* might not possess the same intense bite as its colder counterpart, it still satisfies completely. The *Chikara* topped with *mochi* rice cakes is especially fantastic, as is the *Kitsune* blanketed with sheets of fried, sweetened tofu.

The Serving Spoon, 1403 Centinela Ave., Inglewood, CA 90302; (310) 412-3927; theservingspoon.net; Southern; $$. Opened in 1982 by Harold E. Sparks, The Serving Spoon is a full-service diner serving Southern classics in a brightly lit and energetic room. The restaurant, by the way, is named after a diner that was featured on the soap opera *All My Children*, Sparks' favorite afternoon indulgence. Today the restaurant is run by his daughter and son-in-law. While the menu reads as nearly identical to those at other soul food spots in town, one whiff of the kitchen's careful cooking and you'll see that there's something extra special happening here. Take Cookie's Wings & Waffle, for instance, which brings pleasure that far exceeds the sum of the individual parts. The well-seasoned chicken, expertly fried and outstandingly juicy, pairs like a dream with the cinnamon-dusted waffle that hits an intriguing savory note. Eaten in tandem, the flavors are rounded and harmonious—a thrilling combination of sweet, salty, and umami. Also spectacular is the fried catfish, a boneless fillet battered and beautifully browned. The fish flakes off in tender hunks, while the cornmeal crust crunches just so. Best of all is the slab of corn bread served alongside every main course. Buttered, toasted, and served with a packet of honey, it's Yankee-style all the way and delicious as all get-out. The grits, macaroni and cheese, and clove-imbued yams make for stupendous sides.

Shin Sen Gumi Yakitori, 18517 S. Western Ave., Gardena, CA 90247; (310) 715-1588; shinsengumigroup.com; Japanese; $$. It's loud inside Shin Sen Gumi Yakitori, and fans of this meat-on-a-stick haven wouldn't have it any other way. The entire staff belts out "*Irasshaimase!*" to everyone who walks through the door, a warm welcome that keeps decibels amped up the entire night. Adding to the raucous ambiance are rowdy revelers sipping sake and beer as they indulge in delights from the charcoal grill. Considering that *yakitori* literally means "grilled chicken," expect skewers of every imaginable part from cartilage to gizzards to butt to liver. The grill imparts a smoky blanket that the offal benefits from most. Some of the stronger sticks veer from the poultry path. The bacon-wrapped items, including quail eggs, enoki mushrooms, and tomatoes, are tremendously tasty and understandably popular, as are the pork belly, octopus, and beef tongue. In true Hakata fashion, the skewers are seasoned in either salt or teriyaki sauce and served with *ponzu* (citrus-seasoned vinegar) and *yuzu kosho* (a condiment made from chile peppers, *yuzu* citrus peel, and salt). As with all of the city's hot spots located in cramped quarters, arrive early or expect a long wait.

Torihei, 1757 W. Carson St., Torrance, CA 90501; (310) 781-9407; torihei-usa.com; Japanese; $$. Torihei is the collaborative effort of chefs Masataka Hirai and Masakazu Sasaki. While the former is charged with the chicken-centric yakitori menu, the latter narrows in on Kyoto-style *oden* dishes. Before going to town on an endless parade of meats-on-a-stick, begin with a salad of Chicken Skin with Ponzu; it's an excellent excuse to eat chicken skin straight up. The homemade chicken liver pâté served with toasted bread and honey should be hoarded upon arrival because the kitchen often runs out before service is completed. Moving on to the yakitori items, chicken and beef hearts, chicken gizzards, chicken tails, and chicken cartilage are all fine options, as is the mishmash of chicken meatballs. Every table is outfitted with *shichimi togarashi* (Japanese spice blend) and *sansho* (Sichuan pepper powder) to further season each grilled item. The *oden* offerings are a treat as well, especially the soft-boiled egg garnished with salmon roe and the whole tomato topped off with a slab of mozzarella. Make reservations ahead of time or be prepared to drool in line.

FURTHER EXPLORATION: KOKEKOKKO

For an equally exceptional chicken-heavy yakitori experience, try **Kokekokko** in Little Tokyo (360 E. 2nd St., Los Angeles, CA 90012; 213-687-0690), where Tomohiro Sakata grills everything from hearts to necks to wings. Tomo-san offers special off-menu dishes to regulars, so that's motivation to return again and again.

L.A. *Landmarks*

Pann's, 6710 La Tijera Blvd., Los Angeles, CA 90045; (323) 776-3770; panns.com; American; $$. When George and Rena

Panagopoulos opened Pann's in 1958, they hired architects Louis Armet and Eldon Davis to design a thoroughly futuristic space, a trend that was immensely popular at the time. With its tilted roof, fluorescent sign, exposed stone walls, and wraparound glass windows, Pann's typifies the whimsical, Space Age look of the genre; the restaurant remains one of the best preserved examples of "Googie"-style architecture to this day. Over half a century later, the dining room feels as fresh as ever. From the swivel stool-lined counter to the red patent leather booths, everything in the room has been beautifully preserved through the years. The classic diner fare is equally timeless. Breakfast is served all day; the highlight is the waffles and wings served with clarified butter and syrup. The former are light and crisp, while the latter benefit from the sugary accompaniment. Pann's biscuits, flaky, buttery things that pair well with bacon, sausage, or just plain jam, are worth getting on the side. Ice cream sundaes made with Thrifty ice cream strike the perfect nostalgic note. Come for the architecture and stay for a bite.

Quality Seafood, 130 International Boardwalk, Redondo Beach, CA 90277; (310) 372-6408; qualityseafood.net; Seafood; $$. Summertime in the South Bay means plenty of sunshine and seafood, and the place to be is Quality Seafood on the Redondo Beach boardwalk. With an unbeatable ocean backdrop and picturesque pier, the setting doesn't get any better than this. Since 1953, this Dragich family-run institution has been a destination for local families and groups of friends to gather over the freshest catch. The stellar selection of seafood is displayed over crushed ice; pick your poison and the experts behind the counter can fry or grill your fish or steam your crustaceans and shellfish. Best of all are the creatures that require no cooking at all. Quality Seafood typically carries over 25 different kinds of oysters each day, from Fanny Bays to Kumamotos. Just a squeeze of fresh lemon juice and these briny bites are ready to go. There's also live sea urchin cultivated from local kelp beds and served up while still squirming. Don't be intimidated by its spiky exterior; the *uni* goes down plenty smooth. Things are bound to get messy here, so don't forget to pack plenty of hand wipes for the occasion. Hammers and crackers are available to rent on the premises.

Randy's Donuts, 805 W. Manchester Blvd., Inglewood, CA 90301; (310) 645-4707; randys-donuts.com; Doughnuts; $. Randy's Donuts is most famous for the gargantuan, doughnut-shaped sign perched atop its building on the corner of Manchester and La Cienega Boulevards in Inglewood. Designed by Henry J. Goodwin, the shop was originally part of the now-defunct Big Donut Drive-In chain. For the past four decades, brothers Larry and Ron Weintraub have owned the 24-hour drive-through operation, maintaining the iconic signage with each passing year. The shop offers deep-fried classics including twists, apple fritters, bear claws, and crullers, reasonably priced in the neighborhood of $1 a piece. The bestseller is the yeast-risen glazed doughnuts, simple rings that reach for the sky and stretch with each bite. The jelly-filled and buttermilk doughnuts, as well as the maple-glazed Long Johns, are also worthy of squeezing into your pretty pink pastry box.

Roscoe's House of Chicken and Waffles, 621 W. Manchester Blvd., Inglewood, CA 90301; (310) 981-4141; roscoeschickenandwaffles.com; Southern; $$. For a complete description, see p. 118.

Sakae Sushi, 1601 W. Redondo Beach Blvd., Gardena, CA 90247; (310) 532-4550; Japanese; $. Here at Gardena's Sakae Sushi, one does not have to break the bank to enjoy quality sushi. Owned by the Tani family since 1962, this takeout-only shop specializes in the kind of traditional sushi that Japanese mothers and grandmothers typically prepare at home. While regulars turn to Sakae to fill orders large enough to feed a crowd, the shop also sells sushi by the piece. The concise menu includes six varieties of *oshizushi*, a kind of sushi that is prepared in a wooden box to create a rectangular finished product. There's *Nori-Maki*, a roll made with shiitake mushroom, spinach, *kampyo* (cooked squash), *oboro* (cod paste), and egg; *Inari*, fried tofu pockets filled with marinated rice; *Ebi*, *nigiri* topped with cooked and marinated shrimp; *Saba*, *nigiri* topped with pickled Atlantic mackerel; *Tamago-Maki*, a *Nori-Maki* roll topped with egg; and California Roll made with avocado, shrimp, and roasted sesame seeds. Heavily vinegared rice forms the foundation of each one. Every order is presented in a perfectly arranged white cardboard box wrapped in a paper sleeve with the restaurant's logo; pickled ginger and a pair of chopsticks are tucked into the packaging as well.

Sublime Sweets

Cobblers, Cakes, and Kream, 2323 W. Manchester Blvd., Suite B, Inglewood, CA 90350; (323) 455-1224; cobblerscakesand kream.com; Dessert; $. Pam "The Cobbler Lady" Wright didn't earn her moniker overnight. She opened her first shop, the Cobbler Cafe, in 1989 and has been plugging away off and on, in various locations, ever since. Today, Wright and her cobbler-making crew operate out of a shiny new Inglewood store called Cobblers, Cakes, and Kream. While the cakes and ice creams are new additions, the cobblers are dependably the same. What's special about the cobblers here is the crust. Wright tops each one with a generous piece of dough that's slightly larger than the actual size of the pan, creating rustic folds and pockets not unlike a piece of fabric. Peaches, apples, and blackberries are her fruity fillings of choice. For those veering off the well-worn cobbler path, there are Key lime and sweet potato pies, red velvet and coconut layer cakes, as well as frozen concoctions created using **Fosselman**'s (see p. 184) ice creams.

FURTHER EXPLORATION: SWEET RED PEACH AND SOUTHERN GIRL DESSERTS

Sky-high and wonderfully sweet Southern-style cakes are the specialties at **Sweet Red Peach** in Inglewood (1035 S. Prairie, Unit 2, Inglewood, CA 90301; 310-671-CAKE; sweetredpeach .com) and **Southern Girl Desserts** (3650 Martin Luther King Jr. Blvd., Los Angeles, CA 90008; 323-293-2253; southern girldesserts.com). While the former specializes in red velvet and 7-Up cakes, the latter makes a mean sweet potato pie-inspired creation.

King's Hawaiian Bakery and Restaurant, 2808 W. Sepulveda Blvd., Torrance, CA 90505; (310) 530-0050; kingshawaiian restaurants.com; Hawaiian; $. Transport your taste buds straight to Hawaii with just one bite of the ever-popular Paradise Delight at King's Hawaiian Bakery and Restaurant. It's a three-layered triple threat of guava, passion fruit, and lime–flavored cake with whipped cream, fresh strawberries, and peach filling interspersed between the layers of plush chiffon. Fruity glazes echoing the three primary flavors add the finishing touches. The Paradise Delight is an undeniable stunner, with a sublime texture and flavors to match. While you're at the bakery, try the plain or filled *malasadas*, Hawaii's answer to the mainland's doughnuts, as well as cookies, Danishes, and pies of all stripes.

Mikawaya, 21515 Western Ave., Torrance, CA 90501; (310) 320-4551; mikawayausa.com; Japanese; **$.** For a complete description, see p. 91. **Additional Location:** 1630 W. Redondo Beach Blvd., Gardena, CA 90247; (310) 538-9389.

Patisserie Chantilly, 2383 Lomita Blvd., #104, Lomita, CA 90717; (310) 257-9454; patisseriechantilly.com; Bakery; **$.** Chef Keiko Nojima's French pastries with a Japanese flair are nothing short of spectacular. From the perfectly precise layers on each cake to the delicate cream piping on the famous puffs, immense care and attention to detail go into creating each sweet. While every dessert lining the pastry counter is impeccable, it's the black sesame cream puff that gets all the good press. Each one is filled to order with black sesame–flavored whipped cream, drizzled with honey, and sprinkled with soy powder. The intense and pure flavor that Chef Nojima is able to extract from the black sesame seeds is incredible—neither too much cream nor sugar clouds the main event. Japanese flavors are in full effect with the Le Matcha cake as well. Alternating layers of green tea and condensed milk mousses form the body, while a red bean cake holds down the fort. As with the black sesame cream puff, the flavor of the green tea is absolutely pure. For those whose palates lean more toward traditional, there are classic French fruit and chocolate tarts, as well as the Chantilly Fromage, the chef's signature cheesecake with a honey graham cracker crust.

Sakura-ya, 16134 S. Western Ave., Gardena, CA 90247; (310) 323-7117; Japanese; **$.** Little Tokyo's Fugetsu-Do might be the oldest Japanese confectionary in Los Angeles, but Gardena's Sakura-ya is the best. The sweetened *mochi* and *manju* sold at this family-owned business have been widening smiles since 1960. The selection of *mochi*, which come plain or stuffed with sweetened red bean paste (*an*) or white bean paste (*shiro an*), boast the texture of gentle clouds. Every bite offers a study in unparalleled plushness. While the orange and pink varieties are popular with newbies and children, the older set fancies the bean-stuffed ones, as well as the baked *manju*. The cinnamon-sprinkled *imo-manju* filled with sweet potato puree tastes a little like Thanksgiving.

FURTHER EXPLORATION: CHIKARA MOCHI

Located several doors down from Sakura-ya is **Chikara Mochi** (16108 S. Western Ave., Gardena, CA 90247; 310-324-5256). The shop specializes in *gyuhi mochi,* a softer variety of the sweet that allows for intricate designs (nature is a popular motif) and coloring.

SusieCakes, 3500 N. Sepulveda Blvd., Manhattan Beach, CA 90266; (310) 303-3780; susiecakes.com; Bakery; $. For a complete description, see p. 289.

Tea Station, 610 W. Redondo Beach Blvd., Gardena, CA 90247; (310) 515-2989; teastation.us; Dessert; $. For a complete description, see p. 186.

Specialty Stores, Markets & Producers

Alpine Village, 833 Torrance Blvd., Torrance, CA 90502; (310) 327-2483; alpinevillagecenter.com. Alpine Village brings a slice of Bavaria to an unlikely stretch of the South Bay. Here in this faux German complex, you'll find everything from a wedding chapel to a dentist office and a traffic school. The entire place is kitschy to be sure, but also a whole lot of fun, especially the Village's marketplace. Swing on by the butcher's counter for handmade German sausages including bratwurst, *bockwurst, landjager, weisswurst*, and liverwurst, as well as Polish *kielbasa*. Most are made from scratch using traditional recipes handed down for generations. Toward the back of the market is a wonderfully festive bakeshop featuring European and American baked goods. The *bienenstich*, also known as a "bee sting cake," is a classic German confection composed of two slabs of sweet yeast dough filled with vanilla custard and topped with caramelized almonds. The *dobosh*, a seven-layer Hungarian cake made of yellow cake and hazelnut cream coated in chocolate ganache, is as sweet as it is stunning. Aside from fancy cakes, there are more basic staples like pretzels, breads, and rolls. For the boozy bunch, the market stocks over 150 different brands of beer and European liquors, not to mention imported jams, cookies, coffee, pâté, and pickles too.

Mitsuwa Marketplace, 21515 Western Ave., Torrance, CA 90501; (310) 782-0335; mitsuwa.com/English. Mitsuwa Marketplace is a wonderland of Japanese groceries, prepared foods, and imported products. Of the three locations in Los Angeles, the San Gabriel branch is the smallest and most basic; expect to find groceries, produce, and a few electronics. The outlets in Torrance and West Los Angeles, on the other hand, are sizeable and fascinating places worthy of a half-day excursion. In addition to offering an incredible selection of fresh fish and aisles dedicated to everything from seaweed to Pocky (a popular brand of Japanese sweet and savory snacks), Mitsuwa redefines food court fare. Holding down the fort in Torrance and West Los Angeles is Santouka Ramen, a Japanese *ramenya* founded over 20 years ago by Hitoshi Hatanakain. There are currently seven locations stateside and many more in Japan serving memorable bowls of *shio* (salt) and spicy miso ramen. Only found at the West Los Angeles store is Hannosuke, the first US outlet of this tempura rice bowl specialist from Japan. Several times a year, Mitsuwa plays host to food-centric festivals including the Umaimono Gourmet Fair (featuring specialty foods from various Japanese provinces), Summer Festival (featuring cultural and culinary offerings), and Hokkaido Fair (a celebration of food from the island Hokkaido in northern Japan).

FURTHER EXPLORATION: MARUKAI PACIFIC MARKET

Gardena's **Marukai Pacific Market** (1620 W. Redondo Beach Blvd., Gardena, CA 90247; 310-464-8888, marukai.com), a membership-only emporium of hard-to-find Japanese groceries and products, has one of the best food courts in town. Fortunately, one does not have to be a card carrier to indulge in the offerings including Mammoth Bakery, a Japanese sweets powerhouse, and Shin-Sen-Gumi 2 Go, which prepares ramen, udon, and yakitori to be consumed on the fly.

South Los Angeles

Florence, Jefferson Park, University Park, Vermont Square, Willowbrook

Foodie Faves

Chichen Itza, 3655 S. Grand Ave., Los Angeles, CA 90007; (213) 741-1075; chichenitzarestaurant.com; Mexican; $$. It's impossible not to be taken by Chichen Itza's *cochinita pibil*, a specialty from the Yucatan that's cooked in banana leaves and melds tender pulled pork with *achiote* (a blend of annatto, oregano, cumin, cloves, cinnamon, black pepper, allspice, garlic, and salt) and orange juice. The citrus-tinged meat is terrific tucked inside a *torta* (sandwich) or in a taco, but it tastes best of all heaped onto a platter with black beans, rice, fried plantains, and steamy tortillas. Reach for the restaurant's prized habanero salsa to send the flavors off the charts. Gilberto Cetina opened Chichen Itza in 2001 inside the Mercado La Paloma, a colorful marketplace in historic South Central. Here, the dishes of the Yucatan, which have deep Mayan roots and ties to Spanish, Lebanese, and Dutch cuisines, are celebrated at every turn. Start off with a Mayan *sikil pac*, a roasted tomato, pumpkin seed, and chive dip served with tortilla chips. There's also *kibi*, a close relative of Middle Eastern *kibbeh*, which was brought to the Yucatan by Lebanese immigrants over a century ago. The ground beef and cracked wheat patties seasoned with mint and spices are fried golden brown and served with pickled red onions. The *vaporcito tamales* filled with *achiote*-seasoned chicken, pork, or vegetables and steamed in banana leaves are another specialty unique to the region.

FURTHER EXPLORATION: LA FLOR DE YUCATAN CATERING & BAKERY

La Flor De Yucatan Catering & Bakery in Pico-Union (1800 S. Hoover St., Los Angeles, CA 90006; 213-748-6090; laflordeyucatan.net) specializes in Mayan cuisine and baked goods from the Yucatan region. The famous *hojaldra* (ham and cheese pastry) is a staple, while the *panuchos* (fried tortillas filled with black beans and topped with lettuce, shredded char-broiled turkey, cucumbers, tomatoes, and pickled red onions) and the *cochinita pibil* are mostly available through catering.

Ella's Belizean Restaurant, 3957 S. Western Ave., Los Angeles, CA 90062; (323) 298-1310; Belizean; $. The customers walking out of Ella's Belizean Restaurant can barely see over their stacks of Styrofoam to-go boxes and aluminum catering trays. This is the place to go to feed a crowd without breaking a sweat. Though the place has a certain undeniable charm, its ambiance is mostly nil, while seating is limited to three high tops. Still, the crowds roll in hungry and roll out with enough food to satisfy a family. The menu, messily scrawled onto a wipe board, features Mayan appetizers and Kriol main courses. To start are crunchy little bites like *panades* (meat pies), conch fritters, *garnaches* (Belizean tostadas), and *salbutes* (stuffed tortilla shells). Main courses stay on a stewed and tender path. The well-seasoned oxtails are ladled over rice and beans with a few slivers of fried plantains. A curiously sweet potato salad dotted with corn and peas, as well as a baggie of spiced and pickled onions, is served on the side. The stewed pork, stewed chicken, and curry goat strike a similarly hearty note.

Hawkins House of Burgers, 11603 Slater St., Los Angeles, CA 90059; (323) 563-1129; hawkinsburgers.com; American; $. One bite of the Fat Cheese Burger from Hawkins House of Burgers and you'll wonder why cooks bother with froufrou touches like Gorgonzola, brioche, arugula, and secret sauces. This straightforward setup of Angus beef, shredded lettuce, tomatoes, onions, pickles, and American cheese in between mayonnaise and mustard–slathered commercial buns is an absolute slam-dunk. Cynthia Hawkins inherited this restaurant, as well her burger-making chops, from her father, who came to Los Angeles from Arkansas in 1939. What began as a small food stand has expanded into a good-size operation with an ordering counter up front, seating outside in an adjacent patio, and a kitchen in between. With such unfussy ingredients at play, it is essential that each one shines, especially the meat of the matter. Here at Hawkins, the patties are formed by hand using coarsely ground beef. Each one is cooked to order on a hot griddle that imparts a definite sear, trapping the juices until the burger meets your teeth. Bacon, chili, fried eggs, pastrami, and additional monster beef patties can be stacked on for a nominal fee. Those up for a heart-palpitating challenge ought to try the Whipper Burger, a tower of decadence consisting of two beef patties layered with cheese, egg, pastrami, onions, lettuce, tomatoes, pickles, mustard, mayonnaise, and a deep-fried hot link. Every burger comes with a brown paper bag full of crisp, golden steak fries.

Tamales Elena, South Wilmington Avenue and East 110th Street, Los Angeles, CA 90059; Mexican; $. No one makes tamales quite like Elena Irra. She, along with her husband Juan, owns and operates Tamales Elena in Watts, a white trailer hitched onto a brown pickup truck that's parked on South Wilmington Avenue near East 110th Street Mon through Sat 7 a.m. to 2 p.m. and Sun 8 a.m. to 1 p.m. While the menu includes memorable *tortas* (sandwiches), burritos, tacos, and quesadillas, it's the Guerrero-style tamales that get top billing. Elena has been selling them to friends and neighbors for over a decade, including 5-plus years on the trailer. There are three savory varieties (pork, chicken, and cheese) as well as two sweet tamales (pineapple and strawberry) available each day. While average tamales tend to taste one-dimensional, not to mention mushy, Elena's expertly crafted parcels are seasoned beautifully, with the cornmeal's pleasantly gritty texture front and center. The sweet ones, which have fruit preserves incorporated in the cornmeal batter, benefit from the wonderful texture as well. If you happen to visit on a Saturday or Sunday, pick up a tall cup of *menudo*, a soulful soup laced with red chiles and swimming with tripe. It's known to be an effective hangover cure.

FURTHER EXPLORATION: LOS CINCO PUNTOS AND MAMA'S HOT TAMALES

The tamales at **Los Cinco Puntos** in Boyle Heights (3300 E. Cesar E. Chavez Ave., Los Angeles, CA 90063; 323-261-4084) are a favorite among tamale enthusiasts, as are the ones at **Mama's Hot Tamales** (2124 W. 7th St., Los Angeles, CA 90057; 213-487-7474) in Westlake. Mama skips on the lard, so the meatless tamales are vegetarian.

L.A. Landmarks

Harold and Belle's, 2920 W. Jefferson Blvd., Los Angeles, CA 90018; (323) 735-9023; haroldandbellesrestaurant.com; Cajun; $$$. Harold & Belle's on West Jefferson Boulevard was established in

1969 by New Orleans transplants Harold and Belle Legaux and remains family owned and operated to this day. It was a dream of Harold Sr. to have a place where friends from New Orleans could "gather, talk over old times, shoot pool, and socialize." Over the years, this Los Angeles landmark has undergone several makeovers and expansions; there's no longer a pool table sadly. Most recently, the space was updated with a French colonial theme and a new banquet hall. While the aesthetics have changed with the times, the classic Creole fare has remained dependably constant throughout the restaurant's long history. Everyone loves the po' boys, especially the ones stuffed with jumbo shrimp and flaky fried catfish. Each carefully constructed sandwich is presented on sturdy french bread with just a touch of mayonnaise. The pitch-perfect cornmeal batter makes for an impressively crisp crust. The crawfish étouffée is plenty spicy and reliably good as well. Mix it up real good with rice before digging in. Harold and Belle's famous "File Gumbo" made from a dark roux and ground sassafras is as hearty as they come and generously dished out with plenty of shrimp, sausage, ham, crab, and chicken. It comes in both small and large sizes, but no one ever gets the former.

Roscoe's House of Chicken and Waffles, 106 W. Manchester Ave., Los Angeles, CA 90003; (323) 752-6211; roscoeschicken andwaffles.com; Southern; $$. For a complete description, see p. 118.

Southeast
Los Angeles

*Artesia, Bell, Cerritos, Commerce, Compton, Cudahy, Downey,
Huntington Park, La Mirada, Lynwood, Montebello, Norwalk,
Pico Rivera*

Foodie Faves

**Anticucheria Peruana, 14351 Pioneer Blvd., Norwalk, CA
90650; (562) 929-3398; Peruvian; $.** Anticucheria Peruana, also
known as Anticucheria Danessi, may very well be California's first
restaurant dedicated to grilled Peruvian skewers called *anticuchos*. In
addition to the signature offal offerings, Mario Danessi's brightly lit and
colorfully painted spot also serves *mariscos,* fruits of the sea prepared
with Peruvian flair. The *anticuchos de corazon,* thinly sliced beef hearts
seasoned in a wicked *aji colorado* marinade, is the signature dish. While
the heart of the matter is appealingly chewy, its edges are charred
just so. To dial up the heat, spoon on a bit of pale green *aji verde* or
rocoto sauce with scallions. The *combinado de pancita y rachi* redefines
mixed grill with tender hunks of pork stomach and honeycombed beef

tripe sauced in *aji panca,* a hot but not scorching Peruvian red chili sauce. It can be difficult to hold back when the cooking's this good, but save room for the *picarones* (squash and sweet potato doughnuts) for dessert. Each fried-to-order ring is lighter than expected, startlingly crunchy, and drizzled in an irresistible caramel sauce made of brown sugar, cinnamon, and figs. Grilled offal and doughnuts—what could be better?

Bludso's BBQ, 811 S. Long Beach Blvd., Compton, CA 90221; (310) 637-1342; bludsosbbq.com, Barbecue; $$. Pit master Kevin Bludso brings "a lil' taste of Texas" to the Southland at this lil' Compton eatery. With a couple of windows at which to place and pick up orders and a small waiting area with a few stools, it's mostly a takeout joint, but don't let the size of the place fool you—there's a whole lot of goodness packed in between these four walls. Bludso hails from a long line of barbecue specialists beginning with his great-great-grandfather. Prior to opening Bludso's BBQ in 2008, he learned the craft of 'cuing from his grandmother in Texas. For a glimpse of how the magic happens, take a peek behind the building where the smokers do their slow and low thing. There are pork ribs, beef brisket, rib tips, whole chickens, pork shoulder, and house-made chicken and beef links available every day. Angus beef ribs make an appearance only on Saturday and Sunday. The proteins come dressed to the nines in either a mild or spicy sauce—ask for it on the side if you want to experience the meat in all its natural glory. Each one is exquisitely smoked with a fine bark and pretty pink smoke ring, signaling that the meat and smoke had the proper time to mingle. Order the meats a la carte, or choose two or three and make it a "combo," which comes with two sides. There's also the Texas sampler, which includes a bit of this and a bit of that with two large sides—it's enough fuel to feed a family. Sides-wise, the collard greens with bits of pork are terrific, as is the properly mushy Southern-style macaroni and cheese. Mop up every last bit of sauce with complimentary slices of white bread. Sister restaurant Bludso's Bar & Que is in West Hollywood at 609 N. La Brea Ave., Los Angeles, CA 90036; (323) 931-2583.

FURTHER EXPLORATION: PHILLIPS BARBECUE

Phillips Barbecue (Leimart Park, 4307 S. Leimert Blvd., Los Angeles, CA; 323-292-7613; West Adams, 2619 Crenshaw Blvd., Los Angeles, CA; 323-731-4772; Inglewood, 1517 Centinela Ave., Inglewood, CA; 310-412-7135) has been serving up some of the city's finest pork ribs and rib tips for over 20 years. It's a takeout-only joint, so call ahead to avoid twiddling your thumbs.

The Corner Place, 19100 Gridley Rd., Cerritos, CA 90703; (562) 402-8578; cornerplacerestaurant.com; Korean; $. For a complete description, see p. 21.

El Carriel Bakery, 2405 Randolph St., Huntington Park, CA 90255; (323) 581-7026; Colombian; $. Myriam Sabogal has been serving up snacks from her native Colombia at this strip mall bakery since 1995. Originally from the city of Cali, Sabogal specializes in *arepa valluna*, a gritty cornmeal cake slicked with butter and griddled to a crisp. It tastes even better stuffed with gooey cheese. Also savory and satisfying are the more common flour *arepas* filled with cheese, beef, or chicken, or served plain with a link of chorizo on the side. Traditional sweet breads including *bunenuelo*, cheesy yet light doughnut holes; *pan de bono*, stretchy bread rings made of corn flour, cassava starch, cheese, and eggs; and *almojabana,* cheese bread, are served up wonderfully warm and fresh. Order a mug of *café Colombiano* or *chocolate batido* (hot chocolate) to wash everything down just like they do in Colombia.

Guelaguetza Restaurante, 11215 Long Beach Blvd., #1010, Lynwood, CA 90262; (310) 884-9234; guelaguetzarestaurante.com; Mexican; $$. For a complete description, see p. 30.

Honey's Kettle, 2600 E. Alondra Blvd., Compton, CA 90221; (310) 638-7871; honeyskettle.com; Fried Chicken; $. Vincent Williams, the proud owner of Honey's Kettle in Compton and Culver City, guards his fried chicken recipe close to the vest. He prepares the secret batter off-site and delivers it daily to each location, where the kitchen adds water, mixes until smooth, and hand batters the chicken as orders roll in. Every thigh, wing, breast, and leg is submerged in this downright magical mixture before meeting the hot oil in a stainless steel kettle drum. The result is an insanely crusty and golden batter that's like no other fried chicken on the planet. Every bite unleashes a shockingly loud crunch, while the meat is succulent and genuinely juicy. There's not a single dud on the bird when it's prepared Honey's Kettle style. Served on the side are dimpled buttermilk biscuits that are more cakey than flakey, as well as hotcakes made from the same batter. A drizzle of honey on both chicken and biscuits, along with a few lashes of hot sauce, and you're good to go. The shinier Culver City location offers a more extensive menu with sandwiches, "designer" salads, and pies, but the original Compton restaurant definitely has more soul.

Kyochon Chicken, 123 Los Cerritos Mall, Cerritos, CA 90703; (562) 809-2449; Korean; $. For a complete description, see p. 38.

La Casita Mexicana, 4030 E. Gage Ave., Bell, CA 90201; (323) 773-1898; casitamex.com; Mexican; $$. For the past decade and then some, chefs Jaime Martin del Campo and Ramiro Arvizu have been preparing the dishes of their native Jalisco, along with other Mexican specialties, at La Casita Mexicana in Bell. What sets this restaurant apart from the zillion other Mexican eateries dotting the city's landscape is its serious commitment to capturing the flavors of Mexico and to using only fresh, local, and seasonal produce. In fact, most of the herbs and vegetables served at the restaurant are grown nearby at a communal garden. The result of pairing Southern California's finest ingredients with these chefs' immense talents is food that shines like no other taqueria's in town. Complimentary bowls of tortilla chips drizzled with three different moles and sprinkled with toasted sesame seeds signal the start of every meal. A rainbow of moles can be found on the menu as well, spooned on things like flautas and *enmoladas*. The red *pipian mole* made of pumpkin seeds has a distinct peanut-buttery flair, while the green *pepian* is mild and nutty. The *mole poblano* is richly colored and boasts spicy undertones and unabashed sweetness. Aside from the moles, the restaurant also makes a memorable *chiles en nogada*. It's the national dish of Mexico and consists of a roasted poblano chili stuffed with spiced ground beef, dried fruits, walnuts, and candied cactus. A rich and creamy pecan sauce and a handful of pomegranate seeds provide the finishing touches. The only way to properly end a meal here is with an order of *churros*, two-inch-long sweet rods piped full of *dulce de leche* and served fresh out of the deep-fryer. See chefs Martin del Campo and Arvizu's recipe for **Chiles en Nogada** on page 314.

Magic Wok, 11869 Artesia Blvd., Artesia, CA 90701; (562) 865-7340; Filipino; $. Ask a Filipina where to find the best Pinoy cooking in town and she'll point you to her mother's home. Ask her where to find an adequate substitute and she'll suggest Magic Wok in Artesia. Elena Pulmano converted a former Chinese fast-food outlet into a homey spot for honest Filipino cooking in 1979, but kept the restaurant's moniker out of convenience. After a decade of feeding the community the crispiest *pata* in town, Pulmano handed the reins to her nephew Rudy and his wife, Marivic Abuyen, in 1989. Other than a fresh coat of paint and a few new menu items, not much has changed at Magic Wok since it debuted over 30 years ago. The crowds still go gaga for the crispy *pata*, a bone-in leg of pork that's brined, boiled, and fried till blistered and golden. The *sisig* is also wildly popular. Bits of skin-on pork, carrots, and scallions are sautéed and seasoned with a heavy dose of garlic, black pepper, and citrus. The *binagoongang baboy,* a punchy marriage of deeply fermented shrimp paste (*bagoong alamang*) and fatty bits of pork, isn't for everyone, but if your tastes swing toward the funky, sweet, and fermented, this pig's for you.

Mom's Burgers, 336 W. Alondra Blvd., Compton, CA 90220; (310) 632-6622; American; $. Joyce "Mom" McLaurin opened this hamburger shack over three decades ago to bring simple yet immensely satisfying fast-food-style fare to the neighborhood. Stroll up to the window to place your order, and then wait for a gentle tap on the Plexiglas window to signal when it's ready to be picked up. Waits can be a bit long since everything is made to order, so call ahead for a curbside pickup or better yet, bump to the slow jams blasting from the speakers or partake in an impromptu game of chess. Both work up an appetite quite nicely. Once the goods are in hand, grab a seat at one of the stools along the counter or at the umbrella-shaded tables hidden beside the building. The most basic offering is Mom's Burger, a single beef patty with shredded iceberg lettuce, chopped white onions, ketchup, mustard, mayonnaise, pickles, and a slice of tomato. The bun is of the squishy commercial variety, while the meat is hand-formed and well-seasoned with salt and coarse-ground pepper. Griddled on a flattop, the patty is cooked through and beautifully caramelized. The shop's most popular burger is The Chronic, a double-patty situation with thick-cut bacon and a fried egg in addition to the regular cast of toppings. For those feeling particularly gluttonous, sign up for The Colosso, which piles on a mound of pastrami atop a fully dressed burger. Chili cheese fries ladled with homemade chili and grated cheddar cheese make for a mighty fine but perhaps gratuitous side dish.

Mumbai Ki Galliyon Se, 17705 Pioneer Blvd., Artesia, CA 90701; (562) 860-6699; Indian; $. Mumbai Ki Galliyon Se, which literally means "from the streets of Mumbai," is the only restaurant in Los Angeles specializing in the street foods of Mumbai, the most populous city in India. Here, Sailesh Shah and his wife, Shruti, prepare sweet and savory snacks from their former homeland. The dining room doesn't offer much in the way of ambiance, aside from the handmade signs displaying names of Mumbai Metro stations hung on the walls, but that's what makes this place so charming. The completely vegetarian menu lists close to 100 dishes including specialties from South India and Punjab, and even Indochinese fusion, but stick to the quintessential street food offerings for the most unique dining experience. Nearly everyone orders the *dabeli*, a slider of sorts stuffed with potato patties laced with masala (a spicy mix of chiles, cumin, and cinnamon), onions, green grapes, peanuts, and pomegranate seeds in between buttered and toasted buns. Also popular is the *pav bhaji*, a tomato-based vegetable stew served with toasty garlic bread that Sailesh insists on preparing himself each day, without assistance from his wife and children. The various plates of *puri*, hollow puffed wheat shells filled with potatoes, chutneys, yogurts, and scented waters, are also irresistible. Wash everything down with a tall cup of sweet yet tangy *piyush*, a cooling beverage made from yogurt, saffron, cardamom, pistachios, and almonds that takes 3 days to prepare.

Rajdhani, 18525 Pioneer Blvd., Artesia, CA 90701; (562) 402-9102; rajdhaniartesia.com; Indian; $$. This "Vegetable Restaurant" on Pioneer Boulevard is famous for its 10-course Gujarati-style *thali* buffet. It's a steam table–less affair where waiters dish up flaky breads, hearty lentils, tangy curries, and even dessert tableside until you say mercy. Before the parade of food commences, chilled glasses of water and *chhas* (buttermilk) are delivered in metal cups in preparation for the onslaught of heat. The level of spicing here is suited to local palates, meaning it can be a few notches higher than at more run-of-the-mill Indian establishments. Steamed basmati rice and a variety of breads, along with a trio of spiced legumes and vegetables, are dished up in a metal tray to start. On the side are tins ladled with soupier offerings and additional small bites. The selection changes daily and often includes *dhokra*, spongy steamed cakes made from chickpea flour; *choley,* stewed and spiced chickpeas; *kadhi*, a creamy gravy thickened with chickpea flour; *papad*, thin and crisp crackers; and roti, flakey, buttery flatbreads. Skip the silverware all together and dig in with your right hand, moistening crumbly bits with sauces and gravies for smooth delivery from plate to lips. Ask for more of one particular dish or the whole shebang and your wish will be granted in a snap. For dessert, the standard *gulab jamun*, fried milk powder solids soaked in a cardamom and saffron–laced syrup, is delightful, while the *gajar halwa*, grated carrots simmered in milk, sugar, and cardamom and topped with nuts, is less sweet but just as fetching.

Surati Farsan Mart: Indian Sweets and Snacks, 11814 186th St., Artesia, CA 90701; (562) 860-2310; suratifarsan.com; Indian; $. Tantalizing *methai* (sweets) and *chat* (snacks) are what it's all about at Surati Farsan Mart, a stylish shop specializing in Gujarati-style nibbles since 1986. On the *chat* side of things is pitch-perfect *pani puri*, delicate whole-wheat shells carefully filled with mung beans, potatoes, and *jaljira*, a cool liquid imbued with herbs and spices, and drizzled with chutneys. Attempt to eat it all in one big bite to avoid any *jaljira* dribbling down your chin. Various varieties of *chevdo* or "hot mix" are sold by the pound. The "African Chevdo," a mixture of *tikhi sev* (thin, crunchy noodles), cashews, peas, peanuts, and fried shredded potatoes, is perfumed with a bevy of spices and completely addictive. The *khandvi*, inch-long chickpea flour "noodles" rolled with onions, mustard seeds, cilantro, and coconut, make irresistible appetizers for here or to go. The deep-fried samosas stuffed with vegetables and served with two types of chutney are the quintessential *chat*. To transform these parcels into a full meal, try the *chole samosa* served in a chickpea stew or the *ragda samosa* served in a pea stew. The selection of *methai* includes a rainbow of confections carefully constructed from sugar, nuts, and spices. The shop makes half a dozen varieties of *barfi*, sugary bites flavored with dried fruits and nuts.

Udupi Palace, 18635 Pioneer Blvd., Artesia, CA 90701; (562) 860-1950; udupipalace.net; Indian, Vegetarian; $. Udupi Palace, one of the first restaurants in Little India to specialize in vegetarian cuisine from the southern region, is named after a temple city in owner Uday Shetty's home state of Karnataka in South India. The room is simply appointed with an abundance of natural light, while service is friendly and mostly helpful. Nearly everyone orders one of the restaurant's impressively portioned *dosas*, crisp paper-thin crepes made from a rice and lentil batter. There are a dozen different varieties served here including a *masala dosa* (stuffed with spiced potatoes), *mysore masala dosa* (a *masala dosa* with the addition of coconut and onion chutneys), *sada dosa* (plain), and *paper dosa* (a super-long *masala dosa*). The Butter *Masala Dosa* made with plenty of ghee (clarified butter) and served with *sambar* (a mildly spicy stew of vegetables and lentils) and a cooling coconut chutney offers a fine introduction for those new to the artful and satisfying cooking that is characteristic of the region. The *Chana Batura*, another one of the restaurant's specialties, is centered around an amazingly puffy bread that looks like an inflated balloon with a craggy, lunarlike surface. The chickpea stew and yogurt sauce served alongside are ideal for dipping. The South Indian *Thali* offers the most variety with six different vegetables, stews, and curries, along with rice, breads, pickles, yogurt, and *payasam* (rice pudding) for dessert.

L.A. Landmarks

Dal Rae, 9023 Washington Blvd., Pico Rivera, CA 90660; (562) 949-2444; dalrae.com; American; $$$. There aren't too many places left like Pico Rivera's Dal Rae, where continental fare is served in a dim wood-and-leather setting with a piano bar. Regulars have been filing in nightly since 1958 for Caesar salads prepared tableside and steaks crusted in black pepper. These dependable standbys, coupled with attentive service and strong traditions, have made the Dal Rae an iconic eatery. Sip an old-fashioned or any of the expertly made cocktails at the bar before settling in for supper. Every meal here begins with a tray of raw vegetables served over shaved ice and baskets of cheese toast. Next to arrive are old-school appetizers like shrimp cocktail and oysters Rockefeller, all of which are served without a hint of irony. The aforementioned Caesar salad tastes better than any in memory; maybe it's the tableside service that takes it to the next level, or perhaps it's the anchovy-laced dressing with Dijon mustard, fresh lemon juice, and a splash of Worcestershire. The famous black pepper steak, a tender New York steak topped with cracked pepper, green onions, and fried bits of bacon and mushroom, continues to dazzle decade after decade. Dessert is as deserving of gastro real estate as the starters and mains, especially the banana flambé and cherries jubilee; both are prepared tableside and served for two.

Dino's Chicken and Burgers, 6135 Pacific Blvd., Huntington Park, CA 90255; (323) 585-4444; dinoschickenandburgers.com; Greek, Mexican; $. For a complete description, see p. 71. **Additional Location:** 9367 Telegraph Rd., Pico Rivera, CA 90660; (562) 942-7222.

Mario's Peruvian Seafood, 15720 Imperial Hwy., La Mirada, CA 90638; (562) 902-8299; Peruvian; $$. For a complete description, see p. 74.

Porto's Bakery & Cafe, 8233 Firestone Blvd., Downey, CA 90241; (562) 862-8888; portosbakery.com; Cuban; $. For a complete description, see p. 240.

Sam Woo Barbecue, 19008 Pioneer Blvd., Cerritos, CA 90703; (562) 865-7278; Chinese; $. For a complete description, see p. 82.

Zankou Chicken, 125 N. Montebello Blvd., Montebello, CA 90640; (323) 722-7200; zankouchicken.com; Lebanese; $. For a complete description, see p. 84.

 *Sublime Sweets*

La Monarca Bakery, 6365 Pacific Blvd., Huntington Park, CA 90255; (323) 585-5500; lamonarcabakery.com; Bakery; $. Ricardo Cervantes and Alfredo Livas tapped into an underserved market when they opened the first La Monarca Bakery in Huntington Park in 2006. The two natives of Monterrey, Mexico, were continually disappointed by the Mexican bakeries in town and decided to take matters into their own hands. Here at La Monarca Bakery, traditional Mexican baked goods are produced without lard, trans-fats, preservatives, or artificial ingredients. The duo's organic approach to *pan dulces* resonated with the community from the get-go; a second store was opened in 2009 in Commerce, a third in Santa Monica in 2010, and a fourth in South Pasadena in 2012. Chef Alain Bour, a French native who lived in Mexico for 35 years, oversees the day-to-day operation at all four locations, where everything is baked fresh daily. Begin by grabbing a pair of tongs and

lining a metal tray with tissue, then proceed to grab one (or two) of everything that looks delectable. Robustly plush *conchas* come in vanilla and chocolate, while wedding cookies delight in chocolate, cinnamon, and powdered sugar–dusted plain. Make sure to try the *polvorones* as well, crumbly shortbread cookies made with macadamia nuts. Croissants with a tunnel of *dulce de leche*, chocolate, or cream cheese with guava running through the center pair exquisitely with the house-made Oaxacan coffees. For special occasions, the best-selling vanilla bean chantilly cake with fresh fruit is a winning choice, as is the traditional *tres leches* cake. Look out for seasonal specialties like orange-tinged *pan de muerto* in October and *rosca de reyes* in December and January. **Additional Location:** 5700 E. Whittier Blvd., Commerce, CA 90022; (323) 869-8800.

Los Alpes Ice Cream Parlor, 6410 Rugby Ave., Huntington Park, CA 90255; (323) 587-4246; Ice Cream; $. It's always a good time for a frozen treat here in the land of endless summer. One of the most brilliant ways to cool off is with Mexican popsicles called *paletas*. For the largest, most drool-inducing selection in town, head to Los Alpes Ice Cream Parlor in Huntington Park. Fernando Flores, along with his wife, Margarita, opened the shop in 1979 and now makes over 50 varieties of *paletas de aguas* (water-and-juice-based pops) and *paletas de crema* (milk- or cream-based pops). Today, the popsicles are crafted by the Flores' grandson Israel Mondragon; he's been at it for nearly two decades, introducing new flavors like mango and chile, *nopales* (cactus) and pineapple, and strawberries and cream to the already stellar lineup. The *paletas de aguas,* which come in flavors like tamarind (*tamarindo*), hibiscus (*jamaica*), and alfalfa, are the most refreshing bunch, while the *paletas de crema* are a touch richer with flavors like *arroz* (rice), Mexican eggnog (*rompope*), and vanilla. The *Paletas de Especialidades* are funky as all get-out, especially the *frijol* made from pinto beans, cinnamon, and vanilla—cool beans.

FURTHER EXPLORATION: MATEO'S

With locations in Culver City (4929 Sepulveda Blvd., Culver City, CA 90230; 310-313-7635), Pico-Union (1250 S. Vermont Ave., Los Angeles, CA 90006; 213-738-7288), and Mid-City (4234 W. Pico Blvd., Los Angeles, CA 90019; 323-931-5500), **Mateo's Ice Cream and Fruit Bars** is the most accessible *paletería* in town. In addition to *paletas*, Mateo's also sells *nieves* (ice cream), *licuados* (shakes), and fruit and vegetable juices.

Portugal Imports, 11655 Artesia Blvd., Artesia, CA 90701; (562) 809-7021; portugalimports.net; Portuguese; $. For the past 25 years, Portugal Imports has been the go-to place in Los Angeles for provisions of the Portuguese persuasion including sausages, cheeses, and salt cod. In addition to the assortment of imported goods lining the shelves and refrigerator, the shop offers a stellar selection of made-from-scratch breads and pastries that alone are worth the trek to Artesia. Flaky tartlets called *queijadas* come with a number of sweet fillings such as *amendoa* (almond), *ananas* (pineapple), *caramelo* (caramel), and *coco* (coconut). The smooth and sweet *queijadas de nata* (custard) may be

FURTHER EXPLORATION: NATAS PASTRIES

Fatima Marques, a native of Lisbon, Portugal, opened **Natas Pastries** in Sherman Oaks in 2005 (13317 Ventura Blvd., Sherman Oaks, CA 91423; 818-788-8050; nataspastries.com). In addition to the restaurant's namesake *queijadas de nata*, there's also a savory bistro menu serving traditional dishes like *caldeirada*, a seafood stew, and *Sandes de Chouriço e Queijo*, a grilled Portuguese sausage sandwich with onions, tomatoes, and cheese.

the shop's bestseller, but it's the *queijadas dona amelia* that really pack a punch. A specialty from Terceira Island located off the western coast of Portugal in the Azores archipelago, the *queijadas dona amelia* are dense little pucks crammed with raisins and pineapple, spiced with nutmeg and cinnamon, and finished with heaps of powdered sugar. If a Momofuku Crack Pie and Christmas fruit cake were to have a love child, this pint-size pastry would be it. Portugal Imports also makes gorgeous loaves of *massa sovada*, Portuguese sweet bread, as well as pillowy *malasadas* (doughnuts) that are only available on Saturday mornings.

Saffron Spot, 18744 Pioneer Blvd., Artesia, CA 90701; (562) 809-4554; saffronspot.com; Ice Cream; $. Smita Vasant churns out an exceptional line of ice creams that are inspired by the flavors she grew up with in Mumbai, India. What began as a hobby shared only with friends and family eventually led to a wholesale operation called Neemo's Exotic Ice Creams catering to restaurants and special events. Vasant's product was so well received by the community that she opened this retail store in Artesia's Little India in 2005; her unique and nuanced scoops deserved a wider audience. Saffron Spot's original roster of flavors, which includes "Saffron Silk," "Mango Magic," "Chikoo Crunch," and "Cashew Cream," has since expanded to more than two dozen. While Saffron Silk, an intriguing blend of saffron ice cream, rose, and pistachios, remains the top seller, some of the newer offerings like pomegranate, fig walnut, and *mawa* (cardamom) have garnered devout fans. The shop also makes a refreshing *falooda,* a textured milk shake with Persian roots traditionally composed of rose syrup, vermicelli, and basil seeds. The Saffron *Falooda* served here is made with saffron-infused milk and ice cream, thin noodles, and chewy basil seeds. In addition to ice creams and *falooda*, the shop also offers fresh juices, "exotic milks," *gola* (shaved ice), and Indian snacks.

Tea Station, 11688 South St., Artesia, CA 90701; (562) 860-7089; teastation.us; Dessert; $. For a complete description, see p. 186.

Verdugos

Altadena, Glendale, Pasadena

Foodie Faves

Carousel, 304 N. Brand Blvd., Glendale, CA 91203; (818) 246-7775; **carouselrestaurant.com; Lebanese; $$.** It's all about the *mezze*, a serious spread of hot and cold appetizers, at this three-decade-old Lebanese institution. Greg and Rose Tcholakian opened the original Carousel in a Hollywood strip mall in 1984 serving kebabs, vegetarian specialties, and traditional dishes. In 1998, the couple's son opened the swankier Glendale outlet, which allowed for an expanded menu, live entertainment on weekends, and a moodier ambiance. While *mezze* are traditionally served as an appetizer, Carousel encourages diners to curate a spread fit for a meal, grazing from one dish to the next with thin sheets of pita in hand. The *hammos* (pureed garbanzo beans with tahini, lemon juice, and garlic), *mutabbal* (smoky roasted eggplant spiked with garlic), and *tabbuleh* (chopped parsley and cracked wheat salad) form the foundation of every spread. From there, add on the utterly delightful *muhammara*, a dip made of crushed walnuts, red pepper paste, and pomegranate juice. The *kebbeh orfaliyeh*, Armenian-style steak tartare, is a touch spicy and very satisfying, while the *sarma*, grape leaves stuffed with rice and vegetables, pack a tangy punch. Honing in on hot *mezze*, sample the *fatayer*, pan-fried turnovers stuffed with cheese or spinach, and the *sambousek*, fried meat pies. The pièce de résistance is the *sou-juk flambé*, homemade Armenian beef sausages sliced and threaded on a skewer and flame-broiled tableside. Dinners on Friday and Saturday feature live music, belly dancing, and set menus.

FURTHER EXPLORATION: MAROUCH RESTAURANT AND SKAF'S GRILL

To further scratch your Lebanese itch, head to **Marouch Restaurant** in Hollywood (4905 Santa Monica Blvd., Los Angeles, CA 90029; 323-662-9325; marouchrestaurant.com) and **Skaf's Grill** in Glendale (367 N. Chevy Chase Dr., Glendale, CA 91206; 818-551-5540). The former braises a seriously sumptuous lamb shank, while the latter's grilled kebabs come charred and juicy.

Dog Haus, 105 N. Hill Ave., Pasadena, CA 91106; (626) 577-4287; doghausdogs.com; American; $. Pasadena has become a hotbed for hot dogs in recent years. While Slaw Dogs on North Lake has its proponents, it's Dog Haus on the east side of town that consistently delivers the city's snappiest wieners. The dogs here weigh in at a hefty quarter pound and are creatively prepared with a slew of thoughtful toppings. Alternative diets are satisfied with veggie and turkey varieties. What really makes these dogs the "Best of the Wurst" are the King's Hawaiian buns. These eternally sweet and soft rolls were made to be toasted and paired with something meaty. The most over-the-top dog is the Little Leaguer, which brings together *chili con carne*, Fritos, diced onions, and shredded cheddar. It's a beast of a creation that benefits from the bun's slight sweetness. A thick slice of smoked bacon runs along the side of the Grand Slam, with a fried egg and smashed Tater Tots on top. Pierce the yolk to smother everything in a slick and rich coating before diving in. Every table is smartly topped with a big box of napkins and squeeze bottles filled with yellow mustard and ketchup. For zestier garnishes, walk over to the extensive condiment bar toward the front where several varieties of mustard, curry ketchup, hot sauce, relish, and pepperoncinis can be had. In addition to their signature hot dogs, Dog Haus also serves sausages, burgers, and a handful of sides. **Additional Location:** 93 E. Green St., Pasadena, CA 91105; (626) 683-0808.

DANGER DOGS

Bacon-wrapped hog dogs are an illegal yet prevalent part of L.A. street food culture. Hawkers of these illicit savories can be found after dark throughout the city wherever belligerent revelers congregate; nightclubs, bars, and concert venues in Downtown, Hollywood, and Highland Park are always dependable places for a fix.

Constructed on converted grocery store carts fitted with burners and topped with a sturdy cookie sheet, these street-side beasts never fail to deliver an avalanche of sweet, salty, spicy, and tangy flavors. To start, commercial hot dogs are wrapped in bacon and grilled to a taut and caramelized crisp. Next, they're nestled inside lightly toasted buns and topped with onions and bell peppers that have been sautéed in residual bacon grease. Squiggles of mayonnaise, ketchup, and yellow mustard, along with a seared jalapeño pepper, add the finishing touches.

Perfectly legal renditions of these iconic hot dogs are served up at **Fab Hot Dogs** in Reseda ("L.A. Street Dog") and at **Dog Haus** in Pasadena ("Downtown Dog"). For complete descriptions, see p. 131 and 232, respectively.

Euro Pane, 950 E. Colorado Blvd., #107, Pasadena, CA 91106; (626) 577-1828; Bakery; $. Sumi Chang opened Euro Pane after learning the bread-making ropes at La Brea Bakery under the tutelage of Nancy Silverton. Even though the shop has been around for well over a decade and recently opened a second location down the street, an empty table is still hard to come by when the weekend rolls around. It's a neighborhood ritual to linger over a fresh croissant, relishing each and every flaky, buttery layer, with a cup of coffee and the morning paper. While Chang's classic French pastries are baked to perfection, it's her decadent open-faced egg salad sandwich that draws crowds from near and far. Each sandwich begins with a large slice of bread (the rosemary currant is best) that's schmeared with a terrifically tart sun-dried tomato pesto and topped with mixed baby greens. Then, an ooey gooey egg salad made from soft whites and even softer yolks is mounded on top. It's creamy and rich—absolutely the finest egg salad in all of the land. Finish your meal with a supersize sea salt macaron. **Additional Location:** 345 E. Colorado Blvd., Pasadena, CA 91101; (626) 844-8804.

Kyochon Chicken, 1140 Glendale Galleria, Glendale, CA 91210; (818) 552-2449; Korean; $. For a complete description, see p. 38.

Old Sasoon Bakery, 1132 N. Allen Ave., Pasadena, CA 91104; (626) 791-3280; oldsasoon.com; Middle Eastern (Syrian, Armenian); $. Opened in 1986 by Haroutioun Geragosian, Old Sasoon Bakery is named after the village in Armenia that his grandparents left following World War II. Today, the shop is run by Geragosian's son Joseph and several other family members. The first thing you'll notice when walking into the store is just how good the place smells. Freshly baked breads and pastries perfume the air both inside and outside the shop. The ambiance is homey, yet efficient. On your first visit to Old Sasoon, come hungry and order the *khachapuri*, a Georgian breakfast staple composed of a boat-shaped flatbread topped with a blend of cheeses, one or two runny eggs, and a few pats of melted butter (an original Sasoon touch). On subsequent stops, try a few *beorags* (savory hand pies) that come stuffed with things like mushrooms, *basturma* (cured beef), and *soujouk* (sausage). Another treat that's sure to satisfy is the fluorescent orange flatbread slathered with *zahtar* (a blend of sesame seeds, powdered sumac, and dried thyme), chiles, onions, and red pepper sauce.

FURTHER EXPLORATION: GARO'S BASTURMA

Garo's Basturma (1088 N. Allen Ave., Pasadena, CA 91104; 626-794-0460), which is located on the same street as Old Sasoon, is a small, but mighty grocery store that supplies Armenian restaurants nearby with quality basturma and soujouk. Both are made from scratch using family recipes and are available for purchase by the pound.

Raffi's Place, 211 E. Broadway, Glendale, CA 91205; (818) 240-7411; raffisplace.com; Middle Eastern (Persian, Armenian); $$. Every meal at Raffi's Place begins with *sabzi*, or "something green"—sprigs of basil, chopped parsley and white onions, and whole radishes served on a plate, along with pats of butter and a basket of unleavened *lavash* (flatbread). When pulled together, along with a sprinkling of *somagh* (powdered sumac), these aromatics and herbs make for a uniquely Persian appetizer. The *sabzi* to start, as well as the bougainvillea-shaded dining room, have been a part of the Raffi's experience since 1993, when Rafik Bakijan and his wife, Gohar, opened the restaurant to share treasured family recipes with Los

Angeles' burgeoning Middle Eastern community. For those requiring a heartier starter, try the *tadig,* a prized crispy rice crust served with *ghormesabzi* (stewed greens with beef, kidney beans, and dehydrated limes) and *gheimeh bademjan* (stewed split peas and eggplant). It's a textural powerhouse of epic proportions. The heart of the menu is the kabobs. Raffi's makes over a dozen kinds using beef, chicken, fish, and lamb, including *soltani* (filet mignon and ground beef), *barg* (thinly sliced filet mignon), *shish* (marinated chunks of filet mignon), and most fabulous of all, *koobideh* (ground beef). Every kabob is caramelized and charred to perfection and served on a bed of out-of-this-world fluffy basmati rice with grilled tomatoes and Anaheim peppers. An order of the Yogurt and Mousir, grated shallots combined with rich yogurt, goes amazingly with the kabobs.

FURTHER EXPLORATION: SHAMSHIRI

Shamshiri (1712 Westwood Blvd., Los Angeles, CA 90024; 310-474-1410; shamshiri.com) brings punchy Persian fare to Westwood, Glendale (122 W. Stocker St., Glendale, CA 91202; 818-246-9541), and Reseda (19249 Roscoe Blvd., Northridge, CA 91324; 818-885-7846). The soulful *fesenjan,* a sweet yet tangy stew made of pomegranates and walnuts served over chicken or *tadig,* shines the brightest. The *zereshk polo,* saffron-scented rice dotted with sour barberries, is straight out of Technicolor.

Tibet Nepal House, 36 E. Holly St., Pasadena, CA 91124; (626) 585-0955; tibetnepalhouse.com; Himalayan; $$. The cuisine of the Himalayas, which is heavily influenced by the culinary traditions of India and China, is the specialty at this Old Pasadena find. Opened in 2001, Tibet Nepal House was the first restaurant of its genre to appear in the area. While the restaurant's reasonably priced and varied-enough lunchtime buffets are popular with nearby shoppers, workers, and students, a dinnertime visit is just as swell. A platter of *momo* (steamed dumplings) makes for a solid start. At Tibet Nepal House, the *momo* come filled with vegetables, chicken, or yak and are served with a superfluous dipping sauce. The yak meat dumplings are especially juicy, reminiscent of Shanghai-style soup dumplings. For those in a noodle soupy mood, the *phing* brings together a mild curry broth with soft, linguine-like noodles. Lamb, onions, and soft curds of scrambled eggs add the final touches. Any of the main courses featuring *saag* (spinach) should also be considered. While the spinach's spicing is laced with cardamom, its texture borders on silky. Pair the *saag* with deep-fried Tibetan whole-wheat bread or simple basmati rice. Be on the lookout for the *gaunle khasi*, goat meat stewed in onions, tomatoes, ginger, and Himalayan spices, which is often available during the Sunday champagne brunch buffet or as a dinner special.

Umami Burger, 49 E. Colorado Blvd., Pasadena, CA 91105; (626) 799-8626; umami.com; American; $$. For a complete description, see p. 68.

L.A. Landmarks

Dinah's Family Restaurant, 4106 San Fernando Rd., Glendale, CA 91204; (818) 244-4188; dinahsrestaurant.com; Fried Chicken; $$. Dinah's fried chicken has captured a slice of the South in Glendale since 1967. While the front room is dedicated to serving folks taking their birds to go, a cozy dining room seats those dining in; everyone who steps into Dinah's is treated to genuine Southern hospitality. The secret to the Pearson family's beloved fried chicken lies in the four different flours and 11 herbs and spices that coat each breast, leg, thigh, and wing. The pitch-perfect seasonings, coupled with a pressure cooking deep-fryer, make for superbly moist specimens that are prized for their crispy, grease-less skins. It's no wonder that the restaurant boasts that their fried chicken is "so free from cooking oil." Chicken livers and gizzards are given the same treatment to comparable effect. While Dinah's mostly plays it by the book when it comes to fried chicken, the sides served here are a different story. The sweet and tangy Fruit Mellow, a kind of ambrosia salad with whipped topping and mandarin oranges, as well as the pineapple-dotted coleslaw, pairs exceedingly well with the finger-lickin' clucks. The writing on the packaging says it all: "Nuthin' Could Be Finah!"

The Hat, 491 N. Lake Ave., Pasadena, CA 91101; (626) 449-1844; thehat.com; American; $. For a complete description, see p. 179.

Lucky Boy, 640 S. Arroyo Pkwy., Pasadena, CA 91101; (626) 793-0120; luckyboyburgers.com; American; $. Join the gaggle of local high school students and devoted old-timers at this Pasadena institution for the most important meal of the day. Place your order with one of the gruff fellas at the front window and wait for your number to be called a short while later. Snag a charmingly dated table either outside or in and be prepared for breakfast bliss of the salt and grease–induced variety. Lucky Boy's famed breakfast burrito, jam-packed with hash browns, eggs, cheese, and your choice of bacon, sausage, chorizo, or ham, spans 8 inches in length and weighs in at close to 2 pounds. It's served with a watery salsa that regulars pour on with abandon. This flour tortilla–wrapped gut buster has been fueling Pasadena residents since 1973. **Additional Location:** 581 E. Walnut St., Pasadena, CA 91101; (626) 793-7079.

The Original Tops, 3838 E. Colorado Blvd., Pasadena, CA 91107; (626) 449-4412; theoriginaltops.com; American; $. It's hard to imagine The Original Tops as anything other than a burger joint situated in the eastern reaches of Pasadena, but that wasn't always so. During its early days in the 1950s, Tops flittered around the San Gabriel Valley as a coffee shop and later as a walkup window. Under Steven Bicos' care, it eventually grew into the "homespun" fast-food establishment that it is today. Now owned by Steven's sons John and Chris, Tops still prides itself in making much of the menu from scratch; french fries are cut by hand, while onions and zucchinis are battered to order. Burgers begin quite basic with a quarter pound patty of ground Angus chuck layered with iceberg, tomatoes, pickles, and red onions on a toasted and Thousand Island-sauced bun. Cheese and bacon are available for add-ons. From there, things get a bit fancier with the Kobe Bistro Burger, a half-pound Kobe beef patty with smoked mozzarella, caramelized onions, tomato, mixed greens, and an herb mayonnaise. The Tops Special brings it home with a heap of pastrami piled onto an already decadent cheeseburger. Tops has been the heart and soul of this lonely stretch of Colorado Boulevard for over 35 years.

Pie 'n Burger, 913 E. California Blvd., Pasadena, CA 91106; (626) 795-1123; pienburger.com; American; $. California-style burgers and pies by the slice, dished up with a side of nostalgia, are the specialties at this neighborhood haunt. Grab a seat at one of the wooden swivel chairs along the Formica counter overlooking the grill; they have the best view of the house. Considering the neighborhood, chances are good that a Nobel Prize–winning physicist will be dining to your left and a geeky graduate student to your right. So as long as you don't utter the letters M, I, or T, this set usually plays nice. While there are salads and sandwiches to be considered, as well as a solid patty melt, most everyone orders the two namesake items. The burgers are made in the Golden State tradition with a charred all-beef patty, crisp iceberg lettuce, house-made Thousand Island dressing, and dill pickles. Make it a cheeseburger for a few cents extra. The ingredients are neatly stacked between a griddle-toasted bun, creating a simple yet effective package that's been satisfying Pasadeneans since 1963. The pies are equally well crafted. The ones with flaky crusts and fruity fillings change with the seasons, while those filled with curds, puddings, or cream and topped with a sensational meringue are available year-round. Summer's ollalieberries and spring's rhubarb are among the favorites.

Porto's Bakery & Cafe, 315 N. Brand Blvd., Glendale, CA 91203; (818) 956-5996; portosbakery.com; Cuban; $. Strolling around Porto's Bakery & Cafe on a bustling Saturday afternoon, it's hard to imagine that the shop began over 50 years ago as a home-based business in Manzanillo, Cuba. Since its humble beginnings, Porto's Bakery has garnered a devoted following, outgrowing several locations and eventually settling into a 20,000-square-foot building in the heart of Glendale. The crowds waiting for a piece of the Porto pie can be truly staggering on weekends and during peak lunching hours; thankfully, the staffers on hand at all three locations manage the amusement park-esque lines smoothly and professionally. Before stuffing your face with the famous Cheese Rolls, *Refugiados*, and Potato Balls pastries, try one of the gently priced and simply made Cuban sandwiches. The Cubano, a collection of slow-roasted pork, ham, swiss cheese, and pickles between two slices of Cuban bread, is hard to turn down, as is the *ropa vieja*, a sandwich stuffed with tenderly stewed beef, bell peppers, and onions in a tomato sauce. Every sandwich is served with plantain chips on the side. Now that you've laid down a properly savory base, it's time to dive into the sweets. The Cheese Rolls are reminiscent of breakfast Danishes, while the *Refugiados* pair sweet guava jam and cheese with flaky layers of puff pastry. The mini fruit tarts and crème brûlée taste as good as they look.

Roscoe's House of Chicken and Waffles, 830 N. Lake Ave., Pasadena, CA 91104; (626) 791-4890; roscoeschickenand waffles.com; Southern; $$. For a complete description, see p. 118.

Yang Chow, 3777 E. Colorado Blvd., Pasadena, CA 91107; (626) 432-6868; yangchow.com; Chinese; $$. For a complete description, see p. 84.

Zankou Chicken, 1296 E. Colorado Blvd., Pasadena, CA 91106; (626) 405-1502; zankouchicken.com; Lebanese; $. For a complete description, see p. 84. **Additional Locations:** 1415 E. Colorado St., Glendale, CA 91205; (818) 244-1937. 901 W. Glenoaks Blvd., Glendale, CA 91202; (818) 244-0492.

 *Sublime Sweets*

Berolina Bakery, 3421 Ocean View Blvd., Glendale, CA 91208; (818) 249-6506; berolinabakery.com; Bakery; $. Owned and operated by Anders Karlsson and his wife, Youna, Berolina Bakery has been producing beautiful European-style loaves, cakes, and pastries since 1991. The couple studied pastry arts in their native Sweden and Belgium respectively before marrying and joining forces at this Glendale bakery. Berolina's bevy of breads includes standard varieties like whole wheat and sourdough, as well as European selections like Swedish Limpa, German Black Forest, and Swiss Farmer. Other specialty breads are only available on specific days of the week; look for Potato Dill on Wednesday and Rye Currant on Friday. The shop's fabulously flakey croissants and Danishes are available every day of the week. Berolina's most impressive offering isn't found behind the pastry counter. The Real Brusselse Wafels are prepared to order and served warm and toasty with a light dusting of powdered sugar. The flavor is intriguingly yeasty yet mild, while the texture is impossibly light. Real-deal Brussels-style Belgian waffles are hard to come by in this Liège-leaning town.

Bulgarini Gelato, 749 E. Altadena Dr., Altadena, CA 91001; (626) 627-7640; bulgarinigelato.com; Gelato; $. Just before running into the rugged foothills of Altadena, hit a left into the dingy strip mall with the Rite Aid on the corner for a taste of the best gelato in town. Leo Bulgarini, the shop's dedicated proprietor, learned the tricks of the trade at his uncle's restaurant in Italy decades ago and continues the sweet tradition today. Bulgarini is a stickler about what goes into his gelato. The pistachios are sourced from Sicily, while the milk is from Broguiere's Dairy in nearby Montebello. Unlike traditional ice cream, which contains a good amount of milk fat, the gelato here is quite light, which means that the flavor of the nuts, fruits, and dairy is absolutely paramount. Bulgarini makes anywhere from two to ten flavors each day depending on the season and demand. From the famous pistachio to the dark chocolate with candied orange peels, each creation is sweet, light, and pure.

FURTHER EXPLORATION:
PAZZO GELATO AND GELATO BAR

Michael Buch, the owner and chief gelato-maker at **Pazzo Gelato** (pazzogelato.net) in Silver Lake (3827 W. Sunset Blvd., Los Angeles, CA 90026; 323-662-1410) and Echo Park (1910 W. Sunset Blvd.—lobby of the Citibank building—Los Angeles, CA 90026; 213-353-9263), makes a wicked red velvet flavor with cream cheese gelato and tufts of actual red velvet cake. Gail Silverton at Studio City's **Gelato Bar** (4342 Tujunga Ave., Studio City, CA 91604; 818-487-1717) churns a toffee flavor inspired by the English toffee at Littlejohn's at the Original Farmers Market.

Carmela Ice Cream, 2495 E. Washington Blvd., Pasadena, CA 91104; (626) 797-1405; carmelaicecream.com, Ice Cream; $. Jessica

Mortarotti opened this brick-and-mortar on the edge of Pasadena after years of selling her delightful ice creams from a pushcart at local farmers' markets. Named after her grandmother, who nurtured her love of cooking at a young age, Carmela is dedicated to churning out all-natural ice creams. Every scoop is made using organic milk and inspired by herbs, spices, flowers, and seasonal fruit. The list of flavors changes from day to day, but tubs of the shop's perennial favorites like salted caramel, mint cacao, lavender honey, and brown sugar vanilla bean are always ready for the regulars. If raspberry rose, green tea, or Earl Grey are on offer, make sure to jump on it because these flavors only appear once every blue moon. Carmela makes wonderfully crisp and buttery waffle cones in house, so skip the cup and go straight for a cone. It's worth the extra splurge. **Additional Location:** 7920 W. 3rd St., Los Angeles, CA 90048; (323) 944-0232; carmelaicecream.com.

FURTHER EXPLORATION:
MOTHER MOO CREAMERY

In nearby Sierra Madre, Karen Klemens churns out organic ice creams in interesting flavors like raw honey and salty chocolate at **Mother Moo Creamery** (17 Kersting Ct., Sierra Madre, CA 91024; 626-355-9650; mothermoo.com). The seasonal offerings are always inspired and stretch one's definition of what a proper ice cream flavor can be.

Cool Haus, 59 E. Colorado Blvd., Pasadena, CA 91105; (310) 424-5559; eatcoolhaus.com; Ice Cream; $. For a complete description, see p. 283.

The Gourmet Cobbler Factory, 33 N. Catalina Ave., Pasadena, CA 91106; (626) 795-1005; thegourmetcobblerfactory.com; Dessert; $. Rustic cobblers handmade with locally grown fruit are the star attraction at Pasadena's Gourmet Cobbler Factory. For the past 16 years, the Powell family has been baking their signature sweets at this modest shop located off Colorado Boulevard. Cobblers come in a range of sizes, from single servings to trays large enough to feed a village, as well as a number of flavors including peach, apple, mixed berry (blueberry, strawberry, raspberry, blackberry), cherry, and lemon meringue. While the fruity fillings walk the fine line between sweet and tart, the carefully woven crusts atop each one are golden and flaky; the combination of flavors and textures satisfies to the moon. Cobblers are baked continuously throughout the day, which means that the chances of getting your grubby paws on a fresh-from-the-oven creation are high no matter when you drop in. In addition to the usual lineup of cobblers, the Powells also bake sweet potato and pecan pies and prepare seafood gumbo daily.

La Monarca Bakery, 1001 Mission St., South Pasadena, CA 91030; (626) 403-6860; lamonarcabakery.com; Bakery; $. For a complete description, see p. 227.

Little Flower Candy Company, 1422 W. Colorado Blvd., Pasadena, CA 91105; (626) 304-4800; littleflowercandyco.com; Dessert; $. Christine Moore's Little Flower Candy Company may very well be the happiest place in Pasadena. It's simply impossible not to beam when there are puffy marshmallows and silky caramels to be had. Here at this cozy cafe on the edge of town, this former pastry chef produces positively pillowy marshmallows in flavors like vanilla, cinnamon sugar, coffee, and chocolate. The highlight is the granulated sugar that coats the marshmallows, contrasting wonderfully with their uniquely bouncy texture. They're bundled four to a pack to keep sugar binges in check. The handmade caramels that launched the shop are equally dazzling. If it's too hard to decide between the lemon-, vanilla-, or sea salt–flavored candies, skip the packaged sets and grab a few of each flavor from the jars next to the cash register. The fresh baked goods on hand, including brownies, cookies, and tarts, are just as notable as the candies. Early birds come for the spectacular cinnamon rolls, which are simultaneously gooey and flaky—the best of both worlds.

Pappa Rich, **100 W. Green St., Pasadena, CA 91105; (626) 440-0009; Malaysian; $.** Located on the corner of De Lacey and Green in Old Pasadena, Pappa Rich is the first American outlet of a wildly popular chain of Korean bakeries called Pappa Roti. The shop has an undeniable log cabin vibe due to its bevy of wooden furniture and accents. The air smells strongly of mocha. The thing to get here are the buns, which will forever be likened to breasts thanks to the magnificent prose of Jonathan Gold. They're gloriously soft, inexplicably airy, and somehow crisp pastries that are served warm at all hours of the day.

FURTHER EXPLORATION: COCOHODO

Cocohodo (3500 W. 6th St., Los Angeles, CA 90020; 213-382-8943; cocohodo.co.kr/coco_e), a popular Korean chain specializing in *hodo kwaja* (walnut cakes), is making inroads into the local scene with a branch in Koreatown in the back of Zion Market. The little walnut-shaped pastries are served hot and are filled with a sweet red bean filling. There's a walnut in the center that gives all the homesick Koreans a little hop in their step.

Best of all is the barely melted pat of butter hidden toward the center that seems to meld with the pastry. It's a decadent touch that makes the bun all the better. Sweet, savory, and rich, this is indeed the "Father of All Buns."

Sarkis Pastry, 1111 S. Glendale Ave., Glendale, CA 91205; (818) 956-6636; sarkispastry.com; Bakery; $. Growing up in a family of bakers, it was only natural that brothers Sarkis and Vazken Kolanjian would open a sweets shop after fleeing Beirut, Lebanon, and arriving in Glendale in 1974. The brothers debuted Sarkis Pastry in 1983, offering a bountiful and beautiful selection of Near Eastern and European pastries. Displayed alongside delicate cream puffs, croissants, and éclairs are over a half dozen varieties of baklava, sheets of phyllo dough layered with nuts and sweetened with rosewater-tinged sugar syrup. There's also *maamoul*, dense pucks filled with crushed pistachios or walnuts with a shortbread exterior made from farina and butter; a slight essence of rosewater perfumes this sweet as well. Also delightful are the *lokma*, doughnutlike pastries that are formed into round, bite-size balls or long, extruded bites and soaked in sugar syrup. The pastries that employ *kunafa*, fine filaments of dough that resemble shredded wheat, are texturally fascinating. Try the one filled with a mildly sweetened cream cheese. **Additional Location:** 1776 E. Washington Blvd., Pasadena, CA 91104; (626) 398-3999.

FURTHER EXPLORATION: PANOS PASTRY

Panos and Alberta Zetlian, who opened the first **Panos Pastry** in 1953 in Beirut, reestablished the business in 1981 on Hollywood Boulevard upon immigrating to Los Angeles (5150 Hollywood Blvd., Los Angeles, CA; 323-661-0335; panospastry .com). The Zetlians make 10 varieties of baklava, as well as a plethora of Near Eastern sweets.

Specialty Stores, Markets & Producers

Cook Books by Janet Jarvits, 1388 E. Washington Blvd., Pasadena, CA 91104; (626) 296-1638; cookbookjj.com. Set aside the better part of a day for visiting Cook Books by Janet Jarvits. With over 30,000 used and rare cookbooks tucked away on towering shelves and stacked along every dusty surface, it's easy to lose track of time as you delve into several decades' worth of Betty Crocker tomes and volumes of spiral-bound community fund-raising cookbooks. Jarvits has an encyclopedic knowledge of the collection and is happy to assist you with locating any specific rarities; otherwise, peruse the store's offerings at your leisure. New books are constantly being tracked down at thrift stores, from private clients, and at estate sales, adding to an already robust collection.

FURTHER EXPLORATION: COOKBOOKS PLUS AND CARAVAN BOOK STORE

Mimi Hiller's **Cookbooks Plus** (24267 Main St., Newhall, CA 91321; 661-296-4455) in Santa Clarita offers 17,000 new and used cookbooks for sale either in person or online. While the culinary collection at **Caravan Book Store** (550 S. Grand Ave., Los Angeles, CA 90071; 213-626-9944) in Downtown isn't as vast as Jarvits's and Hiller's, it's still worth poking around every so often for one-of-a-kind finds.

Schreiner's Fine Sausages, 3417 Ocean View Blvd., Glendale, CA 91208; (818) 244-4735; schreinersfinesausages.com. Family-owned by Walt Schreiner and his son Wally since 1952, Schreiner's Fine Sausages boasts one of the best meat counters in town. House-smoked meats including the shop's famous Black Forest–style ham and Canadian bacon are always on hand, as well as sausages of all stripes in flavors like Cajun, chorizo, and Portuguese. Most impressive of all is Schreiner's selection of uniquely Bavarian encased meats that are made in-house, including *landjager* (semidried sausage), *thuringer* (regional German sausage), *bierwurst* (Bavarian cooked and smoked sausage), and knackwurst (overstuffed hot dog). The vast stock can be daunting for the uninitiated, but the dirndl-donning staff is always ready to help. Shopping on an empty stomach is encouraged Mon through Sat 9 a.m. to 5:30 p.m., when the market's teeny restaurant serves up simple sandwiches made from Schreiner's best-selling sausages and meats. The regular meaty lineup includes *bockwurst*, Polish sausages, jalapeño sausages, knackwurst, Black Forest ham, roast beef, and corned beef. All items in the deli case are available too, so pipe up if a favorite isn't scrawled on the wipe board. All sandwiches are served on a crisp french roll with mayonnaise, mustard, and pickles. Order a warm Bavarian pretzel sprinkled with coarse salt and served with yellow mustard to share.

FURTHER EXPLORATION: EUROPEAN DELUXE SAUSAGE KITCHEN

Sausage enthusiasts have been heading to Beverly Hills' **European Deluxe Sausage Kitchen** (9109 W. Olympic Blvd., Beverly Hills, CA 90212; 310-276-1331; germansausages.info) since 1948 for German, Italian, and Polish sausages, as well as *biltong*, South African jerky.

Westside

Beverly Hills, Brentwood, Cheviot Hills, Culver City, Marina del Rey, Mar Vista, Palms, Pico-Robertson, Rancho Park, Santa Monica, Sawtelle, Venice, Westwood

Foodie Faves

A-Frame, 12565 W. Washington Blvd., Culver City, CA 90066; (310) 398-7700; aframela.com; Hawaiian; $$. While Chef Roy Choi's Kogi truck and Chego are as fast and casual as they come, A-Frame is a full-service "modern picnic" channeling the aloha spirit. Communal tables, do-it-yourself silverware, and perfectly sensible enamelware complete the picnicking theme in this once hoppin' IHOP. Everyone starts with a bowl of "Blazin' J's Hawaiian-Style Kettle Corn." Every fistful of buttery kernels brings a hit of sweetness from Corn Pops, sourness from dried pineapples, savoriness from bacon, spiciness from cayenne pepper and chili flakes, and a whole lot of umami from *furikake*. The clam chowder channels Thailand rather than New England with its distinct lemongrass, green curry, and coconut milk notes, and the results are moreish to the extreme. Beth Kellerhals, the queen of sweets at all of Chef Choi's restaurants, whips up pound cake cinnamon *churros* like it's nobody's business. Her seasonal bacon banana cream pie is an in-your-face bacon and banana bonanza. It's impossible not to have a ball at A-Frame.

FURTHER EXPLORATION: SUNNY SPOT

Chef Choi explores Caribbean-inspired fare at **Sunny Spot** (822 W. Washington Blvd., Marina del Rey, CA 90292; 310-448-8884; sunnyspotvenice.com), his "roadside cookshop" a few beats away from Venice Beach. Kick back and relax over Jamaican Roasted Lamb with lettuce wedges and pickled mango, then finish with the We Be Yammin, a sweet potato tart with marshmallow ice cream.

Cut, 9500 Wilshire Blvd., Beverly Hills, CA 90212; (310) 276-8500; wolfgangpuck.com; Steak House; $$$$. Chef Wolfgang Puck's Cut is a cut above the other steak houses in town with its posh setting inside the Regent Beverly Wilshire Hotel, sleek Richard Meier–designed interior, and world-class selection of steaks. While starters and sides are often afterthoughts at protein palaces, here at Cut the appetizers are as memorable as the main event. There's prime sirloin steak tartare with mustard and an herb aioli, as well as warm veal tongue with baby artichokes, marinated shelling beans, and *salsa verde*. Most swoon-worthy of all is the Bone Marrow Flan, a creamier, smoother marrow experience heightened by a mushroom marmalade and parsley salad. When it's time to dig into the meat of the matter, choose from an arsenal of corn-fed USDA Prime cuts aged anywhere from 21 to 35 days. Luxurious cuts of Australian, Japanese, and American Wagyu steaks are also available for a caloric and financial splurge. Every steak is grilled over hardwood and charcoal and then finished under a 1,200-degree broiler. The former infuses the steak with a smoky char, while the latter forms a juice-sealing crust. Side dishes are thoughtful, but quite rich; they include a splashy macaroni and cheese, a potato *tarte tatin* filled with a ragout of leeks and onions, and creamed spinach with a fried organic egg.

Echigo, 12217 Santa Monica Blvd., Los Angeles, CA 90025; (310) 820-9787; Japanese; $$$. The spirit of Sushi Nozawa lives on at this beloved Westside haunt, where the rice is warm and vinegary while the fishes are cool and ultra-fresh. Tucked onto the second floor of a mini-mall, this decade-old restaurant specializing in Edomae-style sushi isn't much of a looker, but the ambiance is beside the point with Chef Toshi at the helm. Ordering piece by piece is perfectly nice, but sitting at the bar for the *omakase* is even better. It's a properly orchestrated affair in which fishes are served from mildest to strongest. *Hamachi* leads off, making way for *toro* (tuna belly), then halibut, scallop, bonito, *kanpachi* (amberjack), and any number of others depending on what's fresh and available at the market. Every *omakase* finishes with a blue crab hand roll that should be consumed as soon as possible to take full advantage of the seaweed's snap. While dinner is reasonably priced compared to other restaurants of similar quality, lunchtime is a straight-up steal.

800 Degrees Neapolitan Pizzeria, 10889 Lindbrook Dr., Los Angeles, CA 90024; (424) 239-5010; 800degreespizza.com; Pizza; $. The students at UCLA just might have it all—pleasant weather year-round, a beautiful sprawling campus, a winning basketball team, and 800 Degrees. Restaurateur Adam Fleischman (**Umami Burger** [p. 68], **Red Medicine** [p. 260], and **Umamicatessen** [p. 69]) debuted this fast-casual Neapolitan pizza concept in 2012, and lines haven't let up since. Whereas most gourmet pies around town are priced well over $10, the ones here start at half that. Even better is how quickly each pizza is constructed. After choosing from a dizzying array of toppings, from artichokes to anchovies to bacon to ricotta, watch as your pizza is blistered in a wood-fired oven—it's ready to go before you can say "mozzarella." Be sure to request an extra well-done crust to avoid soggy centers. Take the guesswork out of dinner by choosing from one of the "specialty pies." The Piccante with gooey gobs of *mozza*, *sopressata* (salami), garlic, and Calabrian chiles is true to its name in the best way possible. The Tartufo with truffle cheese, mushrooms, roasted garlic, and arugula crosses the $10 barrier but is worth the splurge. An array of salads, a burrata bar, "small bites" (meatballs, truffle cheese bread, and the like), and L.A. Creamery gelato round out the menu.

Farmshop, 225 26th St., #25, Santa Monica, CA 90402; (310) 566-2400; farmshopla.com; New American; $$$. Think of Farmshop as Los Angeles' version of Yountville's famed Ad Hoc. Jeff Cerciello, the restaurant's "Culinary Director," spent 13 years with the Thomas Keller Restaurant Group and most notably assisted with the launch and operation of Ad Hoc. With Farmshop, Chef Cerciello draws inspiration from Ad Hoc's concept, style, and philosophy. Top-notch ingredients are sourced locally, service is efficient and professional, and the mood is calm and casual. The restaurant excels at every meal, but weekend brunches (the french toast and pastrami are a must), family-style dinners (featuring four seasonally inspired courses for a set price), and Fried Chicken Sundays are especially of note. If a proper sit-down meal isn't in the cards, Farmshop's larder and bakery offer top-notch takeaways like house-made scones, imported cheeses, and thoughtfully prepared sides and mains.

Fig Restaurant, 101 Wilshire Blvd., Santa Monica, CA 90401; (310) 319-3111; figsantamonica.com; New American; $$$. Hotel restaurants have an unfortunate reputation for being stodgy places with uninspiring fare, but that isn't the case at Santa Monica's Fairmont Miramar Hotel, where Chef Ray Garcia takes the season's bounty and prepares it in as uncomplicated a fashion as possible. "The techniques I use to prepare Fig's signature dishes are simple and straightforward.

Just great ingredients prepared and presented with a minimum of fuss to bring out the best of what nature has already created." The restaurant takes the field-to-fork philosophy even further with an official forager on staff. Kerry Clasby travels from San Francisco to San Diego searching for the region's best ingredients and delivers them straight to Fig's kitchen. To start, there are things like braised beef tongues with tomatillos and breakfast radishes, and the infamous Bacon-Wrapped Bacon, well-marbled pork belly slices draped in bacon on a bed of avocado-dressed lettuce and tomatoes. Main courses are fashioned both heavy and light, from the Pastaless Lasagna to the short rib and pancetta meat loaf. Brunch brings a bevy of thoughtful tacos, gussied up *chilaquiles*, and chorizo and corned beef hash.

Gjelina, 429 Abbot Kinney Blvd., Venice, CA 90291; (310) 450-1429; gjelina.com; New American; $$$. It's hard to say what's prettiest at Gjelina: the chef, the waitstaff, or the dining room. Prettiness matters little though, when the kitchen's cooking is this satisfying. Most everything on the menu is centered on a wood-burning oven, including blissfully blistered pies topped with house-made charcuterie and farmers' market produce. There's one dazzled up with lamb sausage, confit tomato, rapini, pecorino, and Asiago and another with salted anchovy, smoked mozzarella, roasted red pepper, and capers. While both make excellent choices, they barely scratch the surface of the dozen-plus exquisitely dressed pizzas on offer. To pair with the pies, order a few of the simple but exquisitely prepared vegetables, sourced mostly from the Santa Monica farmers' market. Summer's sweet corn is braised and seasoned with cilantro, chiles, feta, and lime, while okra is seared then garnished with black olives, tomato, pine nuts, and mint. Even something as seemingly ordinary as a kale salad is worth raving about; this one is topped with shaved fennel, radish, lemon, ricotta salata, and bread crumbs. Small and large plates like braised pork meatballs and fettuccine with lamb sausage round out Chef Travis Lett's cast of delightful characters. Gjelina Take Away (or GTA), a next-door annex to the restaurant, is a terrific option for pizza, antipasti, and sandwiches for diners on the go.

Hannosuke, 3760 S. Centinela Ave., Los Angeles, CA 90066; (310) 397-4676; Japanese; $. When executed with a deft hand, deep-frying can transform the mundane into the insane. Tokyo's famed Kaneko Hannosuke takes tempura rice bowls (*tendon*) to great heights at its first US outlet inside the West Los Angeles Mitsuwa Marketplace. Whether it's a pristine fillet of fish or a simple slice of sweet potato, the experts behind the fryers make sure that each ingredient is coated evenly in a golden, bubbly crust that's crisp and hardly greasy. Best of all is the slightly sweet and sticky "secret sauce" that coats every ingredient before it lands atop the glossy grains of rice. The Original Tendon includes a flaky fillet of whitefish, shrimp, nori (dried seaweed), *kakiage* (shrimp and scallop), *shishito* pepper, sweet potato, and a downright amazing poached egg. The batter and deep-fry elevates an already dreamy runny yolk to otherworldly status. In addition to the original tempura bowl, there's the Edomae Tendon that replaces the whitefish with *anago* (salt-water eel), Shrimp Style, and Vegetable Style. Every bowl is served with miso soup and *gari* (pickled ginger).

Honey's Kettle, 9537 Culver Blvd., Culver City, CA 90232; (310) 202-5453; honeyskettle.com; Fried Chicken; $. For a complete description, see p. 220.

Kiriko Sushi, 11301 W. Olympic Blvd., #102, Los Angeles, CA 90064; (310) 478-7769; kirikosushi.com; Japanese; $$$$. Ken Namba was destined to be a sushi chef. Born and raised in Tokyo, he spent his formative years in the kitchens of his mother's restaurants inside the famous Tsukiji Market, the largest wholesale seafood market in the world. Chef Namba honed his craft in Ecuador, Bali, and Malaysia

before opening Kiriko in L.A.'s Little Osaka in 1999. Sushi aficionados flock here for dependably delightful fare executed with creativity, flair, and modern flourishes. While ordering a la carte is perfectly acceptable, for the quintessential Kiriko experience, snag a seat at the counter and leave your dining fate in the hands of Chef Namba and his associates. The small plates-focused *omakase* changes with the seasons, as well as marketplace offerings, but expect to be dazzled by house-made tofu sprinkled with bonito in a delicate soy broth, exquisite monkfish liver topped with garlic and soy sauce, and briny sea urchin risotto served in its spiky shell. The house-smoked salmon, sliced thickly and precisely and served atop loosely packed rice, could very well be the best bite of all.

Lotería! Grill, 1251 3rd St. Promenade, Santa Monica, CA 90401; (310) 393-2700; loteriagrill.com; Mexican; $$. For a complete description, see p. 43.

Mayura Indian Restaurant, 10406 Venice Blvd., Culver City, CA 90232; (310) 559-9644; mayuraindianrestaurant.com; Indian; $. Before settling in Los Angeles and opening Mayura in Culver City, Aniyan Puthanpu-Rayil owned a similarly spirited restaurant in his home state of Kerala in the southwest region of India. While the restaurant's menu offers the usual samosas and chicken *tikka masala,* the specialties here hail from South India, specifically Kerala. To accommodate both vegetarian and carnivorous clients, Mayura prepares meaty offerings in a separate kitchen to avoid any possible contamination. For first-timers and regulars alike, the *dosas* are a must. These crisp, paper-thin crepes made from a rice and lentil batter come stuffed with things like seasoned potatoes, spinach, and cheese. The Ghee Roast Dosa arrives perched upright like a tepee and painted with melted butter. A spicy and tangy *sambar* (a stew made of vegetables and lentils), as well as coconut chutney, is served on the side for dipping. Also spectacular here is the *Dum Biryani*, another Kerala specialty combining basmati rice with moist chicken and a ton of spices. Located on the Malabar Coast, Kerala is also famous for its seafood preparations. The Kerala Fish Curry, salmon fillets bathing in a creamy and assertive broth, is served with spongy pancakes made from fermented rice flour (*appam*) that soak up the curry and deliver it with ease.

Mélisse, 104 Wilshire Blvd., Santa Monica, CA 90401; (310) 395-0881; melisse.com; French; $$$$. When Chef Josiah Citrin opened Mélisse in 1999, he aimed to create a fine dining experience without the usual pretense and stuffiness. With its walls a fetching shade of royal purple and suited gents at diners' beck and call, Mélisse achieves a polished yet lively ambiance, just as intended. The setting here, a little modern and a touch traditional, is fitting of Chef Citrin's local, sustainable, and ingredient-driven cuisine. Diners select from a trio of prix-fixe menus, allowing the kitchen to show its stuff in a way that a la carte dining rarely achieves. There's a four-course tasting menu that can be extended with supplements and additional courses, a vegetarian tasting menu, and a carte blanche menu orchestrated by the chef. The restaurant's signature *amuse bouche*, a single grape encrusted in goat cheese and coated with crushed pistachio, is almost always the first bite to land on the table. It's a tart, rich, and creamy mouthful that awakens the palate for what's to come. The Egg Caviar, a soft-poached egg accented with caviar and lemon-chive crème frâiche, is another one of the restaurant's standbys. This egg-on-egg preparation is as satisfying as it is luxurious. The Lobster Bolognese made with fresh capellini, black truffles, and basil satisfies in taste and texture. Nearly all of the restaurant's produce is handpicked by the chef at the weekly farmers' market in Santa Monica, located just down the street from the restaurant.

Musha Izakaya, 424 **Wilshire Blvd., Santa Monica, CA 90401;** (310) 576-6330; musha.us; Japanese; $$. For a complete description, see p. 198.

N/naka, 3455 **Overland Ave., Los Angeles, CA 90034; (310) 836-** 6252; n-naka.com; **Japanese;** $$$$. A traditional Japanese *kaiseki* meal consists of many small courses designed to give a true sense of season and place. Here at N/naka, Chef Niki Nakayama draws upon the genre's traditional elements and infuses it with modern touches, creating an exceptional, original, and thoroughly beguiling experience. Chef Nakayama opened N/naka in 2011 after developing her skills in her hometown of Los Angeles and sharpening them in Japan for three years. The restaurant serves three set menus with no a la carte options, which means that reservations here are not just polite but a must. The most lavish menu is the 13-course Modern Kaiseki priced at $165. Next up are the Chef's Tasting and Vegetarian Tasting, both of which are priced at $110. Each experience includes a gentle, well-orchestrated march of modern and traditional sashimi, fried nibbles, pickled dishes, grain-centered creations, and *nigiri* near the end. The menus change from day to day, but expect to be served thoughtful things like pristine Maine lobster tartare drizzled with *uni* butter and California sturgeon caviar, and spaghetti with clams, roasted garlic, campari sauce, tomatoes, and cream. All of the vegetables are locally grown by Farmscape Gardens specifically for the restaurant, continuing a tradition that Chef Nakayama began years ago with her personal garden in Arcadia.

101 Noodle Express, 6000 **Sepulveda Blvd., Culver City, CA** 90230; (310) 397-2060; **Chinese;** $. For a complete description, see p. 164.

Picca, 9575 W. Pico Blvd., Los Angeles, CA 90035; (310) 277-0133; **piccaperu.com; Peruvian; $$.** After the tremendous success of the original Mo-Chica inside the Mercado Paloma, Chef Ricardo Zarate partnered with restaurateur Stephane Bombet to bring his brand of modern Peruvian cuisine to the Westside. Here at Picca, the music is dialed up to 11, while the crowd is pisco-fueled and boisterous. Adding to the dynamic atmosphere is a lively bar area and a laid-back upstairs lounge. The hottest seat in the house, quite literally, is along the *robata* grill, where cooks provide the evening's entertainment with smoke, flames, and all sorts of skewering. The menu, a lengthy list of ceviches, *causas*, and *anticuchos*, is meant to be shared over several rounds of cocktails. Chef Zarate's ceviches are legendary. The *ceviche mixto* dresses up squid, shrimp, fish, sweet potatoes, and nutty kernels of *choclo* (Peruvian corn) in a punchy citrus marinade. Also fabulous is the sea bass *tiradito* (Peruvian sashimi) served with a sweet potato puree. The *choritos*, steamed mussels bathed in an *aji amarillo* (Peruvian yellow chile pepper) butter broth with salty bits of pancetta, are the very definition of moreish. Another menu must-have are the *causas*, bite-size squares of mashed yellow potatoes topped with things like scallops, snow crab, and spicy yellowtail. After witnessing the *robata* grill in action all evening, a few *anticuchos* are in order. The beef hearts with a *rocoto* (red chile pepper) sauce and the beef fillet with sea urchin butter are especially brilliant. If there's still room to fill after all that nibbling and cocktailing, the flame-licked *arroz chaufa de mariscos* (seafood fried rice) or the *seco de pato* (duck leg confit) with cilantro rice will fill the pit quite nicely.

Piccolo, 5 Dudley Ave., Venice, CA 90291; (310) 314-3222; **piccolo venice.com; Italian; $$$.** This quaint spot located steps from the Venice shore serves refined Italian fare in one of the most romantic settings in town. Vittorio Viotti, a native of Rome, runs the front of the house, while Chef Bobo Ivan, a native of Venice, works his magic behind the stoves. Together the two gentlemen have created the kind of timeless dining experience that keeps Angelenos coming back time and again for special occasions and once-in-a-while splurges. The menu is laid out in traditional Italian fashion: antipasti starters, *primi* pastas, and *secondi* main courses. Begin with the carpaccio, paper-thin slices of seared lamb garnished with celery and shavings of *piave*, a kind of Italian cow's milk cheese, or crispy veal sweetbreads served over polenta and finished with truffles. The pastas, all of which are crafted in house, come filled and folded or tangled in a neat heap. The *tortelli* are prepared Venetian style with dried and salted cod and anchovies, while the squid-ink *tagliolini* is treated to a sea urchin emulsion and *bottarga* (pressed dried caviar) shavings. Even a dish as simple as the *carbonara* tastes divine under Chef Bobo's watch. Perfectly portioned pasta courses mean that everyone has room for a meaty main. The pan-seared wild duck breast with a truffled honey sauce is impressive, as is the roasted rabbit with speck, chestnuts, and figs. The kitchen also offers two "In Bobo We Trust" menus ranging from 6 to 10 courses for a set fee.

Poke Poke, 1827 Ocean-Front Walk, Venice, CA 90291; (424) 228-5132; poke-poke.com; Hawaiian; $$. The Venice boardwalk is better known for its fun-loving parade of hippies and sideshows than its culinary offerings, but Trish and Jason McVearry are changing the perception with their casual cool *poke* (Hawaiian-style tuna tartare) operation. The Venice residents opened Poke Poke directly across from Muscle Beach in 2010. There are four different varieties of "surfer's sashimi" on offer including the Original Hawaiian Poke (ahi tuna, soy sauce, sesame oil and seeds, green and white onions), Spicy Tuna Poke, Wasabi Poke, and Aloha Poke (light soy sauce, rice wine vinegar, crushed red pepper). Diners are encouraged to personalize their *poke* with special add-ons like avocado, jalapeño, and limu seaweed. In Hawaii, *poke* is eaten straight up, but the McVearrys offer brown or white rice to transform a snack into a meal. Enjoy your fresh and well-seasoned marinated ahi at one of the adjacent picnic tables and watch the local meatheads and weirdos do their thing.

Ramen Jinya, 2208 Sawtelle Blvd., Los Angeles, CA 90025; (310) 481-0977; jinya-ramenbar.com; Japanese; $. For a complete description, see p. 133.

Ramen Yamadaya, 11172 Washington Blvd., Culver City, CA 90232; (310) 815-8776; ramen-yamadaya.com; Japanese; $. For a complete description, see p. 199. **Additional Location:** 1248 Westwood Blvd., Los Angeles, CA 90024; (310) 474-1600.

Red Medicine, 8400 Wilshire Blvd., Beverly Hills, CA 90211; (323) 651-5500; redmedicinela.com; Asian Fusion; $$$. It's a crying shame that Red Medicine got off on such an awful foot during its early days after opening. First there was the uproar over the communist propaganda–inspired logo emblazoned with Ho Chi Minh's face, which was followed by the brouhaha for exposing and ejecting the *Los Angeles Times* restaurant critic. These events marred Red Medicine in the eyes of diners, which is such a pity because Chef Jordan Kahn's cooking is some of the most modern, forward, and interesting fare that the city has ever seen. As its manifesto declares, "This is not a traditional Vietnamese restaurant." Instead, Chef Kahn, the former pastry chef at the French Laundry, Per Se, and Alinea, picks and chooses flavors and ingredients from the cuisine that inspire him to create dishes that are as detailed as they are beautiful. Some of his best work is centered on vegetables. Summer's sweet corn is presented in a terrarium prettied with herbs, custard, and frozen sea urchin powder. The crowd-pleasing brussels sprouts, which are served at the bar and in the main dining room, bring caramelized shallots and fish sauce to the vegetal equation. The Heirloom Rice Porridge, adorned with a single egg yolk, hazelnuts, broccoli, and sea urchin, is easily the priciest bowl of *chao* in town, but its richness and depth are unmatched. Desserts, of course, are the chef's forte. The coconut bavarois, a creamy, well-balanced mouthful with hints of coffee, condensed milk, and Thai basil, has been a grand slam since day one.

Rustic Canyon Wine Bar & Seasonal Kitchen, 1119 Wilshire Blvd., Santa Monica, CA 90401; (310) 393-7050; rustic canyonwinebar.com; New American; $$$. While there are plenty of restaurants in town serving seasonally driven farm-to-table fare, no one executes it quite as brilliantly as Chef Jeremy Fox's team. Prior to taking the helm at Rustic Canyon, Chef Fox honed his cooking chops at Michelin powerhouses Ubuntu and Manresa in northern California. The small plates menu, which changes regularly depending on what is produced by local farmers, ranchers, and fishermen, draws on influences from throughout the Mediterranean. During the cooler months of the year, hearty offerings like fried cauliflower and lamb meatballs drizzled with mint oil dominate the menu, while summer and spring bring lighter fare like sweet corn soup and black mission fig crostini. The entire bill of fare is prepared and plated with sharing in mind, making it possible to sample a variety of dishes without ever having to lean over your dining mates' plates. To pair with the kitchen's beautiful

 plates are wines by the glass and bottles from around the world that are hand-picked by Josh Loeb, the restaurant's owner and proprietor. Saving room for a sweet finish is an absolute must when pastry genius Zoe Nathan is involved. The daily selection of trifles, cakes, ice creams, and tarts reflects the seasons as much as the savories do.

Samosa House East, 10700 Washington Blvd., Culver City, CA 90232; (310) 559-6350; samosahouse.net; Indian; $. Samosa House East hasn't been around for nearly as long as its three-decade-old sister restaurant *cum* grocery store Samosa House down the street, but the modern meatless Indian fare found here is just as exquisite, and the comfortable dining room doesn't hurt either. Both places are as casual as they come, with orders taken at the front counter and food dished out onto disposable trays. The combination plates, which include three items from the buffet (curries, kormas, and dals), basmati rice, *raita* (yogurt condiment), and tandoor baked bread (naan, *papadum*, or chapati), are popular with those dining in and taking out. The restaurant's owner Vibha Bhojak uses olive oil and ground nuts in place of traditional butter and cream, making many of the dishes found here vegan. The legitimately smoky Charcoal Smoked Cauliflower is spectacular, as is the cardamom-laced Veggie Chicken. The shredded jackfruit in masala spices is the most complex and intriguing of the bunch. If you're dining with a few friends, make room for some *chaat* (savory snacks) with your meal. The *pani puri*, crisp parcels drizzled with mint and tamarind chutneys and filled with onions, tomatoes, chickpeas, and a splash of mint water, are as fun to construct as they are to eat. And of course, don't forget the signature samosas that are served with two chutneys and a touch of spice. **Additional Location:** 11510 W. Washington Blvd., Los Angeles, CA 90066; (310) 398-6766.

Santouka Ramen, 3760 S. Centinela Ave., Los Angeles, CA 90066; (310) 391-1101; santouka.co.jp/en; Japanese; $. When the temperature's soaring in Los Angeles and pearls of sweat are dripping off one's brow, only the worthiest of noodle soups warrant a sweat bath and change of clothing. Santouka, a no-frills *ramenya* tucked inside the Mitsuwa Marketplace in Torrance and West Los Angeles, makes noodles that defy conventional cravings. Hitoshi Hatanakain founded the chain over 20 years ago in Japan. After opening the first shop in Asahikawa on the northernmost island of Hokkaido, he went on to establish more locations throughout Japan and seven outlets stateside. Santouka offers several varieties of ramen, but the signature bowl is the *shio* (salt). The broth, a blend of pork and seafood stock, has a thin layer of oil on top to keep any heat from escaping. Loved up in the mild and milky soup are curly noodles with the slightest bite, bamboo shoots, wood ear mushrooms, sesame seeds, scallions, tender cuts of *chashu* (pork), and a single pickled plum. It's a well-balanced and satisfying bowlful. The spicy miso ramen is made from the same soup base as the *shio,* but miso and chile are added in place of salt. The burn factor, which is noticeable but not overwhelming, has an addictive quality that will keep one's face buried in the bowl for the duration of the meal—dinner and a facial.

Simpang Asia, 10433 National Blvd., Los Angeles, CA 90034; (310) 815-9075; simpangasia.com; Indonesian; $. Indonesian students studying at local universities flock to Simpang Asia for a taste of home—there's only so much dining hall slop one can endure before taking a stand. Influenced by the flavors of the Middle East, China, and India, Indonesian cuisine is intensely flavorful, stick-to-your-bones fare that veers down a funky path more often than not. For those new to the genre, the *nasi bungkus* offers a swell introduction. Tightly wrapped in a banana leaf, it contains a hodgepodge of several curries and vegetables served over rice. The highlights of the parcel are the beef *rendang*, a dry curry steeped in coconut milk and spices, and the *telur balado*, a hard-boiled egg topped with a sweet chile chutney. The *pepes ikan* (fish in banana leaves), which usually appears on the restaurant's specials menu, is best suited for adventurous eaters who can handle some spice and appreciate fish bones as a textural element. Simpang Asia dedicates a section of its menu to street food classics including the *otak otak*, mellow and smooth fish cakes steamed and grilled in banana leaves and served with a sweet peanut sauce. The *lemper ayam,* which is usually tucked in a basket at the front counter, is a fantastic little snack composed of glutinous rice stuffed with shredded chicken and wrapped in banana leaves. To pair with these brashly flavored dishes, try the *es cendol*, a mung bean jelly drink with coconut milk and palm sugar, or simple avocado juice.

FURTHER EXPLORATION: JAVA SPICE

Java Spice (1743 Fullerton Rd., Rowland Heights, CA 91748; 626-810-1366) in Rowland Heights is another favorite among the local Indonesian population. The *nasi bungkus* and the *ayam kalasan* (marinated chicken in coconut water) are the chief attractions.

Sotto, 9575 W. Pico Blvd., Los Angeles, CA 90035; (310) 277-0210; sottorestaurant.com; Italian; $$$. Southern Italian cooking in all its rustic and hearty glory is celebrated in style at West Los Angeles' Sotto. After years of working together in restaurants across Los Angeles and Orange County, chefs Steve Samson and Zack Pollack finally stepped out on their own in 2011. The menu here, which features blistered Neapolitan pizzas, twisty handmade pastas, and lesser-known regional specialties, is a reflection of the chefs' shared passion for traditional Italian cooking. If you love good bread and aren't afraid of lacquering your lips with a little fat, the *lardo pestato* is a must-order at the start of every meal. Next, dig into a leopard-spotted pizza baked in an 8-ton, 900-degree Neapolitan oven. With this much firepower on hand, pizzas are cooked in 60 seconds tops. Try the *guanciale* pie with house-cured pork cheek, ricotta, scallions, and fennel pollen. Diving into pastas, the buckwheat cavati sauced with a luscious pig's head *ragù* is as satisfying as they come. If you're here for some meat, look no further than the Devil's Gulch fennel-crusted pork chop; it's been pleasing crowds since day one. A swell list of reds and whites has been chosen by Wine Director Jeremy Parzen to pair with the robust fare. The carefully curated list highlights native grape varieties from Southern Italy, of course. There's also a bumpin' cocktail program by Julian Cox. Save room for a cannoli Siciliani to finish. See chefs Samson and Pollack's recipe for **Grilled Pork Meatballs with Snap Peas, Pecorino, and Bitter Greens** on page 302.

Stella Barra Pizzeria, 2000 Main St., Santa Monica, CA 90405; (310) 396-9250; stellarossapizzabar.com; Pizza; $$. Chef Jeff Mahin, a Cal grad who's toiled in many mighty fine kitchens including L2O, The Fat Duck, Nobu, and Arzak, is producing some the city's best pizzas at this steps-from-the-ocean eatery. The key to Stella's stellar pies is the dough, which is made from milled flour from the San Joaquin Valley, filtered water, sea salt, and fresh yeast. The dough rests and ferments for 18 hours in special jars lined along the open kitchen, ensuring a crisp, golden crust with a chewy center when it comes out of the Baker's Pride gas oven. Soggy first bites are all but eliminated with this winning formula. Accenting the one-of-a-kind crusts are a bevy of farm-fresh toppings from the Santa Monica farmers' market and other local purveyors. A favorite among herbivores and carnivores alike is the pizza topped with Bloomsdale spinach, crispy purple kale, young pecorino, cracked black peppercorn, and a drizzle of extra-virgin olive oil. The interplay between the wilted spinach, smoky kale, and mild cheese is a delight. The house-made organic Italian sausage with tomato, fresh mozzarella, oregano, and fennel pollen may very well be the best pie on the menu. Peruse the "For the Table" section of the menu to supplement your spread. The prosciutto plate featuring silky slices of La Quercia's Prosciutto Rossa, house-made bread, and Chilean Olave olive oil fits in nicely with just about whatever you've got going on. **Additional Location:** 6372 W. Sunset Blvd., Los Angeles, CA 90028; (323) 301-4001.

FURTHER EXPLORATION: MILO & OLIVE

Zoe Nathan and Josh Loeb of Stella Rose didn't intend to open a pizzeria when they scooped up the space at 2723 Wilshire Blvd. in Santa Monica. The initial plan was to use the kitchen to relieve the overworked ovens at **Huckleberry Bakery & Cafe** (p. 284), their bustling bakery and cafe a mile away. But one thing led to another, a pizza dough was developed and a wood-burning Mugnaini oven was installed, and thus, **Milo & Olive** (2723 Wilshire Blvd., Santa Monica, CA 90403; 310-453-6776; miloandolive.com) came to be. The pizzas here are top rate, especially the ones featuring house-made pork belly sausage and mushrooms. The crust is reminiscent of Nancy Silverton's at **Pizzeria Mozza** (p. 51). See Chef Nathan's recipe for **Chocolate Hazelnut Scones** on page 318.

Sugarfish by Sushi Nozawa, 4722¼ Admiralty Way, Marina del Rey, CA 90292; (310) 306-6300; sugarfishsushi.com; Japanese; **$$$.** For a complete description, see p. 66. **Additional Locations:** 1345 2nd St., Santa Monica, CA 90401; (310) 393-3338. 11640 W. San Vicente Blvd., Los Angeles, CA 90049; (310) 820-4477.

Superba Snack Bar, 533 Rose Ave., Los Angeles, CA 90291; (310) 399-6400; superbasnackbar.com; Italian; $$. Restaurateur Paul Hibler and Chef Jason Neroni joined forces in 2012 to open Superba Snack Bar, a postmodern take on an Italian *pastaria*. Previously, Hibler was the owner and creator of the popular chainlet Pitfire Pizza, while Chef Neroni was the executive chef at Osteria La Buca. The charming open-air space spills out onto a street-side patio, capturing a slice of Venice life on every plate. The menu here features "Cold Cuts" (house-made charcuterie and accoutrements), "Snacks" (miscellaneous morsels), "From Our Backyards" (farmers' market vegetables), and "From Our Hands" (handmade pastas). Everything is priced just under the $20 mark to encourage communal nibbling over a bounteous spread. The fried duck egg with *papas bravas* (Spanish-style fries), truffle vinaigrette, and prosciutto from the "Snacks" portion of the menu features a wobbly yolk that ties all of the ingredients together with a rich and glossy sheen. The pastas are wildly creative, especially the Smoked Bucatini *carbonara*, which has the distinct essence of burning embers imparted into every strand. There's also the Casarecce, scroll-like pastas served with crispy sardines, preserved lemons, and *bottarga* (pressed dried caviar) bread crumbs. It's the unofficial mascot of the restaurant due to the pasta's distinct "S" shape.

Sushi Zo, 9824 National Blvd., Los Angeles, CA 90064; (310) 842-3977; Japanese; $$$$. Pristine fishes served with a side of 'tude are the specialty at Sushi Zo. While some diners might be turned off by the stern "sushi etiquette" enforced at the restaurant, it's best to think of these guidelines as helpful suggestions to enhance one's dining experience. According to Chef-Owner Keizo Sek, when eating sashimi or *nigiri,* it is best to only dip a small corner of each piece into soy sauce, and to consume each piece fish-side down. Granted, these protocols are a touch neurotic, but one go-round of the chef's *omakase* and you'll see that it's not so bad. In fact, it's damn good. It all begins with Kumamoto oysters served chilled or drizzled with *ponzu*. Up next is a seemingly endless parade of sashimi and *nigiri* punctuated by flourishes of monkfish liver, sea urchin, squid, and scallops. Keizo insists on warm rice with his *nigiri*, which complements the cool cuts of fish in an immensely satisfying fashion. A meal at Zo is a must for sushi aficionados.

FURTHER EXPLORATION: SUSHI HIKO

A former disciple of the venerable Chef Kazunori Nozawa, Chef Shinji Murata serves a strictly sashimi and *nigiri* menu at **Sushi Hiko** in Palms (11275 National Blvd., Los Angeles, CA 90064; 310-473-7688). While the spirit of this restaurant is similar to that of Zo's, the prices are reasonable enough to make it a weekly splurge.

Tar & Roses, 602 Santa Monica Blvd., Santa Monica, CA 90401; (310) 587-0700; tarandroses.com; New American; $$$. Named after the tasting notes characteristic of wine made from Nebbiolo grapes, Tar & Roses serves up wonderfully charred small and large plates in a lively neighborhood setting. The man behind the behemoth wood-fired oven is Chef Andrew Kirschner. He spent the last decade honing his craft at Joe's in Venice, Chadwick in Beverly Hills, Table 8 in West Hollywood, and Wilshire in Santa Monica before opening his own place in early 2012. The modern and rustic menu here is divided into four sections: Snacks, Small, Veggies, and Large. If you're down with grazing over half a dozen plates rather than sticking to a single main course, then this place is just your speed. Take a cue from the restaurant's name and sip a glass or share a bottle of Barolo. The full-bodied red holds up well to Chef Kirschner's cooking. While perusing the everything-sounds-incredible menu, snack on a bowl of caramel corn spiked with chile and dotted with bacon. It's sweet, spicy, salty, and completely addictive. Another little bite that's worth considering is the chicken oysters on a stick served with a cilantro and tamarind sauce. The oysters, round pieces of dark meat on the back of poultry near the thigh, are juicy little things. The roasted bone marrow here is served with a pickled onion marmalade, *gremolata* (a mixture of lemon zest, garlic, and parsley), sea salt, and sourdough. Chef Kirschner has a way of composing plates that are fantastically well balanced, where every yin has its yang. The star of the larger plates is the whole wood-roasted branzino served with a seasonal risotto, like Meyer lemon in the winter or fava bean during spring. In addition to the regular menu offerings, Tar & Roses also serves "T&R Suppers," three-course meals presented family style, for larger parties. Choose from wood-fired goat, whole goose, standing rib back, or a shellfish pot. Advance reservations are required.

Tara's Himalayan Cuisine, 10855 Venice Blvd., Los Angeles, CA 90034; (310) 836-9696; tarashimalayancuisine.com; Himalayan; $$. Here at Tara's Himalayan Cuisine, Tara Gurung Black shares soulful and hearty dishes from her native Nepal with Westside dwellers. Bordered by China to the north and India to the south, Nepal's flavors, textures, and spices are greatly influenced by both countries. Black, a professional dancer and onetime member of the Royal Dance Academy of Nepal, was so taken by Los Angeles when she visited for a performance that she returned years later to open her namesake restaurant here. The *kothey momo*, steamed or pan-fried dumplings stuffed with chicken or vegetables, are a must to start. The essence of cumin and coriander brings out the stuffing's sweetness, while the wrappers possess a pleasant chew. *Thukpa* or "Sherpa's Stew," a kind of Nepalese noodle soup, warms with chiles and satisfies with a combination of heady spices and tender yak meat. The *khasi ko masu*, slow-cooked bone-in goat meat simmered in a fresh tomato sauce with Himalayan spices, is as comforting as it gets either spooned over rice or scooped with chapati. The *aloo bodi tama* (bamboo shoots, potatoes, and black-eyed peas simmered with mountain-grown spices), yak chili, and chicken *korma* are all dependably delicious. Dine with a group and order up a Nepalese storm because 10 percent of the restaurant's profits go toward education in Nepal.

The Tasting Kitchen, 1633 Abbot Kinney Blvd., Venice, CA 90291; (310) 392-6644; thetastingkitchen.com; New American; $$. When Venice's A.K. Restaurant Bar + Grill proved to be a poor fit for the neighborhood, Chef Casey Lane from Clarklewis in Portland was called in to transform the fledgling restaurant into The Tasting Kitchen. Along with his former Clarklewis crew, he morphed the Scandinavian eatery into an ingredient-driven powerhouse featuring a daily changing "Bill of Fare" drawing on Italian, French, Moroccan, and Spanish cuisines. The space, the epitome of California cool, coupled with the kitchen's incredible cooking, has made this one of the toughest reservations in town. Most everything on the menu is made from scratch, from the pickles to the charcuterie. To start are strong cheeses and cured meats, as well as thoughtful small plates featuring clams with chorizo and white beans, and polenta with a truffled egg. Moving on to larger plates, there are fishes prepared a myriad of ways and delicate pastas ranging from classics like *bucatini all'amatriciana* to more unusual creations like the tagliatelle with pork, apple, and sage. Weekend brunch is just as fabulous, especially the savory waffles paired with "Fried Clucks" and the sausage biscuit sandwiches ladled with rich gravy.

Tsujita L.A. Artisan Noodle, 2057 Sawtelle Blvd., Los Ange-les, CA 90025; (310) 231-7373; tsujita-la.com; Japanese; $$. There's a ramen renaissance happening in Los Angeles, and Takehiro Tsujita's namesake *ramenya* is at the center of it all. Located in the Little Osaka neighborhood of West Los Angeles, Tsujita is a branch of Nidaime Tsu-jita, considered one of Tokyo's best noodle houses. It's hard to decide between the restaurant's two signature dishes, ramen and *tsukemen*, which are both only served at lunchtime. The Hakata-style *tonkotsu* (pork bone) ramen is slowly simmered for 60 hours, which results in a viscous, milky broth that sings the song of swine. While it might be a touch excessive to layer on a few slices of *chashu* (braised pork) atop an already porky broth, the tender meat is worthy of a splurge. Heck, add on a seasoned boiled egg while you're at it. The bowl of noodle soup before you may very well be the holy grail of ramen in this town. The *tsukemen* here is also something special. A bowl of cool, curly noodles is served bare, with just a sheet of nori (dried seaweed) and a wedge of lime, along with an uber-savory broth made from bonito (a type of fish), dried sardines, and pork and chicken bones. To eat, dip the noodles into the broth, swirl them around, and deliver them neatly to your lips. Repeat with a dash of black *shichimi* (Japanese chile powder) and a squeeze of lime until your heart's content.

FURTHER EXPLORATION: TSUJITA ANNEX

Forgo the hour-long lines at Tsujita L.A. Artisan Noodle and head across the street to sister restaurant **Tsujita Annex** (2050 Sawtelle Blvd., Los Angeles, CA 90025; 310-231-0222), where the same cult-favorite tsukemen ramen is served at both lunch and dinner. Additionally, the Annex serves tonkotsu shoyu (soy sauce) ramen.

Umami Burger, 500 Broadway, Santa Monica, CA 90401; (310) 451-1300; umami.com; American; $$. For a complete description, see p. 68. **Additional Location:** 1131 Westwood Blvd., Los Angeles, CA 90024; (310) 943-8626.

Urasawa, 218 N. Rodeo Dr., Beverly Hills, CA 90210; (310) 247-8939; Japanese; $$$$. When Chef Masa Takayama departed Los Angeles to open his eponymous restaurant in New York City, his pupil Hiroyuki Urasawa took over the diminutive second-floor restaurant to continue the tradition of serving peerless Japanese fare. Here at this 10-seat cypress counter, Chef Urasawa orchestrates a world-class *kaiseki* experience that wouldn't be out of place in Tokyo's famed Ginza district. Every meal begins with a series of intricate seasonal dishes, followed by traditional sushi that are utterly enchanting. Signature dishes like the tableside *foie gras shabu shabu* and seared *toro* wrapped around monk-fish liver with caviar, as well as masterfully prepared *nigiri*, have made Urasawa a premier dining destination for gourmands across the globe. A meal here ends simply with fresh fruit, a composed dessert, and a bottomless mug of *hojicha* (roasted green tea). Urasawa provides an exquisite feast for the senses, exhibiting truly unparalleled professionalism, dedication, and attention to detail. This experience comes at a premium, but it is as worthy a splurge as there ever was.

Waraya, 11678 W. Olympic Blvd., Los Angeles, CA 90064; (310) 478-3090; Japanese; $$. For a cool spot to drink, eat, and revel the night away with a group of friends, head to West L.A.'s Waraya, where Japanese *izakaya* meets Korean-kissed fare. While establishments specializing in late-night carousing aren't usually of the highest caliber, Waraya is an exception to the rule. Here, beer, sake, and *soju* flow freely, while small plates are prepared with care. Grab a seat at the sushi bar or mosey on back to one of the larger tables. Start with a few pieces of sashimi, *nigiri,* or a simple *maki* roll or two, then progress to hot plates that run the gamut from kimchee pancakes to deep-fried Jidori chicken (*karaage*) to Berkshire pork sausage to sizzling *bulgogi* (marinated beef). Place an order for everything at once or play it by ear like the regulars do, selecting a few choice plates at a time. Among the menu highlights is a Korean-style beef tartare garnished with julienned pear and topped with pine nuts and an egg yolk; a hit of sesame oil brings it all together. The warmth of the *agedashi* tofu, deep-fried silken tofu in a savory broth, is just the thing to settle tummies full of liquor.

L.A. Landmarks

The Apple Pan, 10801 W. Pico Blvd., Los Angeles, CA 90064; (310) 475-3585; American; $. If you're lucky enough to snag one of the 26 red patent swivel chairs lining The Apple Pan's horseshoe counter, then you're in for burger bliss. Alan and Ellen Baker opened the diner in 1947, and very little has changed over the years—the antique cash register still cha-chings when orders are rung up, while sodas are served in conical paper cups with metal holders. The behind-the-counter brigade even still dons paper hats and white aprons. Despite the changing times and neighborhood, this beloved institution clings on tightly to these treasured traditions. The Apple Pan's two signature burgers were developed by Alan Baker in 1905 while in Cleveland, Ohio. The Hickoryburger is composed of a crumbly, well-seared beef patty with mayonnaise, pickles, lettuce, and a tangy house-made barbecue sauce. Add a slice of Tillamook for a few cents extra. It's a saucy and thoughtful creation that's been charming the pants off burger lovers since opening day. The Steakburger is nearly identical to the Hickoryburger save for the secret sauce. In its place is a smashing relish that brightens the entire meaty package. The Apple Pan bakes over 100 pies a day using age-old family recipes. The famous banana cream pie dates back to

1886 and was developed by Alta Spear Gamble in Ravenwood, Michigan. Every slice is masterfully constructed from a mountain of thinly sliced bananas, vanilla pudding, and a buttery crust.

Bay Cities Italian Deli & Bakery, 1517 Lincoln Blvd., Santa Monica, CA 90401; (310) 395-8279; baycitiesitaliandeli.com; Italian; $. Bay Cities Italian Deli & Bakery has been delighting Santa Monica residents since 1925 with its well-stocked aisles of Italian, Argentine, Greek, French, and Middle Eastern specialty foods, fresh pasta made on-site, full-service deli, and crusty loaves of house-baked bread. While the groceries are top-notch, what really brings all the boys to the yard is the famous Godmother sandwich. The hype surrounding what amounts to a gussied-up hoagie is nothing short of tremendous. Legions of passionate patrons endure long lines, nightmarish parking, and gruff South Philly–style customer service for the pleasure found between two slices of hefty Italian bread. Add some sauce and spice to the Godmother by ordering

FURTHER EXPLORATION: CLARO'S ITALIAN MARKET

Claro's (claros.com) has been providing fancy imported Italian goods to Eastside dwellers since 1948. The market's deli is especially of note, with made-to-order sandwiches, prepared foods, cold cuts, and desserts for the taking. Three locations in the Los Angeles area (and three others elsewhere):

19½ E. Huntington Dr., Arcadia, CA 91006; (626) 446-0275
159 E. College St., Covina, CA 91723; (626) 339-3333
1003 E. Valley Blvd., San Gabriel, CA 91776; (626) 288-2026

it with the works, which includes mayonnaise, yellow mustard, onions, pickles, tomatoes, lettuce, Italian dressing, and a hot pepper salad, in addition to the mountain of Genoa salami, mortadella, coppacola, ham, prosciutto, and provolone that's already included. To avoid the chaotic crowds, place your order online (bcdeli.com/order.html) 8 a.m. to 4:45 p.m. Tuesday through Sunday.

Border Grill, 1445 4th St., Santa Monica, CA 90401; (310) 451-1655; bordergrill.com; Modern Mexican; $$$. Chefs Mary Sue Milliken and Susan Feniger, longtime luminaries in the Los Angeles culinary scene, opened the very first Border Grill restaurant in 1985 after a life-changing road trip through Mexico where they learned traditional recipes and techniques from street hawkers, market vendors, and home cooks. Their temple of modern Mexican cuisine has since expanded to Downtown Los Angeles and to Las Vegas at the Mandalay Bay Hotel & Casino, in addition to the original location that relocated to Santa Monica. Every meal begins with complimentary warm tortilla chips served with a trio of salsas. While it's very possible to fill up on those alone, you'd be remiss not to try the green corn tamales served with sour cream and *salsa fresca*, as well as the quinoa fritters drizzled with *aji amarillo* (Peruvian yellow chile pepper) aioli. The slow-roasted Yucatan pork served with handmade corn tortillas, yams, brussels

FURTHER EXPLORATION: SUSAN FENIGER'S STREET

Chef Feniger struck out on her own in 2009 to open **Susan Feniger's Street** (742 N. Highland Ave., Los Angeles, CA 90038; 323-203-0500; eatatstreet.com), a vibrant restaurant set in Hollywood with a menu drawing inspiration from around the globe. You won't be able to resist the Singaporean kaya toast, which expertly teeters between sweet and savory.

sprouts, and pineapple jicama salsa has been the restaurant's best-seller and signature dish since the early days. For a less formal taste of the "Too Hot Tamales'" unique brand of Mexican food, follow the Border Grill Truck on Twitter (@BorderGrill) to see if it's in or around your neighborhood. See chefs Milliken and Feniger's recipe for **Quinoa Fritters with Aji Amarillo Aioli** on page 304.

Father's Office, 1018 Montana Ave., Santa Monica, CA 90403; (310) 736-2224; fathersoffice.com; New American; $$. Father's Office, which was founded back in 1955, didn't make a splash in the Los Angeles culinary scene until Chef Sang Yoon took it over in 2000 and transformed the dingy haunt on Montana Avenue into a European-inspired bar serving seasonal fare and world-class beers. Chef Yoon's early efforts paved the road for the mushrooming gastropub scene in the city today. While the list of tipples served here is truly stellar, it's the Office Burger that dominates the headlines. This dry-aged beef burger topped with caramelized onions, gruyère and Maytag cheeses, bacon compote, and arugula and served on a soft roll has been declared the best gourmet burger by local and national press. It's hard to live up to hype this grand, but in the case of the Office Burger, the superlatives are merited. Don't ask for ketchup to

---

FURTHER EXPLORATION: LUKSHON

Chef Yoon's latest restaurant, **Lukshon** (3239 Helms Ave., Culver City, CA 90232; 310-202-6808; lukshon.com), is located in the same Culver City Helms Bakery complex as the second outpost of Father's Office. The menu takes a modern approach to Southeast Asian cuisine. The shrimp toast, spicy lollipop chicken, and sour sausage-stuffed squid pack 'em in, as do the gratis desserts at the end of the night.

go with your burger and fries; Chef Yoon detests the stuff and refuses to carry it at either of his two Father's Office locations. Same goes with substitutions; leave your picky palate with the bouncer at the door. Food and drink orders are placed at the bar and will be delivered to your table as soon as they're ready. **Additional Location:** 3229 Helms Ave., Los Angeles, CA 90034; (310) 736-2224.

La Serenata de Garibaldi, 10924 W. Pico Blvd., Los Angeles, CA 90064; (310) 441-9667; laserenataonline.com; Mexican; $$$. For a complete description, see p. 111.

Lawry's the Prime Rib, 100 N. La Cienega Blvd., Beverly Hills, CA 90211; (310) 652-2827; lawrysonline.com; American; $$$. Crowds have been lining up for Lawry's famous standing rib roast since 1938, when Lawrence L. Frank and Walter Van de Kamp opened the carvery. Today, the restaurant is still operated by the founding families and remains as popular as ever. The menu includes Atlantic lobster tails, a fresh fish of the day, and even a vegetarian special, but most everyone who walks through the doors zeroes in on the flesh served upon polished silver carts. The restaurant offers five different prime rib cuts of varying heft and girth ranging from the petite California Cut to the double-size, bone-in Beef Bowl Cut. Every prime rib dinner includes Lawry's "Famous Original Spinning Bowl Salad," a blend of romaine, iceberg, spinach, beets, chopped eggs, and croutons in a "vintage" dressing, decadent mashed potatoes, Yorkshire pudding, and a side of grated fresh horseradish and seasoned whipped cream. If additional sides are in order, the creamed corn and spinach are excellent choices.

Matsuhisa, 129 N. La Cienega Blvd., Beverly Hills, CA 90211; (310) 659-9639; nobumatsuhisa.com; Japanese; $$$$. Drawing from 20 years of experience working in sushi bars from Tokyo to Lima, Nobuyuki "Nobu" Matsuhisa opened Matsuhisa in 1987. Here at his first namesake restaurant in Beverly Hills, Chef Nobu introduced South

American flavors to Japanese cuisine, gussying up austere dishes with assertive ingredients like garlic, chiles, and even butter. There are straightforward sashimi, sushi rolls, and tempura, of course, but it's the Matsuhisa Special Dishes that set this institution apart from the countless sushi counters in town. Slices of utterly fresh yellowtail are adorned with paper-thin jalapeño, while *toro* tartare is decadently topped with caviar. Black cod steeped in sweet miso and baked to flaky perfection is the restaurant's sweet and savory signature dish. For the ultimate Matsuhisa experience, request a seat at the sushi bar and opt for the *omakase* (chef's choice), which starts at $90 per person and includes traditional sushi, as well as a tour of the chef's greatest hits.

Pacific Dining Car, 2700 Wilshire Blvd., Santa Monica, CA 90403; (310) 453-4000; pacificdiningcar.com; Steak House; $$$. For a complete description, see p. 77.

Spago, 176 N. Canon Dr., Beverly Hills, CA 90210; (310) 385-0880; wolfgangpuck.com; New American; $$$$. Chef Wolfgang Puck arrived in Los Angeles in 1975 to head the kitchen at Ma Maison, Los Angeles' most fashionable restaurant at the time. After making a name for himself at this storied French restaurant, he moved to open Spago on the Sunset Strip in 1982. Here, he topped pizzas with smoked salmon and caviar and paired goat cheese with roasted beets, shaping a distinct vision of California cuisine that influenced a generation of culinarians including chefs Nancy Silverton, Quinn Hatfield, and Suzanne Goin. Spago relocated to its current flagship in Beverly Hills in 1994. In true Los Angeles fashion, the restaurant celebrated its 30th anniversary in 2012 with a little nip and tuck. The dining room was given a sleeker and more modern makeover, while the menu transitioned to small plates with an emphasis on farm-to-table fare. Chef Puck's longtime confidant Chef Lee Hefter is charged with executing the menu's newest additions. Appetizers fall under "Raw, Wild & Organic" or "Decadent & Indulgent." Filed under the former category is a solid rendition of Chirashi Sushi made with bluefin tuna, yellowtail, salmon pearls, and sea urchin,

while the Aonori Soba Pasta with Dungeness crab and Matsutake mushrooms is the highlight of the latter group. The agnolotti stuffed with the
season's bounty is a relic from the original Spago menu. Main courses
come "From the Sea," "From the Pasture," and "From the Garden." The
Hong Kong–style steamed Maine lobster for two, as well as the whole
roasted Chinese duck, are as delicious as they are luxurious.

FURTHER EXPLORATION: CHINOIS ON MAIN

A year after launching Spago, Chef Puck opened **Chinois on
Main** in Santa Monica (2709 Main St., Santa Monica, CA
90405; 310-392-9025; wolfgangpuck.com/restaurants/fine-
dining/3654). The menu featuring Asian fusion dishes prepared
with California ingredients and French culinary technique was
a wonder at the time. For a taste of the classic Chinois experience, order the famous chicken salad, barbecued baby pork ribs
with soy-honey glaze, and a whole sizzling catfish with ginger
and *ponzu* sauce.

**Tito's Tacos, 11222 Washington Pl., Culver City, CA 90230; (310)
391-5780; titostacos.com; Mexican; $.** From Oaxaca to Jalisco to
Nayarit, the cuisine of nearly every Mexican state can be found somewhere in Los Angeles. Even with the rising awareness and occurrence of
regionalized Mexican fare, there's still a soft spot in Angelenos' hearts
for hard-shell tacos, preferably from Tito's Tacos in
Culver City. Since 1959, the folks at Tito's have
been serving a stream of regulars a steady
diet of crunchy corn shell parcels layered
with seasoned and shredded beef, iceberg
lettuce, and grated cheddar cheese. It's
an all-American taco with a Los Angeles

soul. Aside from the classic tacos, there are burritos, beef and chicken tamales, enchiladas, tostadas, and *chili con carne*. Eat at the picnic tables, either inside or out, or take everything to go.

Valentino Ristorante, 3115 Pico Blvd., Santa Monica, CA 90405; (310) 829-4313; valentinorestaurants.com; Italian; $$$. It's hard to imagine that Valentino, a bastion of Italian fine dining, began in a run-down bar on an unsavory stretch of Santa Monica back in 1972. Under the careful management and direction of Owner Piero Selvaggio, the restaurant that once served heavily sauced American-Italian fare in a not-so-nice part of town evolved into a world-class dining room that shaped Italian food in California. Valentino was one of the first restaurants in town to import Italian rarities like fresh mozzarella and black and white truffles to create dishes with an inspired Italian soul. Today the kitchen is helmed by Sardinian-born Chef Nicola Chessa, who offers a prix-fixe menu, as well as a la carte selections. He has a way with pasta, and the *Pappardelle al Cioccolato con Salsa d'Aragosta* with lobster and cherry tomatoes is exemplary, as is the lasagna with duck *ragù* and porcini mushrooms. Every dish is deep-rooted in traditional Italian cooking, but with modern touches that make it quintessentially Valentino. The wine cellar is as robust as ever. Selvaggio has been passionate about discovering great wines from all over the world since the restaurant's early days, and Valentino has been the recipient of the *Wine Spectator* Grand Award every year since 1981.

 **Sublime Sweets**

Bulgarini Gelato, 8686 Washington Blvd., Culver City, CA 90232; (310) 815-1723; bulgarinigelato.com; Gelato; $. For a complete description, see p. 242.

Churros Calientes, 11521 Santa Monica Blvd., Los Angeles, CA 90025; (424) 248-3890; churroscalientes.com; Spanish; $. Indulge in Spanish-style *churros* served with a mug of thick, amaretto-laced hot chocolate at Churros Calientes, a jewel box of a cafe owned by Sandro Finoglio and chef'd by Eric Bonillo. Grab a seat at the bar or at one of the sidewalk tables while your order is being prepared. *Churros* are always fried to order, assuring that each one is evenly golden, crisp, and ready to be eaten straight up or dipped in bittersweet chocolate first. *Churros* drizzled with *dulce de leche*, strawberry, and chocolate sauces are a touch less rich, but really just as satisfying. A savory Spanish-Venezuelan menu of panini, *bocadillos* (sandwiches), salads, and soups is also served here.

Clementine, 1751 Ensley Ave., Los Angeles, CA 90024; (310) 552-1080; clementine online.com; Bakery; $. Chef Annie Miler isn't reinventing the wheel at her Westside bakery, just executing classic pastries to exacting standards. Come in for a seasonal salad, soup, or sandwich for lunch and stay for exceptional sweets. Or better yet, arrive early for the most robust selection of baked goods and take lunch to go. Chef Miler, who opened the adorably named Clementine in 2000, trained in London at Le Cordon Bleu and in the kitchens of Mark Peel's Campanile, Wolfgang Puck's **Spago** (p. 278), and Nancy Silverton's **La Brea Bakery** (p. 73). Here at Clementine, she prepares her grandmother's treasured recipes using professional know-how and technique, and the results are tremendous. Cookies range from simple chocolate chips and molasses crinkles to fancier cranberry-walnuts with brown butter icing. The bevy of breakfast breads, including wonderful apricot-ginger scones, Apple-Dapple cake, and Saturday-only cinnamon rolls, never fail to put a little skip in everyone's step. The best sweet of all is the banana cake with cream cheese frosting—it's moist, but not too dense, and decadent yet restrained somehow. The savory pastries including quiches, flatbreads, and buttermilk biscuits with ham are equally dreamy. **Additional Location:** 9346 Civic Center Dr., Beverly Hills, CA 90210; (310) 461-0600.

Compartes Chocolatier, 912 S. Barrington Ave., Los Angeles, CA 90049; (310) 826-3380; compartes.com; Candy; $. Founded in 1950 on the principle of bringing European chocolate techniques, recipes, and artistry to the United States, Compartes Chocolatier continues to make its mark on the city's sweets landscape even after 60 years in the business. Much of the credit goes to Jonathan Grahm, a chocolate "prodigy" who took over his family's shop at the age of 15. Here at the Brentwood chocolate factory and storefront, Grahm hand makes chocolates from scratch daily using the best ingredients available including single-origin chocolate from South America, fruits from local farmers' markets, and locally sourced organic nuts. Visit the store on a weekday to catch a glimpse of the magic in process. The flavors of Compartes' chocolates and truffles range from traditional to daring. From the original line of confections are roasted choc-olate-covered nuts, chocolate turtles, chocolate-covered caramels, home-made marshmallows, and choc-olate-dipped apricots. Influenced by his global travels, Grahm has added wildly inventive flavors to the lineup including smoked sea salt, mango and saffron, Kaffir lime and lemongrass, and olive oil and rosemary. It will be interesting to see what the next generation of chocolatiers has in store for this confectionary institution.

Cool Haus, 8588 Washington Blvd., Culver City, CA 90232; (310) 424-5559; eatcoolhaus.com; Ice Cream; $. Cool Haus, which explores the intersection between food and architecture, deconstructs ice cream sandwiches into a cookie roof and floorboard with ice cream walls. After introducing these quirky frozen wares at the Coachella Valley Music Festival in 2009 out of a broken-down postal truck found on Craigslist, founders Natasha Case and Freya Estreller took the Los Angeles gourmet food truck scene by storm. Today, the Cool Haus gals have a fleet of four trucks in Los Angeles (follow @CoolHaus on Twitter for location updates), two trucks and a cart in New York City, two trucks in Austin, and stores in Culver City and Pasadena. "Farchitecture," as it turns out, offers mass appeal. Choose from sandwiches named after famous architects and designers like the Richard Meyer Lemon Ginger and the Frank Behry, or create your very own Cool Haus. The brown butter and candied bacon ice cream on chocolate chip cookies isn't architecturally significant, but the flavors are through the roof. With a dozen varieties of cookies to choose from, like double chocolate sea salt, peanut butter, and red velvet, and even more ice cream flavors, including dirty mint, fried chicken and waffles, and Peking duck, the combinations are endless. Every ice cream sandwich is wrapped in an edible, calorie-free wrapper.

Harajuku Crepes, 9405 S. Santa Monica Blvd., Beverly Hills, CA 90210; (310) 285-3946; harajukucrepe.us; Japanese; $. Rio Hirashima wasn't taken with the crepes he encountered in Los Angeles when he arrived in 2005. Instead of the springy, stretchy, conical specimens that he was used to in Japan, he found traditional French ones that were perfectly nice, but hardly a taste of home. Rather than wait for sporadic trips back to Japan or for someone to fill the niche, Hirashima took matters into his own hands and opened Harajuku Crepe in 2009. While French crepes are mostly sit-down affairs, the Japanese style is a portable creation wrapped in paper and rolled into a cone. The batter, which is available in green tea, Earl Grey, buckwheat, and original, is made from glutinous rice powder (*mochi*), which yields a crispy and elastic texture like no other crepe around. Fruits (bananas, strawberries, blueberries, raspberries, apples), sauces (Nutella, chocolate, caramel, peanut butter, jam), ice cream (vanilla, chocolate, green tea, strawberry), and homemade whipped cream add the final flourishes. It's hard to go wrong mixing and matching the various toppings, but for the ultimate Japanese experience, go with a green tea crepe garnished with red beans, *mochi*, green tea ice cream, and whipped cream.

FURTHER EXPLORATION: FOUR LEAF

Little Tokyo's **Four Leaf** (318 E. 2nd St., Los Angeles, CA 90012; 213-621-2559; fourleaftearoom.com) serves a diverse selection of sweet and savory Japanese-style crepes, including one that straddles both categories—the "Garden of Eden" with fig chutney, brie, and honey whipped cream.

Huckleberry Bakery & Cafe, 1014 Wilshire Blvd., Santa Monica, CA 90401; (310) 451-2311; huckleberrycafe.com; Bakery; $. Following the tremendous success of **Rustic Canyon Wine Bar & Seasonal Kitchen** (p. 261), husband-and-wife team Zoe Nathan and Josh Loeb opened Huckleberry Bakery & Cafe a stone's throw away. While the breakfast, lunch, and brunch menus are all perfectly pleasant, especially the Green Eggs & Ham made with La Quercia prosciutto, pesto, and arugula on an English muffin, it's the counter lined with freshly baked goods that's worth all the fuss. There are always seasonal fruit crostatas and tarts on hand, as well as dozens of menu mainstays with a devoted following. The salted caramel bar with its buttery shortbread crust and silky, salt-flecked caramel is the stuff of dreams. The impossibly flaky maple bacon biscuits deliver on both sweet and savory fronts. Shmearing softened butter on their surface is probably going overboard, but these biscuits make you want to live a little. Come early to snag one of the city's best croissants; options include plain, Valrhona chocolate, or prosciutto gruyère. See Chef Zoe Nathan's recipe for **Salted Caramel Bars** on page 316.

FURTHER EXPLORATION:
SWEET ROSE CREAMERY

Dessert wiz Zoe Nathan churns her way into ice cream lovers' hearts at **Sweet Rose Creamery** in the Brentwood Country Mart (225 26th St., Ste. 51, Los Angeles, CA 90402; 310-260-2663; 826 Pico Blvd., Santa Monica, CA 90405; 310-260-2663; sweetrosecreamery.com). The bite-size bonbons and decadent sundaes never fail to elicit a smile.

Jin Patisserie, 5741 Buckingham Pkwy., Ste. D, Culver City, CA 90230; (310) 399-8801; jinpatisserie.com; Dessert; $. With hand-crafted chocolates, artisanal teas, and spectacular cakes, it's no surprise that Jin Patisserie is a major chick magnet. Kristy Choo, the shop's proprietor, was passionate about food while growing up in Singapore, but didn't think to make it a career until she began tasting sweets from around the world as a flight attendant. She left her mile-high days behind to attend San Francisco's California Culinary Academy, where it was reaffirmed that artful cakes, cookies, and chocolates were her true calling. Choo's globally influenced sweets are meticulously crafted and showcased at Jin Patisserie. Chocolates come in flavors like lemongrass, passion fruit, jasmine, and ginger, while cookies highlight lavender, matcha, and chocolate chip. Also try the Ye Yek, a melt-in-your-mouth Singaporean shortbread cookie. Best of all are the cakes, which could be mistaken for works of art. The Inspiration matches caramel with bittersweet chocolate with a touch of sea salt, while the Spring Bouquet, which is only available on weekends, meshes fluffy meringue with sweet cream and fresh mangoes and strawberries.

K Chocolatier by Diane Krön, 9606 Santa Monica Blvd., Beverly Hills, CA 90210; (310) 248-2626; dianekronchocolates.com; Candy; $. Diane and Tom Krön first took the chocolate world by storm in the 1970s with their Budapest Crème Truffles and chocolate-covered strawberries at Krön Chocolatiers. The business was sold in the 1980s in order for the couple to have time off with their children. Itching to make chocolate again after a decade-long hiatus, the Kröns opened K Chocolatier in Beverly Hills in 2000. The chocolates made here are inspired by age-old family recipes dating back to four generations of Hungarian chocolate makers. The cacao beans are sourced from a range of international suppliers depending on what is best at the moment. In line with tradition, added sugars are kept to a minimum, while fruits, nuts, marzipan, and mint bring a bit of sparkle to each jewel. The famous Budapest Crème Truffles, which are made daily using the finest whipped cream, dark chocolate, cacao powder, and rum, are as timeless as ever. The boozy chocolates filled with tequila, vodka, and scotch are irresistibly potent. **Additional Location:** 3835 Cross Creek Rd., Malibu, CA 90265; (310) 317-0400.

La Monarca Bakery, 1300 Wilshire Blvd., Santa Monica, CA 90403; (310) 451-1114; lamonarcabakery.com; Bakery; $. For a complete description, see p. 227.

Le Bon Garçon, lebongarcon.com; Candy; $. Justin Chao launched the Le Bon Garçon gourmet caramel company online in 2010 after studying pastry arts in Paris at the Bellouet Conseil and at Michelin three-star Le Meurice. His French training greatly influenced his craft. All of Le Bon Garçon's caramels are made from scratch using the best ingredients and no preservatives. Every batch is painstakingly stirred by hand and meticulously wrapped. The resulting candies are incredibly silky and pleasingly chewy without being overly sticky. Molars are left scot-free at the end of a caramel binge, which is quite a feat in the world of soft candies. It's quality you can really sink your teeth into. Le Bon Garçon's suite of flavors includes rich and buttery Salted, bright and tangy Mango-Passion Fruit, sweet and nutty Macadamia, and boozy Rose.

Primo's Westdale Donuts, 2918 Sawtelle Blvd., Los Angeles, CA 90064; (310) 478-6930; primosdonuts.com; Doughnuts; $. Celia and Ralph Primo purchased a failing doughnut shop on a whim for $2,000 back in 1956. The impulsive decision turned out to be a perfect fit for the couple, who nursed the shop back to health and transformed it into a doughnut destination. Today, deep-fried dough seekers descend upon this homey mom-and-pop shop to fill up on old-fashioned buttermilk bars, dense little pucks full of crags and brushed with a sweet glaze. Primo's cake doughnuts, which come plain or iced in chocolate, cherry, or maple, are sensationally moist and hardly bogged down by oil; they're some of the very best cake doughnuts the city has to offer.

FURTHER EXPLORATION: STAN'S DOUGHNUTS

Serving the Westwood Village community since 1965, **Stan's** (10948 Weyburn Ave., Los Angeles, CA 90024; 310-208-8660; stansdoughnuts.com) offers over 75 varieties each day, from standard rings and bars to signature specialties like The Huell, a yeast-risen doughnut filled with peanut butter and topped with chocolate icing and chocolate chips. The Custard Puff pairs cool, smooth, and vanilla-tinged custard with soft dough and a thin coat of chocolate frosting.

Saffron & Rose Ice Cream, 1387 Westwood Blvd., Los Angeles, CA 90024; (310) 477-5533; Ice Cream; $. While there are many vibrant Persian establishments in Tehrangeles, the stretch of Westwood Boulevard between Olympic and Wilshire, none are quite as sweet as Saffron & Rose Ice Cream. The shop is named after its signature flavor, a creamy and floral amalgam tinged with saffron and dotted with pistachios. There's a nutless version available as well, but the man scooping behind the counter always insists on the one with the bright green pistachios. Nearly everyone who walks through the door orders a scoop of the saffron rose, which can be sandwiched between two thin crispy waffles upon request. In addition to its namesake flavor, the shop offers over a dozen other options ranging from fascinating (orange blossom, white rose, date) to familiar (chocolate, strawberry, vanilla). Try a scoop of poppy seed slush or *faloodeh*, a semi-frozen dessert consisting of thin cornstarch noodles in a sugar and rosewater syrup, with your ice cream for extra Persian flair. Aside from its perfumelike profile, Persian ice cream is also notable for its one-of-a-kind texture. Whether eaten with a spoon or one's tongue, the ice cream seems to push back with each bite. These scoops play hard to get, so proceed with extra napkins to avoid a messy breakup.

Schulzies Bread Pudding, 1827 Ocean Front Walk, Venice Beach, CA 90291; (510) 783-3464; schulziesbreadpudding.com; **Dessert; $.** Warm, gooey, and rich bread pudding is just about the last thing that one wants to eat while donning a bikini, but that didn't stop Sarah Schulz from launching Schulzies Bread Pudding in the heart of Muscle Beach. Here, at this casual walk-up a few steps from the bustling boardwalk, bread pudding is reimagined with the weather and local tastes in mind. Schulz has created 108 different bread pudding flavors that are served chilled, just like ice cream. A scoop of Salted Caramel Sutra gets drizzled with sweet and salty caramel, while the Cookies N Creme Dream is topped with real cream. The Essential Earl Grey, which is one of Schulz's favorite flavors, is served straight up. The dozen or so flavors featured each day change often and usually reflect what's in season. Come autumn, the Pumpkin Pie in the Sky! is a must. San Francisco's famed Blue Bottle Coffee is brewed on the premises.

Scoops, 3400 Overland Ave., Los Angeles, CA 90034; (323) 405-7055; Ice Cream; $. For a complete description, see p. 94.

Sprinkles Cupcakes, 9635 S. Santa Monica Blvd., Beverly Hills, CA 90212; (310) 274-8765; sprinkles.com; Dessert; $. Husband-and-wife team Charles and Candace Nelson launched the West Coast cupcake craze in the heart of Beverly Hills when they opened Sprinkles back in 2005. While cupcakes are not as hot to trot as they were a few years ago, there's no denying that the ones baked here are fabulous enough to transcend trends. The bestseller from the start has been the red velvet, a flavor that Candace developed as an homage to her husband's Oklahoma roots. The deeply hued cake is made with Callebaut cocoa, while the frosting is a well-balanced cream cheese number. The nostalgia of childhood birthday cakes is captured beautifully in the Vanilla Milk Chocolate cupcake, Madagascar bourbon vanilla cake frosted with fudgy milk chocolate cream cheese and adorned with French chocolate sprinkles. Slowly but surely, the Nelsons are taking over this stretch of S. Santa Monica Blvd.: Sprinkles ATM and Sprinkles Ice Cream debuted in 2012. While the former delivers a sweet fix to cupcake lovers 24 hours a day via robot claw, the latter churns out organic ice creams with a Sprinkles twist (red velvet ice cream on a red velvet cone, anyone?), as well as a line of Momofuku Milk Bar–esque cookies. **Additional Location:** 735 S. Figueroa St., #210, Los Angeles, CA 90017; (213) 228-2100.

SusieCakes, 11708 San Vicente Blvd., Los Angeles, CA 90049; (310) 442-2253; susiecakes.com; Bakery; $. Susan Sarich celebrates her grandmothers' baking traditions with all-American cakes, cupcakes, and cookies made from scratch using only the best ingredients around at this Westside bakery. The store's glass case is lined with carefully frosted layer cakes in flavors like red velvet, German chocolate, carrot, and coconut. Each one is available by the slice, as well as in miniature cupcake form. The tender cakes and thick frostings are equally sugary, so be prepared for an avalanche of unbridled sweetness either way. Also special here are the velvety smooth, hand-stirred puddings topped with fresh whipped cream. There's banana pudding with vanilla wafers, butterscotch toffee pudding, and classic chocolate pudding. For those in no mood for cake or pudding, Susie offers a fetching collection of pies, cookies, and bars too. The baseball-size Whoopie Pies sandwich a generous dollop of vanilla frosting in between two soft yet substantial chocolate cookies, while Susie's Nutty brings together chewy peanut butter cookies with peanut butter buttercream. These utterly rich and decadent baked goods are meant to be enjoyed with a tall glass of cold milk, just like Susie did years ago while hanging out in her grandmothers' kitchens after school.

Sweet Lady Jane Bakery, 1631 Montana Ave., Santa Monica, CA 90403; (310) 254-9499; sweetladyjane.com; Bakery; $. For a complete description, see p. 97.

Specialty Stores, Markets & Producers

Mitsuwa Marketplace, 3760 S. Centinela Ave., Los Angeles, CA 90066; (310) 398-2113; mitsuwa.com/english. For a complete description, see p. 210.

Surfas, 8777 W. Washington Blvd., Culver City, CA 90232; (310) 559-4770; surfaslosangeles.com. Professional chefs and serious home cooks have been shopping for hard-to-find equipment, ingredients, and supplies at Surfas since 1937. The Culver City warehouse showroom carries everything under the culinary sun from the mundane to the seemingly strange. There's an extensive selection of baking supplies (fondant, pastry tips, prefabbed flowers, etc.), cutlery, and cookware, of course, not to mention seriously obscure ingredients like "meat glue," carrageenan, and xanthan gum. Truly, this is a one-stop shop to stock your modernist pantry. Come in for a sauté pan and leave with cans of imported anchovies, a chef's coat, and a tart pan—it's that kind of a place.

Recipes

Guelaguetza's Mole Negro

Guelaguetza has expanded and contracted since its opening in 1994, but the stellar cooking by matriarch Maria Monterrubio has remained dependably delicious over time, especially her Oaxacan moles. This pitch-black mole negro is rightfully famous with its 26 ingredients and unparalleled sweet and savory depth. In the restaurant, it's sauced over chicken, stuffed in banana leaf–wrapped tamales, and ladled atop enchiladas.

Serves 12

For chicken broth:

1 whole chicken	½ garlic clove
1 onion, trimmed and peeled	2 Hoja Santa leaves

For mole negro:

250 grams chilhuacle chiles	1 teaspoon marjoram
250 grams mulato chiles	1 cinnamon stick
250 grams ancho chiles	1 tablespoon anise seed
250 grams pasilla chiles	100 grams pumpkin seeds
1 cup vegetable oil	1 teaspoon ground cloves
2 onions, chopped	1 teaspoon allspice
1 garlic clove, minced	Dash cumin
2 plantains, peeled and sliced	1 kilogram red tomatoes
300 grams pan de yema	500 grams green tomatillos
100 grams sesame seeds	250 grams Oaxacan chocolate
150 grams almonds	100 grams granulated sugar
100 grams raisins	1 nutmeg, grated
2 teaspoons oregano	Salt
2 teaspoons thyme	1 teaspoon black pepper

Prepare chicken broth

Place chicken in a large pot and cover with water along with onion and garlic clove. Cook on high heat until bubbles begin to break through the surface of the liquid. Turn heat down to medium low so that stock maintains a low, gentle simmer. Skim the scum from the stock with a spoon or fine-mesh strainer every 10 to 15 minutes for the first hour of cooking and twice each hour for the next 2 hours. Add hot water as needed to keep the chicken submerged. Simmer uncovered for 6 to 8 hours. Add Hoja Santa leaves after the broth has finished cooking. Set aside.

Prepare mole negro

Remove the seeds from the chiles and place on a griddle over low heat. Roast the chiles until crispy and dark brown, almost black in color. Rinse the chiles in hot water then place in a bowl of cold water to soak for 30 minutes. Puree chiles in a food processor and set aside.

In a large saucepan over medium-high heat, heat ½ cup of vegetable oil until it shimmers. Add onion, garlic, plantains, pan de yema, sesame seeds, almonds, and raisins and sauté until ingredients are golden brown. Then, add oregano, thyme, marjoram, cinnamon, anise, pumpkin seeds, cloves, allspice, and cumin to lightly toast. Puree the mixture in a food processor and set aside.

In a large pot over medium heat, cook the whole tomatoes and tomatillos until juices are released and skins are loosened. Be sure to stir continuously. Once the liquid has come to a boil, remove from heat and set aside.

In a small saucepan over medium-high heat, combine the chocolate with 4 cups of water. Whisk continuously until the chocolate fully dissolves and the mixture is perfectly smooth. Remove from heat and set aside.

In a large pot over medium-high heat, heat the remainder of the vegetable oil until it shimmers. Add the pureed spice mixture and stir for 10 minutes, then add in the chiles and stir for 10 more minutes. Add the tomato and tomatillo mixture and stir for 5 minutes. Bring the mixture to a boil and add the chocolate, sugar, and nutmeg and stir for 5 more minutes.

Strain the chicken broth and slowly add it to the mole sauce along with the carved chicken. Add salt and pepper to taste.

Let the mole boil for an addition 15 minutes, stirring constantly. Serve immediately.

Recipe courtesy of Guelaguetza Restaurant (p. 30)

Lotería! Grill's Salsa Verde Chilaquiles

After devoting nearly 2 decades to an advertising and film production career, Jimmy Shaw left the Hollywood scene behind to open Lotería! Grill at the Original Farmers Market on Third and Fairfax in 2002. His aim from the start was to share the regional dishes of his native Mexico in a modern and comfortable setting. Traditional Mexican breakfast is served all day here, including three versions of chilaquiles, smothered tortilla chips garnished with queso fresco and crema. This recipe for Salsa Verde Chilaquiles is tangy, comforting, and just the thing to cure a hangover.

Serves 4

For salsa verde

8 medium tomatillos (1½ pounds), husked and rinsed

1 serrano chili or jalapeño, stemmed

½ white onion, trimmed, peeled, and halved

2 garlic cloves, trimmed and peeled

½ bay leaf

Pinch of dried oregano

Pinch of dried thyme

½ teaspoon salt

¼ cup low-sodium chicken broth

1 tablespoon corn oil

For fried corn tortillas

Vegetable oil, for frying

12 corn tortillas (6-inch)

For chilaquiles

2 large eggs, beaten

½ cup shredded Monterey Jack cheese

2 tablespoons crumbled queso fresco or mild feta

3 tablespoons finely chopped white onion

1 tablespoon finely chopped fresh cilantro

Crema fresca or sour cream, for garnish

Prepare salsa verde

Place the tomatillos, chili, onion, and garlic in a medium-size pot and cover with water. Bring to a boil. Simmer for about 15 to 20 minutes, until the vegetables are soft and the tomatillos turn pale green. Remove from heat to cool slightly.

Transfer the boiled vegetables, along with the cooking water, to a blender. Puree for a few seconds to blend; be sure to hold down the lid with a towel for safety. Add the herbs, salt, and broth and puree until smooth. This should produce about 1 quart of salsa verde. Set aside.

Put a pot over medium-high heat and coat with the oil. When the oil is hot, pour in the tomatillo sauce; it will bubble a bit. Reduce the heat to medium and simmer for 10 to 15 minutes until the sauce is slightly thickened, stirring occasionally. Keep warm while assembling the chilaquiles.

Prepare fried corn tortillas

Pour about 2 inches of oil in a heavy-bottomed pot or countertop deep fryer and heat to 375°F. Stack the tortillas and fan them with your thumb to separate. Cut the tortillas into triangles, 8 per tortilla.

Working in batches, fry the tortilla chips, turning them with a skimmer or slotted spoon so they don't stick together, until golden brown, about 2 to 3 minutes. Transfer the chips to a paper towel–lined baking pan or brown paper bag to drain. Return the oil to the proper temperature between batches. Set fried corn tortillas aside to cool.

Prepare chilaquiles

Pour the salsa verde into a wide pot or pan over medium heat. Just when it starts to bubble, stir in the beaten eggs. Cook and stir for about 5 seconds until the egg feathers into the sauce to thicken and bind.

Immediately add the chips, tossing gently until they have absorbed enough sauce and become soft. Take care not to break the chips. Sprinkle with Monterey Jack cheese on top. To serve, pile the chilaquiles on a large platter or onto 4 individual dishes. Sprinkle with queso fresco, onion, and cilantro, and garnish with crema fresca.

Tip: *This dish can be made with store-bought unsalted tortilla chips.*

Courtesy of Chef Jimmy Shaw of Lotería! Grill (p. 43)

Good Girl Dinette's
Chicken Curry Potpie

American diner meets Vietnamese comfort food at Good Girl Dinette, a High-land Park treasure. The good girl behind the operation is Chef Diep Tran. Her most popular creation is this chicken curry potpie that marries traditional Vietnamese curry with an all-American buttermilk biscuit. The deep-yellow madras broth pairs masterfully with its flaky, buttery hat.

Serves 5

For buttermilk biscuits

3½ cups all-purpose flour, or as needed

2 teaspoons kosher salt

3½ teaspoons baking powder

11 tablespoons very cold unsalted butter, cut into 1-inch cubes

1¼ cups buttermilk

For chicken curry

2 tablespoons canola oil

2½ pounds bone-in chicken thighs, skin removed

¼ cup madras curry powder

2 lemongrass stalks, tops trimmed, bases halved lengthwise and smashed

3 white onions, cut into ¾-inch dice

½–¾ cup fish sauce

4 large carrots, peeled and cut into ¾-inch dice

3 large Yukon Gold or baking potatoes, peeled and cut into ¾-inch dice

1¼ cups coconut milk

Prepare buttermilk biscuits

Have ready 5 24-ounce oval (or 7-inch round) gratin dishes.

In a large bowl, whisk the flour, salt, and baking powder to combine. Transfer 1 cup of the dry ingredients to a food processor, and sprinkle with the cubes

of butter. Pulse 5 to 7 times until the butter pieces are pea-size. Transfer to the bowl with the remaining dry ingredients, and stir to distribute the butter evenly.

Make several depressions in the flour mixture with your fingers; add the buttermilk a little at a time, mixing with your fingers, until it is all incorporated. Gently work the dough just until it comes together. Cover lightly, refrigerate 1 hour.

Prepare chicken curry

Warm the oil in a 5-quart saucepan over medium-high heat, then add the chicken thighs, curry powder, and lemongrass. Cook, stirring, until the thighs are seared on all sides and the curry powder is chestnut brown, 3 to 5 minutes. Add the onions and ½ cup fish sauce, and cook over medium heat, stirring and scraping the bottom of the pot, for 15 minutes.

Add the carrots and enough water to cover. Bring to a boil, reduce heat, and simmer uncovered until the carrots are tender, about 20 minutes. Transfer the chicken to a plate and discard the lemongrass. Add the potatoes and coconut milk to the pan, and bring to a simmer. Pull meat from chicken thighs in bite-size pieces. Return the meat to the curry and continue to cook, uncovered, until potatoes are tender, about 20 more minutes. Taste sauce and, if needed (fish sauces vary in saltiness), season with up to ¼ cup additional fish sauce.

Assemble chicken curry potpie

Heat oven to 425°F. Divide the biscuit dough into 5 portions. On a lightly floured work surface, roll out each portion so it will cover the top of a gratin dish to within ½ inch of the edges. Distribute the chicken curry among the 5 dishes and top each with dough. Bake until the biscuits are golden, 15 to 20 minutes.

Courtesy of Chef-Owner Diep Tran of Good Girl Dinette (p. 123)

Sotto's Grilled Pork Meatballs with Snap Peas, Pecorino, and Bitter Greens

Southern Italian cooking in all its rustic and hearty glory is celebrated in style at West Los Angeles' Sotto. After years of working together in restaurants across Los Angeles and Orange County, Chefs Steve Samson and Zack Pollack finally stepped out on their own in 2011. The menu here, which features blistered Neapolitan pizzas, twisty handmade pastas, and lesser-known regional specialties, is a reflection of the chefs' shared passion for traditional Italian cooking. Nearly every table starts with an order of these Grilled Pork Meatballs with Snap Peas, Pecorino, and Bitter Greens. The crisp, cool salad pairs spectacularly with the caramelized and charred meatballs.

Makes 20 meatballs

For pork meatballs

1 tablespoon extra-virgin olive oil

1 medium yellow onion, diced

5 garlic cloves, finely chopped

½ tablespoon chopped marjoram

½ tablespoon chopped sage

½ tablespoon chopped rosemary

2 pounds coarsely ground pork shoulder

2 whole eggs plus 3 yolks

5 ounces grated pecorino Sardo

½ tablespoon chopped fennel seeds

4 ounces unseasoned bread crumbs

2 tablespoons chopped parsley

Salt and black pepper to taste

For greens and snap pea salad

1 bunch wild baby arugula

1 bunch baby mustard greens

20 blanched and sliced snap peas

1 cup grated pecorino cheese

2 sieved hard-boiled eggs

½ lemon

3 tablespoons extra-virgin olive oil

Salt and black pepper to taste

Prepare pork meatballs

In a large skillet over medium-low heat, sweat the onions in 1 tablespoon olive oil until translucent, about 5 minutes. Add the garlic, marjoram, sage, and rosemary and continue cooking until soft, about 3 minutes. Remove from heat and set aside to cool.

In a large mixing bowl, combine the pork, whole egg, egg yolks, pecorino, fennel seeds, bread crumbs, chopped parsley, and cooled onion mixture. Season with salt and black pepper to taste.

Knead the mixture thoroughly to ensure that the meatballs hold together while grilling. Refrigerate the farce at least a half hour before forming meatballs. Portion and shape the meatballs; each one should weigh about 1.5 ounces. Grill the meatballs over medium heat until just cooked through, about 5 minutes per side.

Prepare greens and snap pea salad

Combine first 5 ingredients in a mixing bowl. Dress with a squeeze of lemon juice, olive oil, and season with salt and pepper. Place a small handful of salad on a medium-size plate. Place 3 grilled meatballs on top of the salad.

Courtesy of Chefs Steve Samson and Zach Pollack of Sotto (p. 264)

Border Grill's Quinoa Fritters with Aji Amarillo Aioli

Chefs Mary Sue Milliken and Susan Feniger, longtime luminaries in the Los Angeles culinary scene, opened the very first Border Grill restaurant in 1985 after traveling through Mexico and learning age-old regional recipes and techniques from street hawkers, market vendors, and home cooks. These quinoa fritters drizzled with aji amarillo (Peruvian yellow chili pepper) aioli are one of the most popular appetizers at their temple of modern Mexican cuisine. It's impossible to resist the assertive crunch of the grains and the molten cheese filling.

Serves 6

For quinoa fritters

⅔ cup white or black quinoa, rinsed and well drained (if necessary)

1⅓ cups water

¼ cup all-purpose flour

¼ cup grated cotija or feta cheese

¾ teaspoon salt

Freshly ground black pepper, to taste

4 green onions, white and light green parts only, finely chopped

½ bunch Italian parsley, chopped

1 egg

1 egg yolk

¾ cup canola or grapeseed oil, for frying

Aji Amarillo Aioli (see recipe below), for serving

For aji amarillo aioli

2 egg yolks

1 teaspoon red wine vinegar

Juice and zest of 1 lime

1 clove garlic

½ teaspoon salt

2–3 tablespoons aji amarillo paste, to taste

1 cup extra-virgin olive oil

1 tablespoon chopped parsley

Prepare quinoa fritters

Place a small, dry saucepan over high heat. Add quinoa and toast for about 5 minutes, shaking and stirring constantly to prevent scorching. Transfer to a large saucepan and add water. Bring to a boil, reduce to a simmer, and cook, covered, until water is absorbed, about 10 minutes. Set aside to cool.

In a large bowl, combine cooked quinoa, flour, cheese, salt, and pepper. Add onions, parsley, egg, and yolk. Stir thoroughly with a spoon until the mixture has the consistency of soft dough.

Heat oil in a large skillet over medium heat. Using 2 soup spoons, press batter into egg-shaped ovals and gently slide into the hot oil, or use a small ice cream scoop. Fry until the bottoms are golden and brown, less than a minute. Turn and fry the second side until golden, less than a minute. Drain on paper towels and serve warm, topped with Aji Amarillo Aioli.

Prepare aji amarillo aioli

In a blender, combine egg yolks, vinegar, lime juice and zest, garlic, salt, and aji amarillo paste. Blend until smooth.

With the motor still running, drizzle in olive oil very slowly until mixture is the consistency of mayonnaise (adding too much oil will cause the aioli to break). Stir in parsley, taste, and adjust seasonings as necessary.

Courtesy of Chef-Owners Mary Sue Milliken and Susan Feniger
of Border Grill Restaurants & Truck (p. 275)

Park's BBQ's Bulgogi

Jenee Park of Park's BBQ was one of the very first chefs in Koreatown to serve higher quality meat in magically smokeless environs. While the Kobe-style prime beef, prime brisket, and slabs of pork belly are rightfully popular with carnivorous patrons, it's the sweet and savory bulgogi, thin cuts of marinated beef, that graces every table. To re-create the Park's BBQ experience at home, serve over steamed rice along with a plethora of banchan that can be procured at Korean supermarkets like the Koreatown Galleria on Olympic.

Serves 2–3

- 2 tablespoons soy sauce
- 1 tablespoon sugar
- 1 tablespoon sesame oil
- 1 tablespoon water
- 1 tablespoon chopped green onion
- 1½ teaspoons minced garlic
- 1½ teaspoons sesame seeds
- ⅛ teaspoon black pepper
- 250 grams (about 9 ounces) beef sirloin, thinly sliced

Combine the soy sauce, sugar, sesame oil, water, green onion, garlic, sesame seeds, and black pepper in a small bowl. Transfer the beef to a separate bowl and pour the prepared marinade on top. Combine well and let the meat soak for 30 minutes at room temperature.

Heat a wok or skillet over high heat. Add the meat and pan-fry 3 to 5 minutes. Serve over rice along with an assortment of banchan.

Courtesy of Chef-Owner Jenee Park of Park's BBQ (p. 29)

Mo-Chica's Ceviche Mixto

Chef Ricardo Zarate relocated Mo-Chica to swanky Downtown digs after courting legions of admirers with his contemporary Peruvian cooking at the Mercado La Paloma. At Mo-Chica 2.0, the room is as vibrant as the chef's flavors, while the menu has more than doubled in size. Many of the original dishes have carried over to Seventh Street including this ceviche mixto, a well-balanced and refreshing combination of sea bass, prawns, scallops, and squid swimming in a tangy rocoto leche de tigre marinade.

Serves 2

For leche de tigre amarillo

- 2½ ounces onions
- 1 ounce celery
- 1½ ounces ginger
- 1½ ounces garlic cloves
- 1½ ounces aji amarillo paste
- 2½ ounces sea bass, cut into pieces
- 13½ ounces lime juice
- 5 ounces ice cubes
- 1⅓ ounces salt

For ceviche mixto

- 2 shrimp, blanched
- 4 calamari, blanched
- 1 scallop, blanched
- 4 bite-size cubes sea bass, blanched
- 2½ ounces leche de tigre Amarillo
- ½ tablespoon cilantro, minced
- 1 ounce finely shaved red onion
- ½ tablespoon aji amarillo paste
- 1 tablespoon fresh choclo (Peruvian corn kernels)
- 1 ounce camote (sweet potato), cubed and blanched
- ¼ tablespoon garlic paste
- Micro greens

Prepare leche de tigre amarillo

Combine the first 4 ingredients in a blender. Add the aji amarillo and sea bass and blend further to make a paste. Add the lime juice a little at a time until the consistency is properly creamy. Finally, add in the ice and salt and blend until smooth.

Prepare ceviche mixto

Combine the seafood and the leche de tigre with the cilantro, onions, aji amarillo paste, and choclo in a bowl. Add cubed camotes and garlic paste, and garnish with micro greens like shiso.

Courtesy of Chef Ricardo Zarate of Mo-Chica (p. 50) and Picca (p. 258)

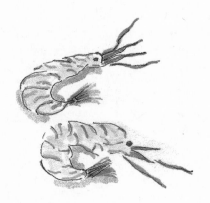

Rivera's Tortillas Florales with Indian Butter

Celebrated Chef John Rivera Sedlar pays homage to 3,000 years of Latin American cuisine in all its enchanting forms at Downtown's Rivera. With three distinct rooms each serving a unique menu, diners are taken on a tequila- and mescal-fueled gastronomical tour across three continents and countless regions. In the Playa Room, the chef serves a Mexican- and Southwest-inspired menu including his famous tortillas florales, which are adorned with wildly colorful flowers and served warm with "Indian butter," a guacamole-like spread. Californians referred to avocados as "Indian butter" in the early 20th century.

Serves 6 to 8

For tortillas florales

1¼ pounds dried corn

4 quarts water for cooking the corn plus ¾ cup for mixing the masa

1½ tablespoons slaked lime (calcium hydroxide, called cal in Latin Markets)

1 tablespoon sea salt

Organic edible flower petals (pansies, roses, nasturtiums, or squash blossoms)

Olive oil

For Indian butter

3 ripe Hass avocados, halved and pitted

½ cup chopped cilantro leaves

1½ tablespoons chopped serrano chiles

1 tablespoon minced yellow onion

1 tablespoon fresh lime juice

¼ tablespoon minced garlic

1 teaspoon salt, plus extra as needed

Prepare tortillas florales

Sort through corn kernels to remove debris, rinse under cool water, and drain. Place corn in a large, deep saucepan and add water and slaked lime. Stir gently until lime dissolves. Bring to a simmer over medium heat, then reduce heat to maintain simmer, stirring occasionally until corn is tender but slightly firm, 2½ to 3 hours. Take care not to overcook. Remove from heat and drain in colander.

Rinse and lightly rub handfuls of corn under cold running water until skins are removed. Transfer skinned kernels (nixtamal) to a bowl and refrigerate overnight.

To make the dough for the tortillas (masa), pass nixtamal through grinder attachment of a stand mixer 2 or 3 times, until it reaches a soft, doughlike consistency that still feels coarse-textured. Transfer ground nixtamal to a large bowl and add sea salt and ¾ cup water. With clean hands, mix ingredients until fully blended, forming a ball of soft dough that holds together.

With fingertips, pull off 2 generous tablespoons to form a sphere slightly smaller than a Ping-Pong ball. Roll dough between palms until ball is perfectly smooth and even. Place ball on baking tray lined with parchment paper. Repeat with remaining masa. Cover completed balls with damp kitchen towel.

Cut 26 6-inch squares of parchment paper. Set aside. Cut plastic bag from produce section of supermarket into 2 9-inch squares. Place 1 piece of plastic on bottom plate of tortilla press. Place masa ball in center. Top with second piece of plastic.

Gently close tortilla press to form a still-thick cake that is not quite the final diameter. Open press and peel off top plastic. With a few flower petals, form an attractive design on top of maize cake. Replace top sheet of plastic and gently close press to seal in petals and spread maize cake to final diameter of 5 to 5½ inches. Place on top of sheet of parchment paper and top with another sheet of parchment. Repeat process with remaining balls of masa, petals, and parchment paper to make a stack of maize cakes.

Heat well-seasoned, heavy cast-iron griddle or skillet over high heat until lightly smoking-hot. Pour olive oil on a bunched-up paper towel and lightly slick griddle. Lift a maize cake with parchment paper beneath it and carefully slap it on griddle, maize side down, then carefully peel off and discard paper. Repeat with as many maize cakes as will comfortably fit at one time in pan. Cook until undersides form dark-brown blisters, then flip with spatula and repeat, about 1½ minutes per side. Remove and stack tortillas inside folded napkin or kitchen towel to keep warm. Repeat with remaining cakes. Makes about 25 tortillas.

Prepare Indian butter

With a tablespoon, scoop the avocado pulp from the skins into a food processor fitted with a stainless-steel blade. Add the cilantro, chili, onion, lime juice, garlic, and 1 teaspoon salt. Process until smooth, scraping the work bowl with a rubber spatula as often as necessary. Taste and, if necessary, pulse in more salt to taste.

Transfer to a nonreactive bowl and cover with plastic wrap, pressing down against the surface of the puree to guard against oxidation. Refrigerate until serving.

Courtesy of Chef John Rivera Sedlar of Rivera (p. 61)

M.B. Post's Green Curry Steamed Mussels with Chinese Sausage

It's loud, fun, and unbelievably delicious at Chef David LeFevre's M.B. Post. A former industrial engineer, Chef LeFevre honed his cooking chops at Charlie Trotter's in Chicago before earning a Michelin star at Water Grill in Downtown Los Angeles. These days, he's ditched fine dining for family-style fare at this beachfront "social house." The rustic and communal dishes coming out of the kitchen, like these green curry steamed mussels, reflect the style of food that Chef LeFevre personally enjoys preparing and eating. Found under the "Seafood . . . Eat Food" section of the menu, the mussels are steeped in a fragrant, made-from-scratch broth along with plenty of Chinese sausages and served with rice.

Serves 4

For green curry paste

- 1 stalk lemongrass
- 3 Thai chiles
- 1 jalapeño
- 2 cloves garlic
- 1 shallot
- 1 ounce ginger
- ½ cup cilantro leaves
- ½ cup Thai basil
- 1 Kaffir lime leaf
- ½ teaspoon ground cumin
- ½ teaspoon coriander
- 3 tablespoons fish sauce
- 1 tablespoon lime juice
- 1 teaspoon shrimp paste
- 1 teaspoon brown sugar

For steamed mussels

- 1 ounce canola or soybean oil
- 2 links Chinese sausage, casing removed and sliced thin
- 2 ounces green curry paste
- 4 ounces coconut milk
- 4 ounces vegetable stock or water
- 14 ounces PEI black mussels, trimmed and cleaned
- 2 Kaffir lime leaves
- 8 Thai basil leaves
- ½ lime for juice
- ½ lime cut into rounds for garnish
- 4 cilantro sprigs

Prepare green curry paste

Put all ingredients into a blender and pulse until a coarse paste forms.

Prepare steamed mussels

Heat oil in a medium-size pot. Add the sliced Chinese sausage and render some of the fat. Add the green curry paste and lightly toast for 15 seconds. Add the coconut milk and vegetable stock and bring to a simmer. Finally, add the cleaned mussels along with the herbs and steam with a lid until all of the mussels open completely. Transfer the mussels and all of the sauce to a large bowl and serve with steamed rice. Finish the dish with fresh lime juice, lime slices, and cilantro sprigs.

Courtesy of Chef David LeFevre of M.B. Post (p. 197)

La Casita Mexicana's Chiles en Nogada

For the past decade and then some, Chefs Jaime Martin del Campo and Ramiro Arvizu have been preparing the dishes of their native Jalisco, along with other Mexican specialties, at La Casita Mexicana in Bell. In addition to their signature moles, La Casita composes a memorable chiles en nogada. It's the national dish of Mexico and consists of a roasted poblano chili stuffed with spiced pork, dried fruits, and almonds. A rich and creamy walnut sauce and a handful of pomegranate seeds provide the finishing touches.

Serves 8

For filling

- 4 tablespoons vegetable oil (or as needed)
- 6 garlic cloves, peeled and finely chopped
- 1 cup diced onion
- 2 pounds boneless pork shoulder, cut into 1 inch cubes
- Salt
- ½ cup water
- 1 pound ripe tomatoes, blended and strained
- ½ cup peeled and chopped almonds
- ¾ cup raisins
- 2 tablespoons fresh chopped parsley
- 2 dried cloves, finely ground
- ½ teaspoon cinnamon
- 30 black peppercorns, finely ground
- 1 cup diced preserved citron or candied fruit
- 3 medium-size plantains, peeled and cut into ¼-inch cubes
- 2 small apples, peeled, cored, and cut into ¼-inch cubes
- 2 small pears, peeled, cored, and cut into ¼-inch cubes
- 2 small peaches, cored and cut into ¼-inch cubes
- ¼ pound pine nuts
- 1 tablespoon sugar
- 2 tablespoons white vinegar
- 8 poblano chiles, roasted, peeled, and deveined

5 cups cold water

1 pound goat cheese or fresh
Mexican cheese

4 cups walnuts

2 tablespoons sugar

For garnish

2 cups pomegranate seeds

Fresh parsley, chopped

Prepare filling

In a large skillet over medium heat, pour 2 tablespoons of vegetable oil and heat until shimmering. Add the garlic and onion and sauté until translucent.

Add the meat, salt, and a little bit of water and continue to sauté for 5 minutes or until the meat is halfway cooked through. Add the tomatoes and bring everything to a boil. Add the almonds, raisins, and parsley and cook for an additional 7 minutes.

Add the cloves, cinnamon, pepper, preserved citron, plantains, apples, pears, peaches, and pine nuts and cook for 5 more minutes. Lastly, add the sugar and vinegar. Take the filling off the heat and let it cool completely.

Prepare nogada sauce

Place all the ingredients in a blender and pulse until creamy.

Assembling Chiles en Nogada

Carefully fill the poblano chiles with the cooled filling. Make sure to pack in enough filling so that the chile regains its original shape.

To serve individual portions, place a single chile on a plate and spoon over the room-temperature nogada sauce generously. If the sauce is too thick, add in a little milk. Lastly, sprinkle the stuffed chili generously with pomegranate seeds, garnish with the parsley, and serve immediately.

Courtesy of Chefs Jaime Martin del Campo and Ramiro Arvizu of La Casita Mexicana (p. 220)

Huckleberry Bakery & Cafe's Salted Caramel Bars

Following the tremendous success of Rustic Canyon Wine Bar & Seasonal Kitchen, husband-and-wife team Zoe Nathan and Josh Loeb opened Huckleberry Bakery & Cafe a stone's throw away. While the breakfast, lunch, and brunch menus are all perfectly pleasant, it's the counter lined with freshly baked goods that's worth all the fuss. There are always seasonal fruit crostatas and tarts on hand, as well as dozens of menu mainstays with a devoted following. This salted caramel bar with its buttery shortbread crust and silky, fleur de sel–flecked caramel, is the stuff of dreams.

Makes 12 bars

15 tablespoons unsalted butter	2¼ teaspoons kosher salt
2¼ cups heavy cream	1 10x8-inch blind baked tart
1 vanilla bean	shell or something similar
2¼ cups sugar	Fleur de sel for topping

Cube the butter and place in a small bowl. Set aside.

Place the cream in a small saucepan. Split the vanilla bean and scrape the seeds into the cream. Add the scraped pod to the cream as well. Bring to a boil, whisking occasionally, and set aside to steep.

Place the sugar, salt, and 2 tablespoons water in a large saucepan. Combine with a wooden spoon and cook over medium heat. Stir only if the sugar is melting unevenly.

Allow the sugar to cook to a deep golden brown color, then immediately turn off the heat and cautiously add the cream in a few additions. It will bubble up; do not be alarmed, but do be careful. Once all the cream has been added, add the butter.

Return to a medium flame and continue to cook until the mixture reaches 238°F on a candy thermometer. Then remove from heat, discard the vanilla pod, and pour the caramel into your shell.

Refrigerate until completely set. Top with fleur de sel.

**Recipe courtesy of Chef Zoe Nathan of Huckleberry Bakery & Cafe (p. 284),
Rustic Canyon Wine Bar & Seasonal Kitchen (p. 261), Sweet Rose Creamery (p. 285),
and Milo & Olive (p. 266)**

Milo & Olive's Chocolate Hazelnut Scones

Zoe Nathan and Josh Loeb didn't intend to open a pizzeria when they scooped up the space at 2723 Wilshire Blvd. in Santa Monica. The initial plan was to use the kitchen to relieve the overworked ovens at Huckleberry, their bustling bakery and cafe a mile away. But one thing led to another, a pizza dough was developed and a wood-burning Mugnaini oven was installed, and thus, Milo & Olive came to be. In addition to the top-rate pizzas, the restaurant boasts a magnificent bakery brimming with freshly crafted breads and pastries, like these Chocolate Hazelnut Scones.

Makes 10 scones

- 1¾ cups plus 2 tablespoons all-purpose flour (235g)
- ½ cup ground, toasted hazelnuts
- 1 tablespoon plus 1½ teaspoons baking powder
- 5 tablespoons sugar, plus additional for sprinkling
- 1 teaspoon kosher salt
- 18 tablespoons cold unsalted butter
- 6 tablespoons cold buttermilk
- 1 teaspoon vanilla extract
- 1 cup chopped dark chocolate
- egg wash (1 egg beaten with 2 tablespoons water or milk)

Combine flour, ground nuts, baking powder, sugar, and salt in a very large bowl. Set aside.

Throw in the cold butter and work it with your fingertips until the pieces are pea- and lima bean-size. Add buttermilk, vanilla, and chocolate. Lightly toss to distribute.

Immediately, dump everything out onto a clean surface, allowing more than enough space to work the dough. Using only the heel of your palm, quickly flatten out the dough. Gather it back together in a mound and repeat the flattening gesture. After 2 or 3 repetitions, the dough should begin holding together. Be sure to avoid overworking. You should still see some pea-size bits of butter.

Shape into a foot-long cylinder, lightly flatten the top, and cut into 10 triangles. Freeze for at least 2 hours or up to 1 month before baking.

Preheat oven to 350°F. Place the triangles of dough on an ungreased sheet tray with plenty of breathing room. Do not allow to thaw. Brush with egg wash and sprinkle liberally with sugar. Bake for about 30 minutes, until baked through and nicely browned.

Serve with very lightly sweetened whipped cream. These are best served the day of.

Courtesy of Chef Zoe Nathan of Milo & Olive (p. 266)

Kogi's Kimchi Quesadilla

Chef Roy Choi sparked a nationwide gourmet food truck trend when he fused Korean and Mexican cuisines aboard the Kogi truck. At Kogi, tacos, quesadillas, and burritos come stuffed with Korean marinated proteins like short ribs and pork and garnished with a light and bright slaw tossed in a chili-soy vinaigrette, sesame oil, and fresh lime juice. "This dish started as a fun food for us to enjoy in the truck and it just hit the streets with a force," said Chef Choi of the kimchi quesadilla. "Its spirit comes from Koreatown."

Serves 4

- **2 cups chopped kimchi**
- **8 tablespoons butter**
- **4 tablespoons canola oil**
- **4 12-inch flour tortillas**

- **4 cups shredded cheddar-jack cheese**
- **8 fresh sesame or shiso leaves**
- **4 tablespoons sesame seeds, toasted**

First cook kimchi with butter and continue to stir over medium heat until caramelized and charred; set aside.

Oil pan or griddle, place tortilla on pan, and add 1 cup of cheese on 1 half, covering to make it look like a black and white cookie.

Add ½ cup kimchi, layer on 2 ripped sesame leaves, and sprinkle with 1 tablespoon sesame seeds.

Fold over the empty half of the tortilla to create a half moon. Continue to cook and flip over. The quesadilla should look blistered like a Neapolitan pizza. Cut and enjoy the drippy goodness . . .

Courtesy of Chef Roy Choi of Kogi (p. 44), Chego (p. 21), A-Frame (p. 249), and Sunny Spot (p. 250)

Beth Kellerhalls' Sriracha Ganache

Beth Kellerhalls, the queen of sweets at all of Chef Roy Choi's restaurants, is the mastermind behind the fabulous pound cake cinnamon churros at Culver City's A-Frame and the not-to-be-missed sweet potato tart with marshmallow ice cream at Venice's Sunny Spot. This Sriracha Ganache is reminiscent of the Sriracha candy bar served aboard the Kogi trucks and at Chego.

1 cup chopped chocolate   **1½ teaspoons Sriracha sauce**
1½ cups heavy cream

Cook the chocolate, heavy cream, and Sriracha sauce in the top of a double boiler over simmering water until smooth and warm, stirring occasionally. Serve over vanilla ice cream.

Courtesy of Pastry Chef Beth Kellerhalls of Kogi (p. 44), Chego (p. 21),
A-Frame (p. 249), and Sunny Spot (p. 250)

Appendices

Appendix A: L.A. Eateries by Cuisine

American
Apple Pan, The, 273
Bill and Hiroko's, 136
Cole's, 80
Dal Rae, 226
Derby Restaurant, The, 177
Dog Haus, 148, 232, 233
Du-par's, 104
Fab Hot Dogs, 131, 233
Grill 'Em All, 43
Grilled Cheese Truck, 43
Hat, The,179, 238
Hawkins House of Burgers, 219
Johnnie's Pastrami, 179
Lawry's the Prime Rib, 277
Lucky Boy, 238
Moffett's Family Restaurant and
    Chicken Pie Shop, 180
Mom's Burgers, 222
Munch Box, The, 137
Musso and Frank Grill, 75
Nickel Diner, 95
Oinkster, The, 125

Original Pantry, The, 76
Original Tommy's Hamburgers, 77
Original Tops, The, 238
Pann's, 203
Philippe the Original, 80
Pie 'n Burger, 239
Short Order, 105
Umami Burger, 68, 136, 237, 272

Argentinian
Carlitos Gardel Restaurant, 168
Rika's Empanadas, 167

Armenian
Panos Pastry, 246

Asian Fusion
Chinois on Main, 279
Lukshon, 276
Red Medicine, 260

Bakery
Berolina Bakery, 241
Bottega Louie, 86
Bread Lounge, 87

Providence, 58
Trois Mec, 68
Valentino Ristorante, 280

Food Trucks
Buttermilk Truck, 42
Cool Haus, 283
Egg Slut, 42
Gastrobus, The, 43
Grilled Cheese Truck, 43
Grill 'Em All, 43
India Jones Chow Truck, 44
Jogasaki Truck, 44
Kogi, 44
Lobsta Truck, 45
Ludo Truck, 45
Mariscos 4 Vientos, 109
Mariscos Jalisco, 108
Ricky's Fish Tacos, 60
Rico's Mar Azul Mariscos
    Truck, 126
Salinas Churros, 112
Tacos Leo, 67
Waffles de Liege, 96

French
Bottega Louie, 86
Canelé, 122
'Lette Macarons, 87
Little Next Door, 41
Ludo Truck, 45
Mélisse, 256
Patina, 79
Trois Mec, 68

Fried Chicken
Chicken Day, 39
Dinah's Family Restaurant, 237
Farmshop, 252
Flossie's Southern Cuisine, 192
Harry's Chicken, 191
Honey's Kettle, 220, 254
Kyochon Chicken, 38, 220, 234
Ludo Truck, 45
Roscoe's House of Chicken and
    Waffles, 82, 118, 205, 216, 240

Gelato
Bulgarini Gelato, 242, 280
Caramia Gelato Tropicale, 127
Gelato Bar, 242
Pazzo Gelato, 242

German
Alpine Village, 209
European Deluxe Sausage
    Kitchen, 248
Schreiner's Fine Sausages, 247

Greek
Dino's Chicken and Burgers, 71,
    177, 226
Papa Cristo's, 79

Guatemalan
Amalia's, 61
La Cevicheria, 40
Rinconcito Guatemalteco, 60

Hawaiian
A-Frame, 249

Korean

A-Won, 16
Beverly Soon Tofu House, 65
Bud Namu Korean BBQ, 24
Byul Gobchang, 20
Chego, 21
Chicken Day, 39
Cocohodo, 245
Chosun Galbee, 28
Corner Place, The, 21, 219
Dan Sung Sa, 26
Don Day, 23
Dongbu Live Fish, 149
Dwit Gol Mok, 25
Genwa Korean BBQ, 28
Hae Jang Chon, 24
Ham Ji Park, 31
Hite Kwang-Jang, 53
Jae Bu Do, 34
Jeon Ju, 35
Jun Won, 36
Kobawoo House, 38
Kogi, 44
Kyochon Chicken, 38, 220, 234
Ma Dang Gook Soo, 47
Mapo Kkak Doo Gee, 47
Mirak, 50
OB Bear, 53
Ondal 2, 55
Park's BBQ, 28
So Kong Dong, 64
Soban, 37
Soot Bull Jeep, 83

Wako Donkasu, 196
Yu Chun Chic Naeng Myun, 22

Lebanese

Carousel, 231
Marouch Restaurant, 232
Skaf's Grill, 232
Zankou Chicken, 84, 139, 227, 241

Malaysian

Pappa Rich, 245

Mexican

Bar Amá, 18
Border Grill, 71, 275
Cacao Mexicatessen, 121
Cemitas Don Adrian, 130
Chichen Itza, 212
Coni's Seafood, 191
Cook's Tortas, 147
Dino's Chicken and Burgers, 71,
    177, 226
El Borrego de Oro, 30
El Huarache Azteca, 122
Flor Del Rio, 107
Gish Bac Restaurant, 29
Guelaguetza Restaurante, 30, 220
Guisados, 107
La Azteca Tortilleria, 113
La Casita Mexicana, 220
La Flor De Yucatan Catering &
    Bakery, 213
La Mascota Bakery, 110
La Monarca Bakery, 227, 244, 287

Appendix B: L.A. Eateries by Neighborhood

Alhambra
Aloha Food Factory, 170
Banh Mi & Che Cali, 143
Boiling Crab, The, 145
Dog Haus, 148
Dong Nguyen Restaurant, 181
Fosselman's Ice Cream Co., 184
Hat, The, 179
Lunasia, 150
Noodle Guy, 162
Old Country Café, 165
101 Noodle Express, 164
Sam Woo Barbecue, 180
Savoy Kitchen, 180
Shakas, 169
Tasty Garden, 173
Tea Station, 186

Altadena
Bulgarini Gelato, 242

Arcadia
A&J, 148
Boiling Point, 147

Claro's, 274
Daikokuya, 148
Derby Restaurant, The, 177
Din Tai Fung, 177
Doe Jon Station, 153
J.J. Bakery, 183
Moffett's Family Restaurant and
    Chicken Pie Shop, 180
101 Noodle Express, 164
SinBala, 171
Tasty Garden, 173
Tofu King, 175

Arlington Heights
Gish Bac, 29
La Cevicheria, 40
Natraliart Jamaican Restaurant and
    Market, 51

Artesia
Magic Wok, 221
Mumbai Ki Galliyon Se, 223
Portugal Imports, 229
Rajdhani, 223

La Caridad, 39
Pazzo Gelato, 242
Xoia, 70

El Sereno
Mariscos Los Lechugas, 109

Encino
Katsu-Ya, 138
Versailles, 39

Exposition Park
Ella's Belizean Restaurant, 213

Fairfax
Angelini Osteria, 14
Animal, 15
Bennett's Ice Cream, 104
Bob's Coffee and Donuts, 104
Du-par's, 104
Egg Slut, 42
Littlejohn's English Toffee
    House, 105
Milk, 92
Original Farmers Market,
    The, 104
Pampas Grill, 105
Pink's Hot Dogs, 81
Shaky Alibi, 95
Short Cake, 96, 105
Short Order, 105
Singapore's Banana Leaf, 105
Sprinkles Cupcakes, 289
Umami Burger, 68

Gardena
Boiling Point, 191
Chikara Mochi, 209
Eatalian Cafe, 192
El Rocoto, 51
Harry's Chicken, 191
Marukai Pacific Market, 211
Mikawaya, 208
Otafuku Noodle House, 195
Sakae Sushi, 205
Sakura-ya, 208
Sanuki No Sato, 201
Shin Sen Gumi, 23
Shin Sen Gumi Yakitori, 202
Tea Station, 209

Glendale
Berolina Bakery, 241
Carousel, 231
Dinah's Family Restaurant, 237
Porto's Bakery & Cafe, 240
Raffi's Place, 235
Sarkis Pastry, 246
Schreiner's Fine Sausages, 247
Skaf's Grill, 232
Shamshiri, 236
Zankou Chicken, 241

Glendora
Donut Man, The, 178
Hat, The, 179
Rika's Empanadas, 167

Chicken Day, 39
Chosun Galbee, 29
Cocohodo, 245
Corner Place, The, 21
Dan Sung Sa, 26
Don Day, 23
Dwit Gol Mok, 25
Guelaguetza Restaurante, 30
Hae Jang Chon, 24
Ham Ji Park, 31
Hite Kwang-Jang, 53
Jeon Ju, 35
Jun Won, 36
Kobawoo House, 38
Koreatown Galleria, 102
Kyochon, 38
Ma Dang Gook Soo, 47
Mapo Kkak Doo Gee, 47
Mirak, 50
OB Bear, 53
Park's BBQ, 29
Pollos a la Brasa, 81
Soban, 37
Soot Bull Jeep, 83
Taylor's Steakhouse, 78
Wako Donkasu, 196
Yu Chun Chic Naeng Myun, 22

La Crescenta
Chicken Day, 39

La Mirada
Mario's Peruvian Seafood, 227

Larchmont
Rinconcito Guatemalteco, 60

Lawndale
Rincon Chileno Deli, 200

Leimert Park
Phillips Barbecue, 219

Little Tokyo
Anzen Hardware, 99
Cafe Dulce, 88
Daikokuya, 22
Four Leaf, 284
Fugetsu-Do, 88
Hama Sushi, 67
Kagaya, 37
Kagura, 196
Kokekokko, 203
Lazy Ox Canteen, 90
Mikawaya, 91
Shin Sen Gumi, 23
Spice Table, The, 65
Sushi Gen, 67

Lomita
Gaja, 194
Patisserie Chantilly, 208

Long Beach
Phnom Penh Noodle
    Restaurant, 116
Roscoe's House of Chicken and
    Waffles, 118
Siem Reap, 117

Shin Sen Gumi Yakitori, 170
Tasty Garden, 173
V.P. Tofu, 187
Yunkun Garden, 176

North Hollywood
Zankou Chicken, 139

Northridge
Bombay Spiceland, 130
Brent's Deli, 137
Katsu-Ya, 138

Norwalk
Anticucheria Peruana, 217

Palms
Bucato, 262
N/naka, 257
Scoops, 289
Simpang Asia, 263
Sushi Hiko, 268
Tara's Himalayan Cuisine, 269

Pasadena
Carmela Ice Cream, 242
Cook Books by Janet Jarvits, 247
Cool Haus, 243
Dog Haus, 232, 233
Euro Pane, 234
Garo's Basturma, 235
Gourmet Cobbler Factory, The, 244
Hat, The, 238
'Lette Macarons, 87
Little Flower Candy Company, 244

Lucky Boy, 238
Old Sasoon Bakery, 234
Original Tops, The, 238
Pappa Rich, 245
Pie 'n Burger, 239
Roscoe's House of Chicken and
    Waffles, 240
Sarkis Pastry, 246
Tibet Nepal House, 236
Umami Burger, 237
Yang Chow, 241
Zankou Chicken, 241

Pico-Union
Beverly Soon Tofu House, 65
Dino's Chicken and Burgers, 71
Mateo's Ice Cream and Fruit
    Bars, 229
La Flor de Yucatan, 213
La 27th Restaurante Familiar
    Nicaraguense, 41
Papa Cristo's, 79
So Kong Dong, 64

Pico-Rivera
Dal Rae, 226
Dino's Chicken and Burgers, 226

Pico-Robertson
Picca, 258
Sotto, 264
Versailles, 39

Rancho Park
La Serenata de Garibaldi, 277

Index